THE
Wild Bears

BOOKS BY GEORGE LAYCOCK

The Deer Hunter's Bible
The Shotgunner's Bible
The Bird Watcher's Bible
The Sign of the Flying Goose
The Flying Sea Otters (with Ellen L.)
Big Nick
King Gator
Never Pet A Porcupine
Never Trust A Cowbird
The Alien Animals
The Diligent Destroyers
The Pelicans
The Animal Movers
Wild Refuge
Air Pollution
Water Pollution
The World's Endangered Wildlife
America's Endangered Wildlife
Strange Monsters/Great Searches
Mysteries, Monsters, Secrets
Alaska, Embattled Frontier
Autumn of the Eagle
Squirrels
The Camels
Wild Animals, Safe Places
Wild Travelers
Wingspread
People and Other Mammals
Beyond The Arctic Circle
The Complete Beginner's Guide To Photography
Does Your Pet Have a Sixth Sense?
Death Valley
Caves
Islands And Their Mysteries
Wild Hunters
Exploring the Great Swamp
Tornadoes—Killer Storms
How The Settlers Lived (with Ellen L.)
How To Buy And Enjoy A Small Farm
Bats In The Night
The Ohio Valley—Your Guide To America's Heartland (with Ellen L.)
The Kroger Story
North American Wildlife

THE
Wild Bears

BY
GEORGE LAYCOCK

The story of the grizzly, brown and black bears, their conflicts with man, and their chances of survival in the future.

PUBLISHED BY OUTDOOR LIFE BOOKS

DISTRIBUTED TO THE TRADE BY STACKPOLE BOOKS

Published by
    Outdoor Life Books
    Grolier Book Clubs, Inc.
    380 Madison Avenue
    New York, NY 10017

Distributed to the trade by
    Stackpole Books
    Cameron & Kelker Sts.
    Harrisburg, PA 17105

Picture research by Imagefinders, Inc. Washington, D.C.

Library of Congress Cataloging in Publication Data

Laycock, George.
  The wild bears.
  Bibliography: p.
  Includes index.
  1. Bears—North America.   2. Mammals—North
America.   I. Title.
QL737.C27L39   1986   599.74'466   86-18055
ISBN 0-943822-79-3
Second printing, 1988

Manufactured in the United States of America

Design by John Romer

Acknowledgments

Biologists are studying bears in every part of the country. During my research for this book I found these professionals, without exception, courteous and generous with their time and information. Elsewhere, scientists, librarians, archivists, and hunters offered assistance. Among those due my special thanks are Larry Agenbroad, Gary Alt, John Beecham, Gary Brown, Bill Cook, Patsy Goodman, Steve Herrero, Charles Jonkel, Dick Knight, Ray Koontz, Cliff Martinka, Steve Mealey, Dale Nuss, Mike Pelton, Lynn Rogers, Larry Roop, and Chris Serveen.

G. L.

Contents

Preface

Conflicts between men and bears have prehistoric roots and these conflicts continue today for various reasons. The bear once promised meat and oil, a robe for the bed, a bragging trophy, and the thrill of taking a large and possibly dangerous animal. Killing bears became the badge of the superior hunter and the mark of the good citizen. Where people built their homes, farms, and villages, there was no longer room for bears.

Fur trappers coming out of Virginia, Kentucky, and Tennessee, bound for the beaver waters of the Rocky Mountains, met the grizzly head on. Sometimes the great bear won, but in the long haul, the grizzly, like his smaller black cousin, was in deep trouble. Mountain man James Ohio Pattie, speaking of the grizzlies encountered during his fur trapping career, said the bears not needed for food were killed anyhow, "to mend their manners." This attitude was typical.

Wherever people and bears have shared this world there has been a special relationship between them. No other animal affects us in quite the same ways. The bears have challenged our dominance, and earned our fear and affection. As long as the bears, both black and grizzly, were abundant on this continent, we attacked them with every method we could devise. Only when their numbers are finally reduced to low levels do we relent and begin searching for ways to save them. Our feeling toward bears reflects our possessive attitude towards all the natural resources around us. We see whatever is here—the bears included—as belonging to us, and therefore being ours to use or dispose of as we choose.

How both bears and people have dealt with each other is the story we explore in this book. The long association between bears and man has taken strange and unpredictable turns, sometimes frightening, sometimes humorous. The bear may win a round or two, but seldom wins the battle.

George Laycock

PART ONE

The Grizzly Bear

Chapter 1

The Rise of the Bears

One July day in 1974, in the little city of Hot Springs, South Dakota, George Hansen's bulldozer turned up several unusually large bones. That evening, as Hansen told his family about finding the bones, his son, Dan, suddenly thought of Dr. Larry Agenbroad, his geology professor at Chadron State College in Chadron, Nebraska. Following Dan's call, Agenbroad hurried to Hot Springs to have a look.

He recognized many of the newly exposed bones as the fossil remains of the long extinct Columbian mammoth, a prehistoric elephant that once roamed parts of North America. The contractor working on the site was caught up in the excitement of the find, and offered to delay development of the project while scientists determined its worth as a paleontological discovery. Although finding abundant remains of elephants—thirty-four in ten years—was itself an important scientific discovery, the most exciting fossil was found in early July, 1983, when the crew's gentle scraping and brushing, after a four-year recess, uncovered a single, long, curved canine tooth. The more Agenbroad and his students studied this tooth, the more excited they became.

At first they thought it might be a grizzly bear that had lived far earlier than any other known grizzly bear for which fossils had been uncovered. As more of the massive skull was exposed over the next few days, Agenbroad knew that, although this was no grizzly, it was an early American bear, one probably extinct for the past twelve thousand years.

What they had found was the fossil remains of the great short-faced bear which appeared in North America a million or so years ago, then spread out across the continent. The bear discovered in the Hot Springs dig is the only one ever found in the North Central Plains. Fossil discoveries elsewhere prove that this early Ice Age bear once lived from Alaska to Mexico and from California to Virginia. Scientists call this extinct bear *Arctodus simus,* and *Arctodus simus* was quite an animal.

Björn Kurtén, a world-famous Finnish expert on prehistoric animal life, has said that the short-faced bear was the most powerful predator of its time. Agenbroad, comparing the canine tooth of the South Dakota skull with that of a mature Alaskan grizzly, says, "The Alaska bear looks like a cub." The short-faced bear, which had a short, broad snout, stood more than five feet high at the shoulders, was at least fifteen percent larger than today's Alaska grizzly, and was even bigger than the Kodiak brown bear. It had long legs and a powerful muscle structure. Everything about the bear suggests to Agenbroad that it lived the life of a swift predator with the ability to bring down a wide variety of large prey.

Why this individual died in a pit along with the other creatures trapped in the hot springs is a mystery. Perhaps it went down into the pit to feast on warm mammoth meat, was injured there, then was unable to climb back up the sheer wall of slippery clay. No one knows. Ordinarily the agile bears, unlike the ponderous mammoths, might have climbed in and out of the pit at will.

This long extinct beast was one of several bears that rose out of the misty past, walked the earth through their alloted time, then vanished.

Scientists have worked for decades to patch together the story of the world's bears and how they evolved to become what they are today. Studying ancient bones, especially skulls and teeth, they have learned that the bear family can be traced back through the history of the earth's creatures for five million years or more to doglike ancestors that lived before the earliest human stood upright and walked the earth. Two million years or so ago, bears that were the predecessors of today's bears were forest dwelling animals of Asia.

People and bears began their long association when the most recent ice age gripped the Northern Hemisphere. During this time, which is recent as geological times are reckoned, the famous European cave bear came into prominence in what is today Germany and France. This enormous creature was hunted, and perhaps worshiped, by Neanderthal man. Dozens of cave bear skeletons have been found in caves in Europe, some of them arranged in burial positions, indicating that early man laid them to rest.

Profile of the prehistoric short-faced bear, reconstructed from a museum skull. The bear appeared in North America over a million years ago and is said to have been the most powerful predator of its time, larger than the Kodiak brown bear.

America too had its cave bear, an extinct beast known today only by its fossil remains and called the Florida cave bear. This bear, which roamed the Gulf Coast across Florida and northward to Tennessee, was also large, but had a heavier build than the short-faced bear. The Florida cave bear was built more like the European cave bear. Although, according to Kurtén, the two were not closely related, they probably evolved under similar conditions. Both the Florida cave bear

Comparison of the skulls of a mature grizzly bear (left) and the newly discovered skull of the giant short-faced bear (right) at the Hot Springs Mammoth Site, South Dakota.

and the short-faced bear seem related to the smaller spectacled bear still living in the Andes of South America.

Today there are bears in many parts of the world. As the internationally known authority on bears worldwide, Dr. Charles Jonkel,

Director of The Border Grizzly Project at the University of Montana, and Chairman of the IUCN Bear Specialist Group, points out, today's bears are grouped into eight species, found in some ninety countries. All but one of these bears are restricted to the Northern Hemisphere.

Aside from the polar bear, only two species of bears live in North America, the American black bear, found continent-wide, and the brown-grizzly bear which in prehistoric times may have lived as far east as Ohio and Ontario, but today is found only in the western part of the continent. These brown-grizzly bears, with the possible exception of the polar bear, are the modern giants of the bear family and the most widespread around the world of all the bear species. In North America, the grizzly and brown bear are closely related subspecies, with the grizzly native to the mainland and the brown, or Kodiak, at home on Kodiak and adjacent islands. Although the peninsula brown

Right profile of the cranium of the short-faced bear.

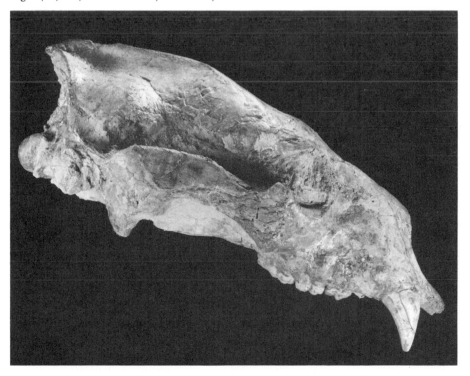

bear is considerably different from the interior grizzly, not all taxono-
mists accept it as a subspecies.

The earliest brown bears probably occurred in China and made
their way to North America during the Ice Ages by crossing the Bering
Strait land bridge. Ancestors of the black bear, also from Asia, were
already here long before the first grizzlies arrived.

Scientists speculate that the polar bear, youngest of the living
species of bears, evolved from the brown bears of the Siberian coast,
specializing to become the most truly carnivorous of all the modern
bear family.

The spectacled bear, the other Western Hemisphere bear, lives in
the high forests of the Andes and some adjacent lowlands. It is the
only bear native to South America. Hunting and destruction of the
forests for timber and agriculture are threats to its future.

In the forests of Asia lives the Asiatic black bear, sometimes called
"moon bear" because of a crescent-shaped white mark between the
front legs. This bear, although locally abundant and widespread, is
threatened by the expanding human population nearly everywhere it
is found.

The slow-moving sloth bear lives in India and adjacent countries.
It sometimes reaches weights of two hundred pounds or more. These
bears too are now extremely rare animals in Sri Lanka and other parts
of their native range.

Smallest of all the modern bears are the sun bears that live in the
forests of east Asia and seldom weigh more than a hundred and forty
pounds. Their name comes from the yellow patch on their chests.
Their numbers are believed to be decreasing steadily.

The rare giant panda is also now generally considered a bear. It
lives in a restricted range in western China where its major food, the
local bamboo, periodically fails. Bears, large and powerful, have been
important to people since man and bears first met. Many cultures have
assigned the bears religious roles in their societies and credited them
with super-natural powers.

As long as bears and men have shared the earth there has existed
between them a special adversary condition. Although we sometimes
ignore the small wild animals around us and let them go their way, the
bear is a special case. Until recent years we have, almost universally,
looked upon these animals as if they somehow threaten our territorial
dominance.

Throughout the ages, men, even those equipped only with stone
axes and spears, have been unable to resist the sometimes fatal appeal
of pursuing these powerful beasts. The lure of the bear hunt is still
strong in men. We have found many reasons to pursue these animals,

Range of the Grizzly and Brown Bears

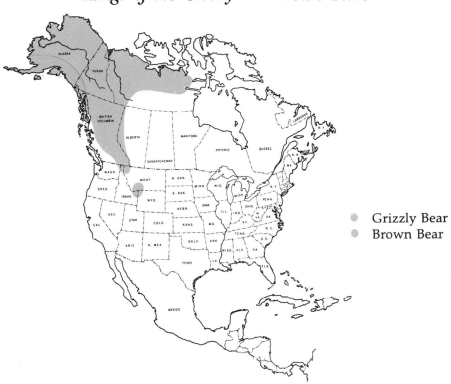

Grizzly Bear
Brown Bear

Range of the Black Bear

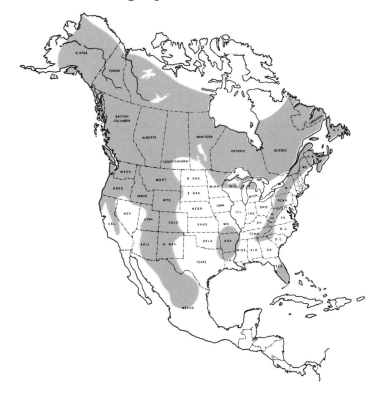

including the need for food, fur, and oil, and we have killed them in defense of our lives and property. Besides, bears have always been hunted for the thrill and excitement of the taking. Whether we hunt them or not, knowing that we are in the presence of bears adds spice to the outdoor adventure. Whenever we go where the wild bear lives, we feel a keen sharpening of the senses, an unforgettable level of alertness.

Especially when we walk in the land of the grizzly.

Chapter 2

The Grizzly Discovered

For early explorers pushing deep into the wild regions of this broad continent, each new day brought unforgettable discoveries of sweeping prairies, spectacular mountains, wild rivers, and amazing wildlife. We will never know who among these pioneering traders, trappers, and explorers became the first to encounter the grizzly bear. Francisco Vasquez de Coronado, as he rode north in 1540 into what would one day become New Mexico, then on across the plains to the north and east, must surely have seen these giant bears in the two years of his travels.

More than sixty years later, in the final weeks of 1602, grizzlies were recorded from the present site of Monterey, California, when explorer Sebastian Vizcaíno noted that bears came to feed on the carcass of a whale stranded on the beach. These bears, according to the late Dr. Tracy I. Storer, for thirty years Chairman of the Department of Zoology at the University of California, Davis, were certainly grizzlies. Black bears did not live in that part of California.

KELSEY'S JOURNEY

But still, word of these early discoveries of North America's largest carnivore did not reach the outside world. For another ninety years European people would know little about the giant bears found in the western half of the New World. Then came Henry Kelsey.

Kelsey was born in England in 1670 and was probably seventeen years old when he came to North America as an apprentice with the Hudson's Bay Company. Little was known about the vast untouched region beyond Hudson Bay, the region from which the furs came for shipment back to Europe.

Kelsey listened to the tales of the trappers, and made friends with the Indians living around the post. Hearing of the Arctic skies, thinning spruce-fir forests, open tundra where caribou and wolves roam, and lakes with giant trout and char, he began to dream of going north. The Hudson's Bay Company needed an agent to explore the distant North Country and young Kelsey attracted the attention of company executives.

The major problem was that the adventuresome Kelsey had no experience as a wilderness traveler. This, however, was corrected by a number of shorter trips until, in the summer of 1690, at the age of twenty, he was ready for his great adventure by foot and canoe into the unknown wilderness to the northwest.

For the next two years, he traveled through that wilderness, among the Indians, marveling at what he found. Kelsey kept a journal, sometimes writing in a kind of primitive verse, and what he wrote includes the earliest description we have in English of the grizzly bear. In one sense, Kelsey was like many who have encountered the grizzly bear, right up to recent times; whenever he spotted one of the giant bears, he wanted to reduce it to possession. Writing of the beast he said,

> Another is an outgrown Bear whc. is good meat
> His skin to gett I have used all the ways I can
> He is mans food & he makes food of man

LEWIS AND CLARK

The next important discoverers of the grizzly bears were still a century away. On April 28, 1805, Meriwether Lewis and William Clark were deep into their epic journey, moving along the Missouri River in what is now Montana, when one of the party fired on a brown, or yellow, bear. The animal was injured but not killed. Their early encounters with the grizzly soon impressed Lewis and Clark with the true nature of this beast whose hair was so grizzled and silver-tipped that they called it "the white bear". They had heard warnings from the Indians, but still lacked close personal experience with the great bear.

Here is the drama of one of their early encounters, according to

Lewis and Clark encountered the grizzly in the early 1800s, on their historic journey up the Missouri River and across the Rockies. Patrick Gass, a member of the expedition, made these drawings of two incidents he witnessed and included them in his journal, published in 1807.

Clark's journals as edited by Elliott Coues: "We proceeded early, with a moderate wind. Captain Lewis, who was on shore with one hunter, met about eight o'clock two white bears. Of the strength and ferocity of this animal the Indians had given us dreadful accounts. They never attack him but in parties of six or eight persons, and even then are often defeated with a loss of one or more of their party. Having no weapons but bows and arrows and the bad guns with which the traders supply them, they are obliged to approach very near to the bear; as no wound except through the head or heart is mortal, they frequently fall a sacrifice if they miss their aim. He rather attacks than avoids a man, and such is the terror which he has inspired, that the Indians who go in quest of him paint themselves and perform all the superstitious rites customary when they make war on a neighboring nation. Hitherto those bears we had seen did not appear desirous of encountering us; but although to a skillful rifleman the danger is very much diminished, yet the white bear is still a terrible animal. On approaching these two, both Captain Lewis and the hunter fired, and each wounded a bear. One of them made his escape; the other turned upon Captain Lewis and pursued him 70 or 80 yards, but being badly wounded the bear could not run so fast as to prevent him from reloading his piece, which he again aimed at him, and a third shot from the hunter brought him to the ground. He was a male, not quite full grown and weighed about 300 pounds."

Clark then adds his description of the grizzly bear. "The legs are somewhat longer than those of the black bear, and the talons and tusks are much larger and longer. The testicles are also placed much farther forward and suspended in separate pouches from two to four inches asunder, while those of the black bear are situated back between the thighs and in a single pouch like those of the dog. [Assuming that the animal Clark examined was typical, he was incorrect in this description of the grizzly bear's testicles.] Its color is a yellowish brown; the eyes are small, black, and piercing; the front of the fore legs near the feet is usually black, and the fur is finer, thicker, and deeper than that of the black bear. Add to which, it is a more furious animal, and very remarkable for the wounds which it will bear without dying."

Lewis and Clark may have over-emphasized the ferocity of the great bear. William H. Wright who hunted, studied, and understood the nature of these beasts, wrote in his book *The Grizzly Bear* that the grizzly does not actually seek trouble. "On the contrary," he added, "we have seen plainly enough that the white pioneers, even before they had seen a grizzly, were prepared to meet a dragon, and that, when they peppered a tough old bear or two with their pea-gun ammunition, they found their expectations realized."

From the first grizzlies they met, the Lewis and Clark party seemed unable to resist any opportunity to shoot at the great bears. On a day in May they were moving up the Missouri in their boats when they spotted a large grizzly bear lying in the open three hundred yards from the river. Six of the party's best hunters hurried off in pursuit.

Hidden by a low hill, they slipped up to within forty yards and from this distance four of them fired on the grizzly while the other two held their fire in reserve. Two of the balls went all the way through the bear, piercing both lungs, but the grizzly leaped to his feet and charged the hunters anyhow. The two hunters who had held their fire now took careful aim and shot. One of the balls broke the bear's shoulder, but these shots only served to confirm the hunters location for the grizzly which continued to charge them at frightening speed.

The two hunters, now fleeing for their lives, dropped their muzzleloaders and raced for the river with the bear at their heels. They dived without ceremony or hesitation from the top of the twenty foot cliff into the Missouri River, and the bear went right in after them, splashing heavily into the water and almost submerging the second man. By this time, one of the first to shoot had reloaded and, from the elevation of the bank, now put a ball through the furious grizzly's head. When they dragged the bear from the water and butchered him, they found that eight balls had passed through his body in various directions.

A month or so later, a huge grizzly caught Captain Lewis with his rifle unloaded and ran him into the river before giving up the chase. Others of the party were pursued by the grizzlies also, causing Lewis to write, "I do not think it prudent to send one man alone on an errand of any kind." But even where other game was plentiful, and the bears were not especially needed for food or oil, members of the party continued to attack any grizzly bear they met.

Even after Lewis and Clark met and described the grizzly bear, not much information on the beast reached the general citizen. It remained for the first of the famous beaver-trapping mountain men, who followed closely on the heels of Lewis and Clark, to begin bringing back to St. Louis and the rest of the world new tales about this magnificient bear and its fearsome strength and daring. In 1819 and 1820, Stephen H. Long made an expedition into the Rocky Mountains, then reported on the journey for the government. Included were his descriptions of the grizzly.

"This animal is widely distinct from any known species of bear," wrote Long, "by the essential character of the elongated anterior claws, and rectilinear or slightly articulated figure of its facial profile. The

Hunting of the Grizzly Bear *by Karl Bod-*
mer, a Swiss artist who traveled up the Missouri
with an expedition in the 1830s. Bodmer painted
many scenes of Indian life in the West.

Grizzly Bears Attacking Buffalo by George Catlin. A portrait painter in New York City, Catlin went West in 1832 to study and paint Indians. He also made a number of paintings of grizzly bears. In this one his rendering of the bears is not very accurate.

grizzly bear is not exclusively carnivorous, as has by some persons been imagined; but also, and perhaps in a still greater degree, derives nourishment from vegetables, both fruits and roots; the latter he digs up by means of his long fore-claws.''

PATTIE IN THE SOUTHWEST

One additional early mention of grizzlies may deserve mention. James Ohio Pattie, a Kentuckian who made a trip of exploration across the Southwest beginning in 1824, laced his journals with lurid observations on the great bear. Pattie tells of the attack on his party's horses by a grizzly and the slow death of a fellow-traveler who was caught by the bear. The bear, according to Pattie, tore the flesh from the man's hip, bit and tore his head, broke his jaw, and punctured his windpipe, "the animal in his fury having placed his teeth and claws in every part of his body." Pattie himself terminated the attack by rushing in, placing the muzzle of his gun against the bear and shooting it. The bear died at once, its human victim five days later.

Pattie, like many mountain men, was never one to downplay a grizzly bear's ferocity. He tells of posting a twenty-man guard at night to "prevent the bears from coming in upon us." There can be no doubt that, in those early years, the grizzlies were common, and sometimes seasonally abundant where food supplies were concentrated. About this time too, as the party made its way up the Arkansas River, Pattie counted, "in the course of the day, two hundred and twenty white bears." Even in those years of the great bear's peak abundance, this would seem a banner day for bear watching. Assuming that Pattie

Grizzly Bear and Mouse *by George Catlin. The size of the huge bear is cleverly suggested by the comparison. Note the deadly claws.*

These two maps reveal the loss of the grizzly-bear population over half a century. The map above shows the distribution of the grizzly throughout the Rocky Mountains in 1922. The map opposite shows the remaining patches of bear populations in 1979.

traveled ten hours that day, he spotted an average of more than one grizzly every three minutes. There seems to be no other report in the literature that approaches this, and modern observers find the Pattie bear count for that remarkable day hard to accept.

Whatever the population, the bear's discovery by explorers, traders, and trappers was about to alter the world of the grizzly for all time. Soon, the future of the giant bear, so long dominant across the western half of this continent, would be in question.

Among the grizzly bear mysteries we have inherited is the question of how many of these creatures lived on this continent before the

white man arrived. There may have been, as some have speculated, a hundred thousand of them. Their range stretched from the arctic plains of Canada and Alaska to the mountains of Mexico and from the Pacific eastward to beyond the Mississippi. The western half of the continent was the land of the grizzly, the magnificent truculent beast that zoologist George Ord named *Ursus horribilis,* the horrible bear.

Within its broad range the grizzly bears varied in their appearance, and scientists split them into dozens of individual species. Dr. C. Hart Merriam, of the Smithsonian Institution and Chief of The U.S. Biological Survey, forerunner of the Fish and Wildlife Service, studying the differences between grizzly skulls in the National Museum, published his findings in 1918. He believed that there were at least eighty-six kinds of grizzly bears. Later, scientists decided that all these bears, as well as all other brown bears around the world, belong to a single species.

Throughout much of their range, in many parts of the world, the pressures from people have eliminated the bears, or reduced their numbers drastically. In North America the life and death contest between man and bear started, even before the earliest white people reached this continent.

Chapter 3

Bears and the First Americans

Age-old stories, passed by word of mouth from generation to generation, make it plain that prehistoric people treated the great bears with fear and respect. One legend tells us of an orphaned Eskimo, or Inuit, boy who lived with his aunt on the tundra, south of where the mighty Yukon River meanders across its wilderness delta and into the Bering Sea. The boy once paddled his kayak to a strange village and there the people held him prisoner, beat him, and mistreated him badly. When the boy reached home and told his aunt what had happened, she became very serious and instructed him to bring her a piece of wood.

She shaped the wood into the image of an animal with long teeth and long sharp claws, then painted it red and white, and carrying it to the edge of the stream, she wept and let her warm tears fall upon it. The old lady then placed the totem in the water telling it, "Go and kill the bad people who beat my boy."

The strange carving floated straight across the creek, and crawled up the other bank. There it began to grow and soon it was a gigantic red bear. The bear went to the village where the boy was mistreated and killed everyone he saw. Then one day he came back and stood on the creek bank where he had first come to life. He clawed the ground, and growled, and chomped. He made a terrible noise and showed his long white teeth. Then he began to cross the stream.

The villagers saw the angry beast coming and quickly sent for the woman and pleaded with her to keep her bear from killing them all. She took the bear by the scruff of the neck and told it not to hurt these kind people. She led the bear to her house, sat down with him and explained that she was pleased with what he had accomplished but that he must not injure people anymore unless they tried to hurt him. Since this time there have always been red bears.

This legend, in an official 1899 publication of the Smithsonian Institution, is one of countless bear stories, ceremonies, songs, dances, and customs created by earlier cultures that occupied North America. Their legends tell us plainly that the great bears were the most terrifying of all the wild animals around them.

Even talking about the barrenlands grizzly was considered dangerous by the people of the Barrow, Alaska, region, and one thing the prudent person never said was, "I am not afraid of the brown bear," because, no matter how great the distance the bear would hear it, seek out the braggart and attack him.

The bear caught in a trap was not to be killed by shooting it with arrows. Guns too, once they were added to the northern hunter's arsenal, were supposed never to be used on the great bear. Instead, the hunter, finding a grizzly in his trap, drew his knife and engaged the bear in close combat.

This put the Eskimo hunter into a situation where he often suffered severe mauling and biting, but there was a procedure that promised him fast recovery: a companion, according to legend, must wrap the injured hunter in the skin of the slain bear. Then the wounds would surely heal.

Any deviation from this procedure placed the hunter in extreme jeopardy, and the Inuit reinforced the story by relating examples showing what could happen to the hunter who insulted the bear. One hunter captured a bear in his trap and, instead of dealing with it with his knife, tried to subdue it with his rifle. However, he succeeded in only wounding it and the bear, even with the trap dragging and banging along behind it, quickly overtook the man and gave him a thorough mauling and biting before the hunter killed it with a final shot. If ever there was a time to wrap a friend in the skin of a bear, this was it, but his neighbors wanted no part of this frightening case and refused even to skin the bear. The mauled hunter soon died.

One who came to understand the sensitivity of these northern people toward the great bear was an ethnologist, Robert F. Spencer, who worked among the northern Alaskan Eskimos in the early 1950's. His base was the village of Barrow on the shores of the Arctic Ocean. The people he interviewed were old enough to remember stories handed down in their society over the centuries and tales of grizzlies were plentiful in their folklore.

According to Spencer's report, published by the Smithsonian Institution, the great bear was seen as the most intelligent of the Arctic's creatures and was believed to possess mystic powers against which people had ceremonies to protect them from the bear's wrath. Spencer learned, for example, that these northern people had taboos they must follow when they ate the flesh of the brown bear and to flaunt these sacred rules was to court disaster from the supernatural. Women were forbidden to eat of the brown bear at all, and if men ate the flesh of the grizzly or brown bear, the meat must be cooked in the place where the bear fell. Furthermore, the man who ate of the brown bear must not have sexual intercourse for several days, the duration of his abstinence depending on the sex of the bear.

Bear Dance, Preparing for a Bear Hunt *by George Catlin. For the Indians, a bear hunt was a group affair; they often prepared for it by painting their bodies and dancing.*

To the south, each Indian tribe had its own customs and traditions involving the grizzlies. But even a hunter who avoided the great bear might find himself in an unintentional confrontation. The plains Indians captured eagles to obtain ceremonial feathers, and a common eagle hunting method was for the warrior to crouch in a pit, covered with grass and leaves. On top of the covering was a jackrabbit secured by a thong, attached to the hunter's wrist, so the attacking eagle could be dragged into the pit and subdued by hand. One warrior was in the pit, waiting for an eagle, when a grizzly lunged at the rabbit. The bear tore the top from the pit and killed the man.

Some Indian tribes believed that warriors could gain permanent gifts of courage by eating vital parts of the grizzly bear. Chief Plenty Coups, leader of the Crow Indians, once told of the day the young boys of his group were called together by his grandfather, Coyote-appears, who had, the day before, killed a grizzly. Standing before the awed boys, Coyote-appears held high the dark red heart of the giant bear. Every boy present knew what he must do, and each of them ate a small portion of the heart as others of their people had done many times before. Afterward, each of them could always claim that he had the heart of the grizzly bear. Years later, after he adopted the ways of the white man and lived in a cabin, the aging white-haired Chief Plenty Coups still reminded himself in difficult times, "I have the heart of a grizzly bear."

The most practical and perhaps sensible approach toward sound relationships with the grizzly may have been developed by the Chemehuevis of southern California. These Indians simply declared that they had a standing pact of friendship with all bears. A member of the tribe, when meeting a bear in the mountains always remembered to speak to the bear as "my friend." Addressed in this manner, said the Chemehuevis, the bear lost its hostility at once.

A grizzly bear hunt was typically a group affair. The individual Indian hunter, carrying Stone Age weapons, saw no future in going after a grizzly by himself. Before tackling the great bear these hunters often painted their bodies and prepared for the hunt with special ceremonies. According to a 1916 report on "The Societies of the Plains Indians" by the American Museum of Natural History, in olden times, when a bear was located, the hunter would approach it, saying to the bear, "I am thankful that I found you and sorry that I am obliged to kill you." He attempted to make the situation more palatable to the bear by offering a sacrifice of berries and maple sugar to its spirit. In addition, he cut off the dead bear's nose and kept it for a later sacrifice. Then the head and the brisket, as well as the four paws, were cut off and cooked and this became the basis of a feast for the hunter's guests.

During the feast, an elder of the tribe would explain to the gods that this hunter had killed the bear out of need, after which all the people seemed to relax and everyone ate without fear of retribution by the spirit of the bear.

When the feast was over, the hunter still did not neglect his duties to the spirit of the animal. He carried the nose of the animal, plus assorted other sacrificial offerings, into the forest and hung them up in a secret place.

An Unequal Combat *by H.H. Cross. The artist vividly depicted the ferocity of the grizzly when cornered. It may take three Indians to subdue the bear, but one will not survive.*

Indians on Horseback with Lances *by George Catlin. Here the artist captured the excitement and drama of a bear hunt on horseback using only lances.*

Indians everywhere harbored strong beliefs about any bear, grizzly or black. In at least one tribe, children were prohibited from eating the bear's paws for fear the impressionable youngsters might acquire the bear's savage nature.

Some tribes, including the Maidu people of northern California's mountains, so firmly believed that we are what we eat that they refused to consume the flesh of the grizzly bear because these bears ate people and to eat them, in turn, would be tantamount to cannibalism. There was also a reluctance to eat bears because the body of the bear, especially once it is skinned, resembles that of a human, a feeling that, to this day, is shared by some modern people.

The Chippewas had their own elaborate ceremony of worship for any bear they killed and this was typical of many tribes. Once a Chippewa hunter had killed a bear, he spread a blanket and on it placed the animal's severed head along with its hide. He then decorated the head with beads and ribbons while the body, instead of being carelessly chopped up, was carefully taken apart at the joints in a show of respect, and at the ceremonial feast, all present ate some of the bear. Then, alongside the body of the animal, the people laid out a fine costume, woman's clothes for a female bear and men's for a male, while elaborate assurances were made to the bear that, all bears falling to Chippewa hunters would likewise be shown this respect. Finally, the bones, cleaned of their meat, were carefully gathered and buried.

One group of California Indians who used the hide of the grizzly in ceremonies planned their hunts for early spring when the lethargic bears were about to emerge from their winter dens. The hunt began as the warriors assembled before the den and explained to the grizzly that the time had come for it to come out and stand up where they could get a good shot. By this time, the hunters were all hiding as best they could behind trees. The battle began when one of them ran close to the bear and shot it with an arrow or two before scampering at full speed to the hiding place of hunter number two, who would then take his turn putting arrows into the grizzly before leading it, in turn, to the next hunter. If the hunt went according to plan, the men all escaped injury while the bear, who had become something of a pin cushion, eventually staggered and fell.

Because of its importance in the lives of the Indians, the bear was a popular choice of groups choosing a totem after which to name themselves. According to historian Warren W. William, the Ojibwas of the northern Great Lakes country contained a bear family which was the biggest group within the tribe. The bears were the Smiths of their time. The bear clan, according to the *History of the Ojibwa Nation,* was also known as the most fearless and daring of their people. A

This bear fetish, in the Cincinnati Museum of Natural History, was considered by its Zuni Indian owner to possess special mysterious powers capable of promoting his welfare as long as he worshipped it.

person could acquire membership in the bear clan only by birth.

There were also bear cults in many tribes, and the bear cult was a kind of fraternal organization. with a limited membership that could not be passed on as a heritage. Membership in a bear cult was usually restricted to people who had a special dream involving bear power.

Often the members of the bear cult were the boldest in battle, the strongest, and the most feared even within their own tribes. It was said that they assumed some of the nature of the grizzly itself, were mean-tempered and always itching for a fight. Among the Blackfeet, any hunter coming home with meat might be at the mercy of the bear cult. If the Bears ran out to stop the hunter, he simply stood by silently while the Bears helped themselves to the finest choice cuts, or perhaps the whole carcass. Sometimes, the owner of the meat voluntarily gave the Bears, not only the freshly killed meat, but meekly presented them also his horse and gun. The Bears carried the meat home and spread the word that presents had been received.

Wherever there were bear cults among the tribes they seemed to have similar powers. They were mighty warriors in battle and they possessed the abilities to cure sickness—or at least to treat it.

These people, who gained their status by first dreaming of bear power, had various symbols of their standing and often used these in

their ceremonies. Depending on the tribe, and perhaps the taste and skill of the individual, the Bear warrior might have a special mask worn for ceremonies or for attending the sick. A Bear shamman of the Blackfeet people was described by artist George Catlin in 1832, as wearing a mask made from the actual head of a grizzly bear.

Catlin once painted a picture of the medicine man administering

Assinboin Camp *by Karl Bodmer. In this picture, the Swiss artist showed a tipi with a bear painted on the side, indicating that its occupants were members of a bear cult.*

his brand of aid and comfort to a sick tribesman. The medicine man, in addition to the bear head mask, wore the skin of the bear, complete with the claws dangling from his wrists and ankles. Carrying a rattle in one hand and a special spear in the other, he leaped about while issuing the grunts, growls, chomps, and snarls of the grizzly bear as he pawed and rolled the patient over and over, as Catlin wrote, "in

Medicine Man, Performing His Mysteries Over a Dying Man *by George Catlin.*
Evidently a member of a bear cult, the medicine man wears a bear head mask and bearskin
complete with claws.

every direction." What happened to the patient? In the case Catlin witnessed, the stricken one died.

A member of the bear cult in some tribes might live in his special tipi with a bear painted on either side of the doorway. He usually wore a bear claw necklace and might also own a special bear knife made with a handle fashioned from a bear jaw. The necklace of bear claws was the most treasured symbol of bravery and the most prized possession of the warrior who owned it. The bear knife was also highly prized and was carried into battle for use in close combat. In addition, the Bear warrior might carry a shield showing the image of a bear, and be dressed in special clothing denoting his membership in the bear cult.

When there was no war for the bear cult member to participate in, he might find an outlet for his energies in a special ceremony or feast because the bear dance was a highly important part of certain celebrations in many tribes. This was a dance to welcome the coming of spring, and for other special purposes.

There are numerous legends of how the bear dance was created. One of these appeared in the *American Anthropologist* in 1896. "Long ago the bear was a person. He went about alone and found a cottonwood stump . . . So he danced back and forth, originating the Bear dance." He returned to his village, told the others about his new dance and they liked it but were too bashful to practice it. The Bear did not like this so he said, "I want you to have this dance while I am still inside my house in the winter time. I won't allow it in the summer. If you perform it then, I shall be very angry." The bear further explained that he liked big crowds, that other people should be invited in and that the dancing and feast should last four days.

Another explanation traces the Ute Bear dance to a minor family squabble. "The Indian had a wife and during the performance she danced with a young man. When the dance was over the husband took a club and knocked her down. The Bear came and said to the man, 'I did not tell you to hurt your wife, I told you to be good and to tell the other Indians not to hurt their wives.' He pulled the man outside his lodge and struck him with his paws. The man howled and promised not to hurt his wife thereafter." The man later held another Bear dance during which he was kind to his wife and this is how the Bear dance began.

The real purpose of the bear dance appears to have been to placate the powerful animals and protect the people from harm by bears during the coming season. One person explained, "If you celebrate the ceremony every spring, the Bear will know it and will not bother you

The White Cloud, Head Chief of the Iowas *by George Catlin (opposite page). A necklace of bear claws was the most treasured symbol of bravery. The Winnebago chief in the photo above also wears such a necklace.*

when you are hunting in the mountains. If you do not, he may hurt you. To this was added another condition which may have been inserted by a woman. "If any one won't dance with the woman who chooses him for a partner, the Bear will bite him and is liable to kill him."

Perhaps no tribe reached greater heights of stagecraft in performing bear ceremonies than the Kwakiutl Indians of the Northwest Coast. Their favorite dance portrayed the events that followed the kidnapping of one of their high ranking chiefs. The performance was staged at night with only the dancing shadows of an open fire for illumination.

The kidnapped chief returns. But now his body is possessed by the Cannibal Spirit and the audience is filled with terror. There is only one way to satisfy the spirit's unspeakable hunger: the chief must be fed a human corpse. At this point, the bear, and a bit of subterfuge, figure into the ceremony. The smoked carcass of a small black bear, fitted with a head resembling that of a person, is substituted for the human body. The dancer who has been scurrying about threatening the audience and sometimes actually biting skin from peoples' arms, consumes part of the bear and all relax somewhat when the drama ends with the Canibal Spirit satiated.

Whether the native people met the bear in the forest, in the berry patch, beside the salmon fishing stream, in a dream, or in a ceremonial dance, they could never escape the fact that the bear was always nearby, either in body or spirit.

Chapter 4

The Nature of the Grizzly

O nce you meet the grizzly bear in its own wild country you will always remember what the encounter does to you, the flow of adrenalin, the beating of your heart, and the way the hairs on the back of your neck rise. Even the finding of a broad track in the dust where the grizzly walked is an unforgettable experience. Suddenly you know that you are in the home territory of the most powerful and unpredictable beast on the continent, one that never has really adapted to the human presence and does not give ground gracefully to any creature, human or otherwise.

Both the speed and strength of the giant bear are unbelievable. Never assume that a bear, lacking the trim lines of deer or antelope, is slow afoot. The animal's powerful muscles can push it along at racehorse speed, covering ground at perhaps twice the speed of the human trying to escape. Furthermore, the grizzly can barrel, tanklike, through thick brush that would bring a man to a complete halt, and the bear has stamina to keep up the race. One respected naturalist told of tracking a running grizzly for nearly ten miles.

In a single blow a large grizzly can break the neck of an ox or horse then drag it off if he chooses. Whether or not it is energy efficient we can't be sure, but the grizzly turns over rocks weighing a couple of hundred pounds in search of ants weighing almost nothing. It can enter a cabin through the door, window, roof, or even the side depending perhaps on its mood and where it is at the moment it makes the decision to go in. Once inside, the bear can puncture, crush, or take apart such objects as it chooses. It can crunch cans, squeezing food out the holes it has punctured. There are records of grizzly bears bending gun barrels and one even bit holes through a cast-iron skillet.

The relative sizes of the grizzly and the brown are shown in this drawing. The average grizzly weighs 400 to 600 pounds, the brown 800 to 1200, with occasional bears going up to 1500 pounds or more. The grizzly has a more pronounced shoulder hump and a shorter, dished face, but the skulls are almost identical.

PHYSICAL CHARACTERISTICS

You would probably recognize the great bear at once by the large hump he carries over his shoulders and the dished face that helps set the profile apart from the straight lines of the black bear's face. The grizzly is also known by the size and shape of its front claws, much longer, perhaps four inches long, heavier, and not so curved as those of the black bear. These are the great bear's digging tools as well as the hooks with which he can lift rocks and take logs apart.

The bear's fur is among the most effective insulating coats worn by any wild animal. The fur that serves bears so well in winter is heavy enough to give them cooling problems in summer because bears have no sweat glands and must lose heat through their slobbering tongues, or sometimes by taking refuge in a pool or stream.

The color of the grizzly helps to distinguish it, although this is not always a reliable characteristic because the colors of both black and grizzly bears vary widely. Generally speaking the grizzly is brownish but the shade may vary from pale blond to almost black. To some degree, the silver-tipped guard hairs, for which Old Silvertip got its name, may flash ripples of light when caught in the sun.

Size alone does not distinguish the grizzly. Mature grizzlies of the same region may vary in size, and females are normally smaller than the males. Most people, even experienced outdoorsmen, seem to have difficulty estimating the size of the grizzly bear with accuracy. The

This photo of a grizzly bear shows its characteristic hump, dished face, and extremely heavy fur. In coloration, the bear varies from brown, as here, to pale blond, to almost black.

A very fat, dark grizzly, photographed at the end of a summer's feeding, its claws glinting in the sun. With these tools, the bear digs in the ground, overturns rocks, and tears apart logs to find food.

grizzly is an imposing creature having a tendency to look larger than it is. There is a human "awe" factor involved, and as one observer stated it, the farther the bear is from a scales, the more it seems to weigh. Many of the weights recorded in round numbers—"this bear had to weigh a good eleven hundred pounds"—are suspect. Now and then there is a one-thousand-pound male grizzly, but the average large grizzly comes closer to four to six hundred pounds. Some adult females weigh less than two hundred pounds.

Largest of the species are those of the giant Alaska Kodiak, Peninsula, and Kamchatka (USSR) brown bear subspecies. Large males weigh as much as twelve hundred pounds, more than half a ton of bear in one package, and females weighing up to eight hundred pounds. These are huge and impressive beasts. Standing on its hind feet, a large male brown bear would tower over the tallest of professional basketball players and, in some cases, reach a height of eight and a half feet or more.

The life of the troubled grizzly bear has been studied by many people in recent times, but at least two earlier pioneering naturalists left accounts of their observations and experiences from a time when the bears were more numerous. One of these was William H. Wright. Born on a New Hampshire farm in 1856, Wright became fascinated with bears of all kinds before he was old enough to read, and his interest was so compelling that later he went west and became a noted hunter of grizzlies.

His hunting career peaked one day when he stalked two large bears and killed them with two shots from his twelve-pound, single-shot .45-100 Winchester. He then discovered a female grizzly and two large cubs behind him and shot these as well, five grizzly bears in five minutes and with five shots, which was, as he said, "The greatest bag of grizzlies that I have ever made single-handed."

That episode may have played a major role in changing Wright's relationship with the big bears he pursued. "In the beginning," he wrote, "I studied the grizzly in order to hunt him. I marked his haunts and his habits, I took notice of his likes and dislikes; I learned his indifferences and his fears; I spied upon the perfection of his senses and the limitations of his instincts, simply that I might the better slay him. For many a year, and in many a fastness of the hills, I pitted my shrewdness against his, and my wariness against his, and my endurance against his; and many a time I came out winner in the game, and many a time I owned myself the loser. And then at last my interest in my opponent grew to overshadow my interest in the game. I had studied the grizzly to hunt him. I came to hunt him in order to study him. I laid aside my rifle."

Standing on its hind legs, a grizzly is a fearsome-looking beast.

In those years, Wright also made some of the earliest photographs of grizzly bears. In his book, first published in 1909, Wright described the grizzly bear as he saw it, compared it and its track with that of the black bear, and proved himself such a keen observer that three-quarters of a century later, most of his findings are still viewed as sound.

"I have met the grizzly under many circumstances and in many places", Wright said. "I have hunted him where he has been but little disturbed, and had seldom come into contact with man, and I have seen him change his habits as his range was encroached upon and his existence threatened. But I have never found him the ferocious and ill-natured brute that he has the reputation of being. On the contrary, I have always found him wary and alert, ready to give one the slip if possible and able to tax one's ingenuity in matching his cunning."

Wright explained, however, that it would be risky to assume that the grizzly will not fight if he considers it necessary, and that when the grizzly charges, anyone close to him is in real danger. In dealing with the grizzly, one must always assume that the individual facing him might charge instead of run away. There is no way of knowing in advance how the grizzly will respond to a close encounter with a human.

Another naturalist who studied the grizzly in depth in those years, when there were still vigorous populations of the bears, was Enos A. Mills, who also wrote a book about his thirty years of following the grizzly trails. Mills, who traveled alone and unarmed in grizzly country, wrote that he did not find the grizzly to be "ferocious". "I have repeatedly been outwitted by him," Mills wrote, "but never has he attacked me." These early observations contrast with some of the more recent attacks by grizzly bears, leaving us to wonder how much the nature of the grizzly has changed through its conditioning to the presence of people and the relentless invasion of the great bear's last strongholds.

Mills once had the opportunity to watch three nearly grown, but weaned, cubs whose loyalty to each other gave them an added degree of survival value. One day two men spotted one of the cubs and shot it, but not fatally. The other two cubs surprised the hunters and while one of the young bears put a hunter up the nearest tree minus his gun and missing one ripped off legging, the other cub rolled the second hunter into a ravine, cracked two of his ribs and cut him in the thigh. Then all three cubs made their escape together through the brush.

A month later the trio of experienced cubs met a trapper on a mountain trail, panicked his pack horse and sent the trapper up the nearest tree. This was too much for the trapper, who promptly set a steel trap and baited it with a chunk of well-aged meat.

A pale blond grizzly with a dark cub. The bear gives birth during her denning period, and the cubs stay close to their mother during their first year.

A couple of days later he caught one of the cubs by the toes of one foot. As the trapper approached, he was charged by two healthy young bears rushing him from the nearby bushes, and once more he went up a tree.

Meanwhile, the trapped cub dragged the log to which the trap was anchored, until it lodged between two trees. He kept on pulling until he separated himself from the trap as well as the toes caught in it, then all three bears once more escaped into the forest. The three cubs, now thoroughly conditioned to people, were seen together several times during the following months, but not taken. "It is not known", wrote Mills, "when or where these three loyal cub explorers finally parted."

LIFE CYCLE OF THE GRIZZLY

Life for grizzly bear cubs, begins in midwinter, probably in January when the mother is secure in her winter quarters. For decades there was only speculation about the details surrounding the movement of grizzlies to their winter quarters. Then, in 1959 noted wildlife scientists Dr. John Craighead and his brother Dr. Frank Craighead, Jr., working with their colleagues, with the approval of the National Park Service, began their pioneering study of the grizzly bears of Yellowstone National Park and the surrounding national forest lands. Using a technique then in its infancy, they live-trapped grizzlies, anesthetized them, then equipped them with collars carrying miniature radio transmitters. With the aid of radio receivers and directional antennae, they followed the movements of the bears day and night, uncovering new details about the grizzly bear's habits and travels. The Craigheads and their associates logged thirty thousand hours, radio tracking several dozen Yellowstone grizzlies and recording information on populations, food habits, travels, associations with people, and other details about the lives of these threatened bears.

The Craigheads learned from their radio tracking that when the time comes to go to the winter den, many grizzlies seem to get the message at the same time. Retiring to winter quarters often occurred during a heavy snow storm, perhaps on a stormy night in November, giving the bear the advantage of having its tracks quickly obliterated. The bear normally moves to a previously prepared den on a steep slope, or beneath the roots of a tree or under rocks. The bear often lines the den with grass.

During the following days the lethargic bear gradually becomes increasingly comatose as the heart beat and breathing slow, and the rate of metabolism is reduced. During the long winter sleep, perhaps

for six months, the bear will not eat, defecate, or urinate, and the only nourishment and water it gets will come from the layers of fat it carried into the den.

Its long winter sleep sees it through the season of low food supplies. Arctic winds sweep over the slopes, blankets of snow settle over the land, animals are scarce, and plants stop growing, but the great bear is secure until spring brings on the next season of growth.

Once settled in, the bear drifts off into a sleep that lasts intermittently all winter. It grooms and adjusts the interior of its den for comfort or temperature control, then sleeps for long periods. The hibernating bear, however, can usually be awakened and, if disturbed in his sleep, may come scrambling out of the den.

In April or May when the bear finally rouses from its winter sleep and emerges from its den it is not, as one might expect, ravenous. Instead of rushing off in search of nourishment, the bear usually wanders about, still living off its body fat. The body temperature, metabolism, and heart beat may still not be back to normal as the animal moves about sleepily in what some say is a walking hibernation.

Then gradually the bear begins to feed, perhaps on the carcasses of winter killed elk or other large animals, then the tender new root growth of spring plants.

The female commonly gives birth, during her denning period, to two cubs although the number may vary from one to four. For a mother weighing three or four hundred pounds, the young are remarkably small at birth. Each new-born cub will weigh about fourteen ounces and be blind and nearly hairless. It snuggles into the warm fur of the mother and grows there on her milk until time for the family to emerge from the den in the spring.

During their first summer the young bears stay close to their mother and in their first autumn, they den with her. The following spring, when they are in their second year, some of the young will go off on their own, freeing the female to breed again and begin another family. Often, however, young grizzly bears stay with the mother most or part of a second year and she skips two years without new cubs.

This grizzly is wearing a special collar equipped with a miniature radio transmitter which permits scientists to monitor its movements. This was the technique pioneered by Drs. John and Frank Craighead when they studied Yellowstone Park bears from 1959 to 1971.

A grizzly sow nursing her cubs. A new-born cub weighs about fourteen ounces and is blind and hairless. The mother nurses her cubs through the winter until spring.

Male and female grizzlies normally live apart, except for a few weeks in June when the females come into estrus. The female will accept the company of the male about every third summer and, although the two may stay together, their liaison is tenuous because bears are notably polygamous. The female sometimes accepts two different males in the same day.

Early June is the peak of the mating season for Yellowstone grizzlies, although they may breed from mid-May through early July. The

Craighead studies show that, although female grizzlies as young as three and a half years old may copulate, they usually do not have their first litters until they are at least five and a half. This, plus the fact that their litters come three years or more apart, and that they raise only two or three young per litter, makes it clear that grizzly bears lack the reproductive capacity to replace quickly any sizable loss in numbers. The female may do no more than replace herself the first ten years of her life.

A pair of cubs, their mother in the background, pose by a sign indicating how high grizzlies will climb to reach food.

Grizzly cubs exhibit the instinct for play early, and often can be seen scuffling together like puppies or kittens.

Although some grizzlies in the wild may live to be thirty years old or more, and a grizzly in the Omaha Zoo lived to be forty-four, the average life expectancy, after the loss of young bears is factored in, is closer to five or six years. Once the grizzly bear reaches maturity, it has little to fear from predators, except for man, and their survival rate is high. Nonetheless, any bear past twenty is old.

The home range of the grizzly bear can take the animal over broad expanses of wild country. While the female usually makes her home in a range of twenty to thirty square miles, the male may wander freely over a thousand square miles as he searches for mates and food. When harvesting seasonal foods, however, the bear may remain in the same area for days or weeks at a time. Unlike many wild animals, they do not defend large home territories.

FEEDING

Wherever he roams, food is the key to the grizzly bear's travels, and his choice of foods depends on what is available. The bear, although classed as a carnivore, is an omnivore as surely as man is; an opportunist, consuming both plants and animals ranging from roots to seeds, ants to elk, and what the bear eats depends on what the seasons offer and the moment provides.

On occasion the grizzly may kill large animals. Some individuals are apparently more skilled predators on big game than others are. Killing large animals can be hazardous, even for a grizzly bear. Several years ago in Yellowstone National Park's Lamar Valley, rangers came upon a female grizzly bear that had been killed. There was evidence of a fight with enough footprints and fur to tell the story. The bear had two holes in one side spaced as they should be if a young buffalo gored it. Furthermore, all the bear's ribs on one side were broken. There was no sign of other animals, and this was apparently at least one instance in which the buffalo came up winners. Research in Yellowstone, and observations elsewhere, indicate that today's grizzly, although capable of killing buffalo, does not commonly tackle adult bison.

Grizzly bears can and do attack and kill elk, deer, and moose, especially the young. But they also readily feed on the carcasses of these animals found dead from other causes. The bears become part of the "clean up crew" in spring when large animals that died during the winter are exposed in the melting snow.

The grizzly more commonly attacks miniature prey. A six hundred pound grizzly bear may be seen leaping about in a meadow,

pouncing on grasshoppers, mice, ground squirrels, or licking up a line of ants. The percentage of vegetable matter far exceeds the animal matter consumed. Biologists believe that there are at least two hundred species of North American plants harvested by the grizzly bear. Among vegetable foods they are fond of the starchy roots of numerous plants but also feed on nuts, berries, and grass. Where fish are available, the experienced fishing grizzly pursues them with vigor and readily catches the slippery fish with its mouth. Fish are especially impor-

Although they kill and feed on elk, deer, and moose, grizzlies more often attack smaller prey. The bear at left is about to pounce on a ground squirrel, while the one above devours its prey.

SOME FAVORITE FOODS OF THE GRIZZLY BEAR

Winter-killed Elk

Grass

Blueberries

Spring Flowers

tant seasonal foods where the bears can intercept migrating fish moving through shallow waters.

Bears tend to avoid other non-related bears as they roam their territories. The mature males are loners. Females with cubs must defend their young against old males that, given the opportunity, will kill them. The only bears that travel together are breeding pairs or family groups, either females with cubs or cubs that are weaned but still together.

A concentrated food supply, however, may bring the bears together from miles around to feed on winter-killed animals, garbage in a dump, or migrating fish. Before Yellowstone's dumps were closed, fifty or more bears, both grizzly and black, sometimes gathered to feed at these un-natural food concentrations. Where bear foods are concentrated, whether a patch of ripe berries or a community garbage dump, the bears may assemble from the surrounding hills, because of the food and not because they want to be together. "I have seen as many as nine grizzlies in one berry patch", said Wright, "and as many as five fishing on one riffle of a salmon stream; but they not only came and went singly, but while there, they gave no outward sign of mutual recognition." When concentrated at such food sources, however, the bears establish their own pecking order with dominant individuals in control.

Under normal conditions berries are a staple in the summer diet. In some areas the yield of huckleberries may even influence the grizzly bear birth rate, with females sometimes bearing fewer cubs in years following poor crops of berries. Later, for the grizzlies of the Rocky Mountains, the seed of the whitebark pine becomes important bear food, and in seasons when there is a poor crop of pine nuts the bears may wander more widely.

Instead of harvesting their own pine nuts, the grizzlies seek out the places where the nuts and cones have been stored by the pine squirrels and rob the squirrels as long as the supply lasts, sometimes returning repeatedly to the same food cache. Research biologist Katherine Kendall, working in Yellowstone National Park, observed the bears feeding on pine nuts and described their technique. To get the nuts, they broke the cones both by biting them and stepping on them. Then the broken parts were spread out and licked up so the nutritious nutmeats could be swallowed while the bear forced the inedibles out the sides of its mouth.

Foraging on these small items, and needing to lay on maximum amounts of body fat to see them through the winter, the grizzly bear must feed busily for long hours through the late summer and autumn. A failure of the pine nut crop in Yellowstone can present the big bear

Evidently grizzlies continue to play even as they grow older. These grown bears were seen playing in the river, splashing around and apparently having a good time.

with a crisis and in these times the far-ranging grizzlies may show up around campgrounds and be seen more frequently by people.

We seldom think of grizzly bears, massive truculent beasts, as being capable of their own moments of light-hearted fun, but Enos Mills once watched a giant grizzly he called "Timberline" play in the snow. Observing from a wooded ledge, Mills saw the bear come to a steep slope, sit down, put his hands on his knees and begin sliding down. The bear dropped over a five foot ledge, recovered, and went on sliding, gaining speed until he reached a paw behind him and applied it as a brake then, still gaining speed, flipped over and dug in his claws until he slowed.

Once more the bear assumed the sitting position and shoved off downhill by making backward strokes with both front paws. He slid a hundred feet or so, lost control, and began tumbling, which seemed not to worry him at all, because he then climbed halfway back up the hill and took another slide.

"All grizzlies are scouts of the first order," wrote Mills. "They are ever on guard. When at rest, their senses do continual sentinel duty, and when traveling, they act exactly as though they believed some man was in pursuit."

SENSES

The senses of a bear, with one exception, are not outstanding. Its vision is average and its hearing fairly good, but the bear's nose is superior. A naturalist once watched from hiding as a large grizzly fed along a mountain slope. Occasionally a rock, loosened by the spring thaw, would roll down the hill, but the bear paid scant attention. Then the naturalist purposely rolled a rock toward the grizzly. The great bear walked over and carefully sniffed the rock. He stood up, looked up the hill then lowered himself to all fours and ran. He was still running when the man last saw him, and the naturalist could only assume that the rock had carried the odor of human hands. The olfactory sense of the bears ranks among the keenest in the animal world. A black bear in northern California was once seen to travel upwind three miles in a straight line to reach the carcass of a dead deer.

The bear can see better and get a better reading on the odor that alerts it by standing tall on its hind feet. Up there, a few feet higher, the air moves faster than it does where the bear's nose is at ground level.

This habit of standing up to check out clues has brought death to many a grizzly because the standing bear is a frightening presence as well as an easy target. Many outdoorsmen who did not know better have assumed that the standing bear is attacking. But only in the movies do bears attack by walking on their hind legs. The bear that is going to attack gets down on all fours and charges with its head lowered. From that position it can attain maximum speed and power.

This then, was the independent wilderness king that met the mountain men and other early adventurers coming to the western part of North America.

To use its sense of smell and sight to best advantage, the grizzly often stands on its hind feet.
In this position it can sniff the faster-moving air for any scent of food or danger.

Chapter 5

Grizzly Meets the Mountain Man

Throughout much of the West, the first white men to invade the world of the grizzly bear were those coming in search of beaver. This flat-tailed creature, largest of American rodents, was the prime source of felt for making hats, and in the early 1800s the world of commerce needed a hundred thousand beaver a year to cover the heads of gentlemen and some not so gentle.

This was no new development. Hats fashioned from felt made of the wool from beaver skins had been popular for centuries, but the people of Europe had used up their beavers and now had to look to the American fur trade for new supplies. On this continent, the animals seemed to be unlimited, but no one knew how great the supply might be because so much of the West was still unknown and unmapped.

This was one of the factors prompting Thomas Jefferson to dispatch Meriwether Lewis and William Clark on their Voyage of Discovery. Among other instructions, they were ordered to explore the possibilities of building the fur trade in the West. Their journey became the first chapter in the saga of the mountain men who were drawn to the wilderness beyond the Mississippi, where the grizzly bear reigned in a position of absolute dominance.

These rugged and independent beaver trappers were perhaps the finest outdoorsmen this continent ever knew, their outdoor skills according to some historians even surpassing those of the native people. Many of them came originally from the wilds of the Appalachians where their Scotch-Irish families had pushed back the frontier to establish new homes in the deep forested hollows. They were typically

Mountain Man Joe Walker *by A. J. Miller. Mountain men were rugged and independent beaver trappers whose survival skills were said to surpass even those of the Indians.*

uneducated, brave, brash, and highly skilled in shooting, woodcraft, and living off the land. Sometimes in brigades and sometimes alone, they spent the next few decades pushing into every Rocky Mountain drainage they could find in search of more beaver, and in this manner the mountain men set the stage for opening the great bear's range.

There were no stores, villages, or mail routes where these men

went. They were soon beyond the throaty call of the steamboat whistle, beyond the clatter of wagonwheels on cobblestones, beyond the laughter of children, and into a land of trees, prairies, and wild creatures—a land so broad it was measured in mountain ranges and months of travel.

The mountain man who cut loose from the brigades to become an independent trapper was as nearly free as a man could ever be. He lived and worked beyond the frontier, where there was no one to say where he might go or what he must do. As long as he could survive the hazards, the mountain man had the world to himself. "His nerves must ever be in a state of tension," wrote George F. Ruxton, "and his mind ever present at his call. His eagle eye sweeps around the country, and in an instant detects any foreign appearance. A turned leaf, a blade of grass pressed down, the uneasiness of the wild animals, the flight of birds, are paragraphs to him written in nature's legible hand and plainest language."

The mountain man was self-sufficient. His little collection of possibles included powder, tobacco, salt, knife, and gun. Content with his diet of meat, on a typical day he tasted no bread and savored no vegetables. He survived instead on buffalo, preferably fat cow which was his choice of the herd, cooked in the glowing embers and carved with a butcher knife into slabs from which he chewed while the juices ran down his unkempt beard.

These men in pursuit of beaver discovered wonders new to white people, found new routes through the mountains, and opened the West for the developers who would follow. Inevitably, the grizzly bear would meet these strangers, because the nature of the mountain man's work took him where the big bears lived. Trapper Osborne Russell once wrote of the grizzly in his journal, when trapping in Montana, "I have frequently seen 7 or 8 standing about the clumps of Cherry bushes on their hind legs gathering cherries with surprising dexterity not even deigning to turn their heads to gaze at the passing trapper but merely casting a sidelong glance at him without altering their position."

But the trappers would not allow the grizzlies to roam the plains and mountains in freedom. The average mountain man considered any grizzly to be a source of supplies, as well as an opportunity to test his daring and his shooting skills.

EXPLOITS OF JOE MEEK

Many considered the meat of the bear superior to pork. Besides, an encounter with a grizzly supplied fresh ammunition for the mountain man's story telling, and yarning was a favorite pastime around the trapper's campfire. Among those famous for their yarning was Joe

Joseph L. Meek, a mountain man famous for his exploits in the Rockies. Many of his adventures involved grizzly bears.

Meek, who claimed to come from a prominent Virginia family before he traveled west to St. Louis and spent the next eleven years trapping in the mountains. Meek, tall, broad-shouldered, full-bearded, courageous and full of spunk, was always welcome because of his story telling and practical joking. He is said to have once counted coup by cracking a stick across the skull of a grizzly, then leaping back quickly enough to avoid the lighting-fast swipe of the claws, simply to prove that he wasn't afraid.

Meek told of the day that he and another trapper were moving along a riverbank when they spotted an exceptionally large grizzly bear on the opposite shore. No opportunity to kill a grizzly was to be passed up even when bear and hunter were separated by a river, so the two trappers both took aim and, in unison, shot the bear, which dropped in its tracks and lay still the way a dead bear should.

As much as shooting the bear, Meek and his partner wanted to brag about it back in camp. They needed proof, so they tied their mules to nearby trees, stripped off their clothes, and left them on shore with their rifles. Then, wearing only their belts and knives, they stepped into the cold water and struck out for the opposite shore.

They came dripping up the river bank thinking that this was a mighty handsome bear they had, only to find that they didn't have him at all. Meek is quoted in Frances Fuller Victor's *The River Of The West* as saying, "He sprung up as we came near him and took after us. Then you ought to have seen two naked men run! It war a race for life, and a close one too, but we made the river first."

At this point the bank rose a dozen feet or more straight out of the river and the water was, Meeks figured, ten or twelve feet deep. "But we didn't halt," he said. "Overboard we went, the bar after us."

All three splashed down in the same instant, the bear between the two naked trappers and trying to get to Meek. All fought the current in their frantic efforts to accomplish their individual aims. "You can reckon that I swam!" Meek said, "Every moment I felt myself being swept into the yawning jaws of the mighty beast".

Meek credited the strong current with saving him from those yawning jaws, and in due time all three made shore. By good fortune, the bear came ashore on the same side of the river where he was when first shot, and the two trappers landed on their own side of the stream. Instead of a braggin' trophy to take back to camp, all they had for their trouble was a cold swim and a mile hike in the nude back to their clothes and guns. Joe Meek's stories of his Rocky Mountain adventures with grizzly bears went with him to Oregon where he became a successful farmer, U.S. marshal, and legislator.

JED SMITH

As the legendary Jed Smith once learned to his sorrow, the grizzly is there when least suspected and nothing packs more threat than a grizzly bear taken by surprise. Jedediah Strong Smith, born in south-central New York, went out to St. Louis as a young man. He was drawn there by the promise of adventure in the West, and in 1822 signed on for fur trader William Ashley's pioneering trip up the Missouri. Smith was a restless explorer at heart, searching out the new trails leading to scenes no white person before him knew. Following information supplied by the Indians, he re-confirmed the location of a South Pass through the Rockies, opening an easier wagon route to California as well as the Rocky Mountain trapping areas. He also discovered Great Salt Lake and explored other important western geographical features. Unlike most of the mountain men, Smith was an educated gentleman.

In 1823, the year after his first expedition, Ashley appointed Jed Smith to lead a brigade of about a dozen trappers up the Missouri to open up new beaver trapping country south of the Yellowstone River. Included in his group were some of the best-remembered of all the mountain men, Jim Clyman, Thomas Fitzpatrick, Edward Rose, and William Sublette. Smith was at the head of his little group when, somewhere between the Black Hills and the Powder River, he was attacked by an enraged grizzly.

Years later, Clyman wrote down his recollection of that day's events. The group was moving single file through a thick patch of cover when a massive grizzly bear charged into the line of men. Smith ran to where the bear was and drew the brunt of the attack on himself. Grizzly and Smith met face to face and, as Clyman recalled, "Grissly did not hesitate a moment but sprung on the capt taking him by the head first."

The bear pitched Smith onto the ground and came down upon him then bit into Smith's belly area breaking the blade from the trapper's butcher knife. Eventually, the men managed to run the bear off far enough to shoot it without hitting Smith. By the time the grizzly finished mauling Smith, the trapper had a number of broken ribs, but worse yet, his scalp was torn from part of his head and one ear was hanging by a strip of skin.

With their captain lying on the ground bleeding from his numerous wounds, his men stood around wondering what they might do. None among them had experience in treating such wounds. Clyman eventually asked Smith what he should do and Smith characteristically, took charge and began directing his own treatment.

The Life of a Hunter—A Tight Fix *by Currier and Ives. Conflicts between mountain men and grizzlies were frequent, and were embellished by the campfire as the years went by.*

None of the men wanted to play surgeon but Clyman decided that if Jed Smith could stand up under a grizzly bear attack and still take charge, he should do what he could to help. First Smith sent two of the men running off to bring water from the stream a mile distant. Clyman fetched a pair of scissors from his pack and began cutting off Jed Smith's hair. It was plain from this that when the bear took Jed's head into its mouth, its teeth reached from the eye on one side of the head to the ear on the other. The skull was gleaming white where it was laid bare.

Clyman threaded a needle and began stitching the scalp back in place under Smith's direction. Eventually the needle had done its work as Smith gritted his teeth and clenched his fists. Next, Clyman examined the torn ear more closely. He explained to Smith that there was nothing they could do to save the ear. Smith thought otherwise and asked Clyman to at least try to stitch the ear back on. "Then I put in my needle," said Clyman, "stitching it through and through and over and over."

When this was accomplished, the group decided to move on along the river and make camp, Jed Smith climbed onto his horse and rode to the campsite. There, the crew erected its only tent and Smith began his recuperation.

For the next ten days they stayed in the area while their leader mended and regained his strength. The ear may not have looked quite normal but it was still there. So were the scars on his face and scalp. One eyebrow was missing and there was nothing anyone could do about that. Jed Smith would never again look the same as he had before the grizzly bear attacked. The grizzly bear, of course, had fared even worse and this was the way it was for the big bears almost anywhere that bears and trappers came together.

The disfigured Jed Smith spent nine years in the West before finally being killed by Comanches. Some historians believe that, by then, he was depressed by the insensitivity of the attack the white people were making upon the creatures of a beautiful land. Life was cheap and whatever was in their way they would sweep aside. In a few decades they had eliminated the beaver from drainage after drainage. The buffalo, elk, antelope, and great bears were going. Smith may have sensed that the the future looked grim for these animals that gave the West much of its character.

RUSSELL'S JOURNAL

One of the best accounts of the mountain man's life was the journal of Osborne Russell. By the time young Russell, a farm boy from Maine, reached the Rockies, the beaver trade was already beginning to wind down. Unlike some of the early mountain men, Russell came to his adopted trade with little experience in handling a rifle, a fact he readily admits in his *Journal of a Trapper.* He learned just how incompetent he was with his rifle one August day when the leader of his brigade sent him out to hunt camp meat along the Snake river. The hunter promptly found a number of buffalo and, writes Russell, "I now prepared myself for the first time in my life to kill meat for my supper with a rifle." Even Russell must have been amazed at the results.

After crawling to within eighty yards, he managed to wound a huge bull on his first shot. From there it was all downhill. "I then reloaded and shot as fast as I could," Russell tells us, "until I had driven twenty-five bullets at, in, and about him, which was all I had in my bullet pouch whilst the Bull still stood apparently rivited to the spot. I watched him anxiously for half an hour in hopes of seeing him fall, but to no purpose." Russell finally up and returned to camp without meat, a bad omen for a mountainman about to tangle with his first angry grizzly bear.

Eight days later, again while out hunting for meat, Russell and his partner came upon a large grizzly digging roots in a marsh near a patch of willows. The bear was minding his own business and they could have passed him up and searched for more buffalo. But the grizzly was an irresistible target and when Russell's partner shot it through the shoulder, it let out a loud bawl then escaped into a patch of willows.

The two men stalked around the thicket, rifles cocked, until they came to within ten feet of where the bear stood. The bear growled and came rushing from the cover at these men who had caused him pain. Wrote Russell, "his enormous jaws extended and eyes flashing fire. Oh heavens, was ever anything so hideous?"

Instead of shooting at the bear, the two men took to their heels while the injured grizzly chased first one then the other. Finally, when about to be over-taken by the bear, Russell turned and lifted his gun. "I pulled the trigger and knew not what else to do." There was, of course, precious little more he could do at that point. But the hunter was fortunate and the bear unfortunate. Russell admitted, ". . . that it accidentally happened that my Rifle was pointed towards the Bear when I pulled and the ball piercing his heart, he gave one bound for me, uttered a deathly howl and fell dead." Russell then adds that it was in this moment that he made a solemn vow never again to "molest another wounded Grizzly Bear in a marsh or thicket."

HUGH GLASS

Of all the individual conflicts between the grizzly bear and the mountain man, one story, doubtless embellished with the retelling, remains unforgettable. The story began on a late summer morning in South Dakota as a thirteen man force of trappers under the leadership of the famous Major Andrew Henry moved along the trail leading up the Missouri.

Accouts vary on exactly what happened, but Jim Clyman, who had known Hugh Glass and the others involved, wrote that Glass was so independent in nature that he disregarded the instructions of Henry to stay close to the group. Another account says that Glass was sent out hunting for meat. Whatever the explanation, Hugh Glass was off some distance from the main body when the grizzly attacked him.

Glass was a man of somewhat mysterious origins. He was older than the rest of the party, and is sometimes described as being old and gray at that time. He may have been twice the age of some of the trappers in their twenties, but he was a rugged, resourceful, and independent man.

He arrived in St. Louis and was there drifting around in 1823 without any solid plans for the future when Ashley was looking for more applicants to join his party of trappers, and from this point on we can be somewhat more certain of the events that followed Hugh Glass as he moved toward the saga which some still say is unbelievable.

On the day he met the grizzly that made him famous, Glass was pushing through a wild plum thicket, a dangerous place to be in this season of ripening fruit so favored by bears. Glass came upon the old bear suddenly. One minute he was alone, the next, there she was in front of him. Not only had he interrupted her feeding, but he also encountered her when she was watching over two cubs.

As the old bear rose to her hind legs, to investigate the intruder, he leveled a shot into her chest. Then he tried running while, at the same time, yelling as loudly as he could for the help of his companions. The shot did not slow the infuriated old bear down significantly and Glass had taken only a few swift steps before she was upon him. She swatted him, sent him sprawling, and came down heavily upon him, raking him with her claws and chewing at him with her teeth.

When the others in the party arrived, Hugh Glass and the bear were going at each other in hand to hand combat, Hugh with his knife, which was having little effect, and the bear with her standard tools which had already reduced the trapper to the edge of death. As opportunity presented itself, the other trappers sent round after round into the grizzly until she finally succumbed.

His companions stood around looking at the fallen Glass, shaking their heads, and marveling at the punishment the human body could absorb and still leave a person breathing. They all agreed that Old Hugh's breathing was only temporary and that Glass had fought his last grizzly. A man could hardly be expected to survive long with blood coming from a deep hole in his throat, his face mutilated, and other deep cuts etched into him in so many places.

They decided to make camp for the night and hope that no Indians discovered their presence. Their small number would make them certain prey to any significant band of Arikaras. As soon as Glass finished breathing they could bury him, then move on quickly.

The only thing wrong with this plan was that Glass was too tough to die from the grizzly bear's attack. He neither moved nor talked. But he lived.

He survived all through that night and in the light of a new day Major Henry knew that he faced a tough decision, perhaps the most difficult he had ever made. Where they were, the whole crew was in danger from the Indians. There was little sense in all of them staying there when it seemed that Glass could surely not survive more than a few additional hours. On the other hand, a leader of men did not simply leave behind a helpless member of his party.

Henry wondered if there might be someone among them willing to stay and tend Glass in these his final hours, then hightail it out of there. The first to step forward was a lanky youngster, a newcomer to the trapping business who, some say, was Jim Bridger. Henry said that if two of them would stay, the company would reward them with forty dollars each. All they would have to do was watch over Hugh Glass, bury him, then catch up with the party. That sounded simple, but it was not an assignment that any of the others in the group especially hankered for. The second one who agreed to stay was John Fitzgerald, an experienced mountain man. Nobody can say why Fitzgerald volunteered, although the forty dollars must have been a factor.

As it turned out, the assignment was even more difficult than expected because Old Glass wouldn't go ahead and die. Days passed. Fitzgerald finally decided to leave, even though Glass was still living. Historians have long speculated about how it was that a young man of Jim Bridger's principles might have allowed himself to leave a partner to die, and this point has never been addressed to everyone's satisfaction. Glass still did not talk, although perhaps he understood something of what was happening. He might not, however, have realized that his former friends were also taking his gun and knife. But if Glass had really died, they would surely have been asked about his valuable gun and knife.

According to the abandoned trapper's story, he had no real sound idea of the sequence of events through the following days. Somehow, after he was abandoned, he rolled or crawled to the edge of the river for water. He managed to stay alive on berries, and maintain his strength. This may have gone on for several days while he slowly recovered. One thing was certain, Hugh Glass was not one to give up his life easily. The more clearly he could think, and the stronger he became, the more he told himself that he had a mission—one reason for living. If it was the last thing he ever did, he would track down the two who had abandoned him and deal with them.

One morning he felt strong enough to leave and begin his journey. The trip back to Fort Kiowa would be a slow one. The distance was some two hundred and fifty miles, and furthermore Hugh Glass still could not walk.

This did not stop him. Perhaps in time he would become strong enough to walk. Meanwhile, he would crawl, by God, and every hour would take him that much closer to his surprise party with those two scoundrels that left him to die.

Food was a problem. He had no weapon or tool to help him. There were berries sometimes within reach. There were roots he could dig with a stick or sharp stone. He found a rattler sluggish from a recent meal and battered it to death with a rock, then ate the flesh.

His best break, legend tells us, came the day he heard wolves on the trail ahead of him. The pack had cut a buffalo calf from the herd and brought it down. Glass, watching from the shadows, thought about the best way to get a share of the meat without being attacked by the wolves. Some writers have speculated that he might have struck a fire to scare the wolves away, but there seems a better chance that the experienced mountain man would simply wait for the canines to gorge themselves, then move in yelling and threatening as best he could until the wolves departed.

Glass stayed by the remains of the calf through that day and the next and still did not leave until the meat was too far gone for him to eat more. By this time the abundance of high protein food had given him new strength, and Glass rose to his feet during the coming days and began walking and stumbling forward, always moving along the stream toward Fort Kiowa.

His progress improved and by the middle of October he arrived at the Fort. Almost two months had passed since his scrape with the grizzly. He soon left on the next leg of his journey of revenge. He moved though hazardous Indian country surviving a close call with the Arikaras, and learned along the way that his group had moved on up the Yellowstone. Hugh Glass moved on too, sticking to their trail. By this time, winter had come to the mountains, but the determined Glass was not letting this stop him.

He finally caught up with his party on New Years Eve, at Fort Henry, and stood outside on that dark snowy night pounding on the logs until the gate slowly swung open.

Hugh Glass, tall, lean, bearded, disfigured, scarred, and covered with a dusting of snow, stood in the door for a moment, then limped into the room where silence had suddenly fallen like a blanket over the unbelieving trappers. "Sure enough by gad, it was old Hugh standin' there in the flesh, or what was left of him."

Here was a new ending to the tale they had retold many times, the story of how the grizzly bear killed Old Hugh. Glass grimly announced the purpose of his long and lonely journey in pursuit of the brigade. He hankered to know one thing, the whereabouts of Bridger and Fitzgerald.

Only Bridger was there. Jim Bridger, who was to gain fame as a mountain man in the following years, was tall, bony, and muscular. He had an especially thick neck, high cheekbones, and a prominent nose, and he moved with the grace of a wild creature. Bridger was a master of the outdoors, but he had never learned the letters of the alphabet, nor how to use them. Glass took one look at the gangling kid and let him off with a tongue lashing.

Glass then learned that the one he viewed as the real culprit, Fitzgerald, had recently joined the army. This caused Hugh Glass to give up his design for revenge. Fitzgerald wasn't important enough to him to risk punishment by the military for killing one of its men. Perhaps Hugh Glass had tasted his revenge. He later sought out Fitzgerald at Fort Atkinson. According to one observer, Glass told the mountain man turned soldier, "You was well paid to have remained with me until I should be able to walk. You promised to do so—or to wait my death and decently bury my remains—I heard the bargain—but I say settle the matter with your conscience and your God"

The real problem with the story of Hugh Glass and the grizzly is determining how much of it is fact. Perhaps this doesn't matter either except that the names of Bridger and Fitzgerald have been dragged in and that Bridger at least may have been maligned. One who doubted that it ever happened, at least in the manner usually related, was historian J. Cecil Alter, who wrote an excellent biography of Jim Bridger. Alter makes a good case. He points out that this would have been completely out of character for Bridger, an honorable and dependable man who became one of the most famous scouts in the West and served many years as a government scout. Alter also mentions that there was another trapper named Bridges who could have been the one involved. Even more believable, says Alter, was the possibility that the fantastic case of Hugh Glass and the grizzly was compounded of a less serious bear attack embellished by Glass's vivid imagination. For Alter, the story proved only that Hugh Glass was a creative story teller, a distinguished raconteur. The mountain men were noted for their yarning, and the grizzly was always an inspiration. At any rate, the legend of Hugh Glass remains one of the frontier's most famous stories of encounters between man and bear.

Within two decades after the earliest trapper brigades began spreading out over the western mountains, the beaver trapping business was winding down. Silk hats became the latest fashion and the demand for beaver dwindled. Furthermore, the supplies of North American beaver were already falling off. Unprotected by any laws, the beaver had been taken without restraint. Occasionally, a thoughtful person would regret the disappearance of the beaver, but it was usually regret in one breath and trap in the next. Russell wrote in his journal near the end of the mountain man's reign, "The trappers often remarked to each other as they rode over the lonely plains that it was time for the white man to leave the mountains as beaver and game had nearly disappeared."

To the very last, the grizzly would be fair game wherever encountered, even by those who mourned the passing of the other wildlife. Typically, Russell, in the waning years of the mountain man's beaver trapping, encountered a large grizzly bear sitting outside its den and promptly moved to bring it down. "I approached within about 180 paces," he wrote, "shot and missed it. He looked around and crept slowly into his den. I reloaded my rifle and went up to the hole and threw down a stone weighing five or six pounds." Nothing happened, so Russell rolled into the den a stone which he calculated weighed three or four hundred pounds.

That did it! "The stone had scarcely reached the bottom when the bear came rushing out with its mouth wide open and was on the point of making a spring at me when I pulled the trigger and shot him through the left shoulder which sent him rolling down the mountain."

By 1840, when the colorful era of the freelance trapper was ending, other forces were stirring. Until now the western hunter's single-shot muzzleloading rifle had given the great bear an edge in many a contest. The Kentucky rifles that accompanied the first mountain men west were designed for the smaller animals of the eastern regions and made it important for the hunter to get a close shot at a vital spot if he were to kill a bear or buffalo. Because of the time needed to reload, he usually had only one chance. A poorly placed shot, and often even a well placed one, left the grizzly time and strength to charge.

But in those years between the adventures of the mountain men and the coming of the Civil War, the gun makers' shops were giving birth to modern firearms. At Harper's Ferry, John H. Hall invented the first practical breechloader. It enabled the rifleman to pour black powder and press the bullet directly into the chamber, lock the chamber then fire it, first with a flintlock mechanism and later by precussion. This speeded up the reloading and firing considerably, but faster guns were on the way.

Working in Hall's shop was a skilled and inventive gunmaker named Christian Sharps who left Hall in 1844 to start his own factory. His rifle was to become the most famous on the frontier. The Sharps rifle, patented in 1848, eliminated the need to load a ball and loose powder into the chamber. Instead, the rifleman could now simply insert a paper cartridge containing both. This gun enabled the shooter

The main salesroom of C. C. Shayne Manufacturing Furrier, from their catalog. Although furs continued to be in fashion, the demand for beaver in particular began to decline after 1840 as silk hats became the vogue in America and Europe. The era of the mountain man was winding down.

to use a heavy powder charge, as well as a 475-grain bullet, which gave both power and accuracy. Furthermore, the practiced hunter could load and shoot nine or so shots a minute.

The grizzly was now in much greater trouble than ever before. New gun designs were appearing rapidly and the design that would place the big bear at an impossible disadvantage would soon appear. By 1860, B. Tyler Henry patented a lever-action, breechloading repeating rifle with a tube magazine made to hold fifteen 44-caliber, rimfire metal cartridges, and other advances were to follow. As one writer said, "The Sharps and other single-shot rifles passed sentence on the grizzly, but the repeater finally carried out the execution."

On the heels of the mountain men, thousands of people would be moving westward. Settlers were coming to lands that a few years earlier had been wilderness. Explorers, ranchers, business people, religious groups, the military, were all following trails blazed by the mountain men into remote areas. This opening of the West, and adapting the land to the white man's use brought overwhelming trouble for the grizzly, and nowhere was the fate of the great bear sealed more certainly than it was in California.

Chapter 6

When Grizzlies Ruled California

Col. William Butts was ready to leave for San Francisco on the first leg of a journey to the East when his ranch hand rushed in to report that he had just shot, but not killed, the old grizzly bear suspected of taking their livestock. There really wasn't time to go chasing off after a grizzly, but the colonel rationalized that, because the bear was already badly wounded, finishing the job should take only a short time. That was his first error of the day. The truth was, on that day in 1853, retired U.S. Army Colonel Bill Butts simply could not resist the temptation to kill another grizzly.

The presence of the giant bears had been perhaps the most compelling reason he had for moving to California. After his years of military service in Mexico and on the Plains, life back in Missouri promised to be too dull for a red-blooded outdoorsman. Butts, a quiet man of medium build, was described as "a daring spirit who always courted danger and sought adventure." So he had migrated to California and become a lawyer, rancher, and grizzly bear hunter.

Minutes after he heard the report of the old she bear's presence, Colonel Butts had gathered up his gun and long knife, mounted his favorite horse, and dashed off to dispatch the bear. The trail soon brought him and his ranch hand to the edge of a ravine with near vertical walls. The colonel dismounted and stood, rifle in hand, studying the heavy brush at the bottom of the gully, no doubt thinking that he was looking down upon exactly the kind of cover in which and injured and angry grizzly might be hiding in ambush. As he stood on the edge of the ravine searching the thicket below for the bear, he felt the earth beneath his feet begin to shift, and before he could move, the bank gave way and he went rolling and tumbling all the way to the bottom and the very edge of the heavy vegetation.

After he stopped rolling, Butts wasted no time starting back up the steep incline. He knew grizzly bears well enough to expect this one to be at his heels. Glancing over his shoulder, he saw the furious bear scrambling for purchase in the soft earth as she heaved her bulk up the slope behind him.

The race to the top was a dead heat, and as they pulled themselves onto the plateau, the colonel wheeled to shoot the bear. In that instant, she clamped the barrel of his gun in her mouth, and according to the account given to a reporter for Harper's Magazine, bit it so hard that she bent it "like a leaden rod."

Butts raised the damaged gun above his head and brought it thudding down upon her furry skull, while the grizzly countered by grabbing the colonel's left leg and pulling it into her mouth. This brought man and bear to earth, each one taking a firm grip on the other as they slipped back over the edge of the ravine and began sliding and tumbling to the bottom again.

There was a brief moment during which the colonel was rendered unconscious by hundreds of pounds of bear falling across him. He was soon revived, however, by the crunching upon his leg.

In the following minutes the action was furious. The bear mauled and shook the colonel senseless, then left him for dead only to glance back over her shoulder and find him looking her in the eye again, whereupon she rushed back and mauled him some more. This apparently happened a number of times; the bear was willing to practice until she got it right.

Meanwhile, the colonel was working on her with his hunting knife, the only weapon he possessed. He carved out one of the bear's eyes and stabbed and ripped her repeatedly until both bear and hunter were soaked with the grizzly's blood. After prolonged combat, during which she had taken Butts's head into her mouth and chewed on his scalp, the bear gradually lost consciousness, then expired of multiple wounds.

Butts was not much better off. His hand to hand battle with the grizzly had cost him an ear and part of his scalp. His face was paralyzed on one side and he had a lifelong limp. Besides, he missed a pleasant trip to the East.

This was just one more chapter in an endless war between the grizzly bears of California and the men who had attacked them so relentlessly, with or without cause, ever since European people first moved into this land along North America's west coast. California, blessed with pleasant climate and productive soil, supported a fine population of wildlife, including perhaps as large a concentration of grizzly bears as lived anywhere on the continent. One authority on the California grizzly bear, the late Tracy I. Storer, in his book *California Grizzly,* written with Lloyd P. Tevis, Jr., estimated that there were once ten thousand of the giant bears in the state.

Furthermore, the California bears were among the largest of the grizzlies, and according to some people, possessed the shortest temper of all the grizzlies anywhere. Exactly how large the California grizzly bear grew is difficult to determine at this late date because most of the weights mentioned in old records were estimates. Storer and Tevis, after searching all the old records they could find, believed that the grizzly bears of that state sometimes reached weights greater than twelve hundred pounds.

From their earliest exposure to the giant bears, the invading light-skinned people decided that the bears must go. There was a near universal conviction that grizzly bears deserved death because they were there. Whether the grizzly caused any damage or not, it was condemned because it was big, strong, and capable of causing harm. Ranchers saw grizzlies as mortal enemies of their livestock. If a bear came upon an animal dead from whatever reason, and left a footprint as it partook of carrion, the rancher credited it with making the kill. But doubtless, the grizzly did vary its diet of berries and mice with an occasional serving of beef or mutton, and in some cases developed an ungovernable desire for domestically produced animals.

These reasons, however, were only part of the big bear's adversary status with the men of California, or elsewhere. As long as the bears lasted, they were pursued, sometimes for practical reasons, but more often for the chase. The Plains Indian warrior satisfied this innate urge when he fashioned the claws of his conquered grizzly into a necklace and wore it as the ultimate symbol of human bravery.

This frontier attitude, which is easily deplored by all of us back glancers, is not completely gone yet, but times and attitudes may be changing. Modern hunters are among those who come to the defense of endangered species. Besides, today there is research to help us understand wildlife populations, as well as regulations to control the numbers of game animals that can be legally taken. Modern game management and enlightened thinking, however, came along too late to help the grizzly bear in much of its range.

By the time there was widespread concern about the future of the grizzly bear, its fate was already sealed in state after state. Records passed down to us from those critical years of mortal conflict between white men and grizzly bears in California reveal some of the attitudes that threatened the big bear everywhere, and offer clues that might

California Grizzly *by Charles Nahl. At one time, California had a large grizzly population —one estimate put the number at ten thousand. As this painting suggests, the grizzlies in that state were unusually large.*

help us adjust our thinking toward wildlife in general. But nowhere was the campaign against the grizzly more bizarre and determined than in California.

ROPING THE GRIZZLY

Among the riskiest hunting ever practiced in California, or anywhere, was the hunt with lassoes as introduced by early Spanish colonists. On special religious holidays the Spanish Californians staged galas with fights between the most powerful bulls available and the biggest grizzly bears to be found, an entertainment form whose roots go back to the bloody games once played by Roman emperors who, for the amusement of the populace, pitted wild animals against each other, and even against people. Such games continued in Rome for several hundred years and, according to Hermann Dembeck in *Animals and Men,* the animals involved included hundreds of bears. The sport disappeared as the bears and other creatures vanished from the hills. The destruction of European bears for human amusement may have reached its pinnacle one day in A.D. 237 when Gordian 1 had a thousand brown bears killed. The bears were captured in pits, the adults hauled off to Rome for the games, and the cubs sold to trainers who could "teach" a bear to dance by forcing it to stand on a heated surface.

Although the procedures for the later fights in California varied in detail, the bear was usually held in a strong cage made of logs and iron until time for its release into the arena amid loud cheering from the crowd. Then, the attendants prodded into the ring a short-tempered range bull, wild-eyed, and equipped with long pointed horns.

The California grizzly was sometimes shackled with a chain perhaps twenty feet long while the bull was unfettered. If there was no arena, the two animals might be thrown and shackled together with a length of chain. A strong bear, and some were said to weigh more than half a ton, usually held the advantage, but there were bets on bear and bull alike. The bear and bull fights were ugly affairs, degrading to both animals and people. By the time the two animals had been mistreated and harassed enough by people, they were more than willing to attack each other at the first opportunity.

The real excitement, however, in these affairs, came to a select minority of hunters who, a few days before the fight, would ride off in search of the the largest, fiercest grizzly bear they could find. Their task was to bring the bear in—alive and unharmed—for the celebration.

This was risky business, calling for the skills of several of the best and most daring horsemen and ropers in the community. As they rode off, amidst appropriate ceremony, to search out a bear, they carried only their lariats, fashioned from tightly braided strips of soaked cowhide. In daytime, the chaparral thickets were the best places to find the beasts but a poor location for roping them. Frequently, the roping of grizzly bears was a sport left for night-time when the bears would be feeding out in the open.

The target for the first man's lariat was one of the bear's front feet, and the next target was the other front foot. With the highly trained horses pulling in opposite directions, the bear could be stretched out so that, amidst the snarling, bellowing, and tearing at earth and brush, added lariats could be thrown about the grizzly's rear feet as well.

Then came the riskiest part. With the horses holding the struggling bear as best they could, one of the riders slid from his horse and

Roping the Bear *by J. Walker. Early Spanish colonists in California practiced bear roping, and staged fights between bulls and bears.*

approached the furious grizzly. He slipped a loop around the bear's jaws and tied them shut. Next, he cautiously dropped a loop around one of the front paws and bound it and its mate together tightly. Finally, the hind feet were also trussed, and the mighty grizzly was rendered helpless and ready for the trip back to the settlement.

This was the work of heroes and the idea was certain to spread inland to the Plains where the American cowboy's reaction was predictable. The cowboy, good with his lariat and willing to admit it, roped many a grizzly bear for the hell of it. But the ropes were used simply to hold the bear in place and render it harmless while it was dispatched with either gun or knife, depending on how close the cowboy was willing to come to the bear and how much he wanted to talk about the episode at the Dry Gulch Saloon the next time he got to town. Rarely if ever did the cowboys go the last mile and hog-tie a bear.

Enos Mills once saw one of these bear ropings in Montana which he said had "rare fighting and adventure in it." Two cowboys managed to chase a grizzly bear up close to camp, and as soon as this was known all the cowboys came riding out, lariats swinging. "They roped the bear," wrote Mills, "But one horse was pulled off his feet and dragged, a cowboy was pitched into a bunch of cactus, another cowboy lost his saddle, the cinches giving way under the strain, and a horse struck in the flank had to be shot. Meantime, the bear got away and stampeded the entire herd of cattle."

Some learned the hard way not to drop a rope around any part of a bear except the front feet. A California grizzly bear once taught this lesson to a young naval officer who came out west in the mid 1800s for the express purpose of lassoing his first grizzly. According to Captain R. B. Marcy, a career U.S. Army officer, western explorer, and map maker, writing in his 1866 book *Border Reminiscence,* the visiting naval officer practiced until he was proficient with rope and horse, then hired a guide and set off into the California mountains searching for his bear.

He soon located one that qualified as a giant among grizzlies and set to work reducing the beast to possession, or so he intended. As the bear chaser rode down on the grizzly, lariat whistling in lazy overhead circles, the old bear suddenly stopped, turned, and stood up. The rope fell gently over the bear's head and was promptly jerked taut by horse and rider, causing the bear to sit down solidly on its haunches.

At this point, the bear was supposed to tumble over into a heap after which he would be led away by the proud horseman. The grizzly didn't know the script, however, and sat there like a giant anchor.

Then, it noticed that it was choking and traced the cause to the rope around its neck.

The bear's response was to begin pulling horse and rider to him, hand over hand, shortening the distance until the rider, realizing that the situation was serious, began yelling to his guide to save him. According to Marcy, the Spanish Californians had even learned to grease their lariats so the bear could not get a grip and also to crop their horses tails and grease them too, to prevent the bear from holding on to the tail and pulling the horse down backward to get to the rider. The naval officer's guide, who had apparently not heard about greasing the lariat, now dashed in at top speed and, in the final instant, slashed the lasso, and both horses carried their riders off in record time to the safety zone. The guide said he was willing to search for a smaller, more manageable, bear but the easterner concluded that he should adopt some alternate hobby.

The same stunt was tried with a more serious outcome one fine day in 1850, in Sonoma County, California, by ranch hand Jim Boggs' partner, who fancied himself handy with the rope. According to *Reminiscences of a Ranger,* written by Horace Bell, Jim saw his friend's lasso settle around the bear's paunch. He then watched with disbelief as the old bear seated himself upon the earth and began hand lining his catch homeward. The problem was intensified by the fact that the rope was securely knotted to the saddle. The horse was no dummy and, somehow, pulled free of the saddle and raced off toward the corral, leaving his rider at ground level in confrontation with a furious ill-treated grizzly bear intent on crunching and clawing all human parts within reach.

Boggs, now deciding to rescue his partner, marched up to the bear, placed his handgun against the animal's head and pulled the trigger. According to Bell, "The bear at once released the partner who took to his heels, leaving Jim and the bear to fight it out."

Boggs lodged one more bullet in the grizzly, then purposely went limp. The bear thinking he had done the job, lumbered off, but turned and double-checked just in time to see Boggs lift his battered head to appraise the situation. The bear wheeled about, pounced on Boggs again and mauled him so terribly that there seemed little chance of his surviving. Although he did live, he was a lifelong cripple. His partner suffered less severe injuries and it is believed that neither Boggs nor his partner nourished any interest in roping more grizzly bears.

For sheer guts, however, no other bear roper could approach Don José Ramon Carrillo. His story was told by W.H. Davis in his 1889 book, *Sixty Years In California.* In hot pursuit of a grizzly one day,

Native Californians Lassoing a Bear *by F.O.C. Darley. From the Spanish, Americans learned the risky and exciting game of hunting bears with lassos. The stunt even spread to other western states.*

Carrillo was close behind the bear when it plunged into a six-foot-deep gully. The bear as well as the horse and rider were unable to avoid the fall, and in the next instant all of them were mixing it up in the bottom of the pit. Since Carillo had no longing for hand to hand combat with a grizzly, and little chance of climbing out of the tight spot into which he had engineered himself, he decided to help the grizzly escape. He grabbed the confused bear by the hind quarters and heaved while the startled grizzly cooperated by clawing his way up the bank and out of the pit.

FAMOUS HUNTERS

In those mid-century years when the Golden State still had a fair share of the grizzly bears that nature granted it, people came for many reasons, some seeking gold, some to ranch, some for the benign climate. Few could leave the bears alone, and occasionally a hunter came just to kill the grizzly bears for which the state was famous. One of these hunters was Colin Preston, a red-bearded lawyer and a black bear hunter who came to California from Arkansas in 1845. By his own count, the free-wheeling Preston killed an unbelievable two hundred and ten California grizzlies in the next ten years. "They are scarcer now," he said, lamenting the fact that there had once been grizzlies close by his ranch and now he sometimes had to go fifty miles to find one.

We have the description of some of Preston's hunting methods from an anonymous journalist who reported on his visit to the hunter's ranch in the mid-1850s. "We make large and dangerous bears drunk," Preston explained. This loathsome practice applied especially to the much-feared sows with cubs. The technique was to locate a fallen tree near the bear's trail, then chop a hole in the trunk large enough to hold a gallon of rum and molasses. The bear finds the liquor, and drinks it rapidly, and is soon rolling and cavorting until, as Preston explained, "he falls at last, stupified and helpless, an easy prey to the hunter." Preston claimed that he had killed many bears in this manner although he didn't really like the idea because of its "treachery."

Another discredited hunting method used by Preston involved baiting the grizzlies to where they could be shot, usually with zero danger to the hunter. He and his ranch hand, also a determined bear hunter, made a scent trail by the usual method of tying part of a calf or deer to the saddle with a rope and dragging the bait across the fields to the base of a large oak tree. The bait was suspended in the lower branches and the hunters perched in the tree above it to wait.

On one such hunt, Preston and his partner waited three nights for the bear to come and sometimes fell asleep in the tree. "Then," as Preston said, "a shadow appeared moving toward us in the direction of the drag. I spoke in a whisper to Antonio. He woke up suddenly and, losing his presence of mind, fell over forward on the ground, his rifle catching and hanging in the tree. He ascended the tree with astonishing ease." The bear was drawing near when, as Preston said, "to my utter amazement, off went Antonio a second time." While Preston berated him for his clumsiness and cowardice, Antonio bounded off into the darkness. He no sooner departed than the hungry bear stood on its hind legs and reached for the bait.

At this point, Preston placed the muzzle of his gun against the bear's ear, shot, and saw him go down. "With the kicking of the gun and my own unsteadiness," Preston admitted, "I too rolled off the branch." He tumbled against the bear. "Terrified now," he added, "I rolled myself off and ran—and didn't stop until I was back at the ranch."

Another famous hunter who pursued the grizzly bears of California in those years as the region approached statehood was mountain man James Clyman. Clyman, who had ranked among the most skilled and successful of the Rocky Mountain beaver trappers when the mountain men were at the peak of their activity, finally reached California in 1845, spent a few months hanging around San Francisco then, in early December, went off on a bear hunt that lasted until Christmas.

There were seven men in the hunting party and they took along half a dozen extra packhorses for hauling back the game. The hunting party crossed the Napa Valley and headed into the mountains. We know the high points of this early California bear hunt because Clyman was the rare mountain man who kept an excellent journal.

On the second day out, according to Clyman's journal, they "saw several Bear at a distance which appeared to be mostly poor and not worth the shooting." Later the same day the party split up and one half of the group shot at and missed a couple of large grizzlies which made the mistake of departing in the direction of Clyman and his partner. "My companion and me dismounted," he later wrote, "and as soon as they came in good rifle distance we fired and dropped both at the first fire. The old shee however did not die Quite so easy but at last gave up after receiving four balls through her vitals."

There were days when they saw no bears. However, when they returned their pack animals were loaded down with nine fat grizzlies and thirty deer.

Clyman brought home some conclusions about the California grizzly bears. All the bears they saw were what he called the "grizzled or grey species". He also mentioned that they "are extremely dangerous" and attack the hunter "without provocation except being interrupted in their lair." Those who know the grizzly well would question Clyman's, "without provocation" claim. Clyman advocated extreme caution in moving around grizzly country and wisely advised against ever trying to drive the bears out of the thickets. Instead, he felt the safest and surest way to take the grizzlies was for two or three hunters to take a stand in a rocky cliff or tree within range of trails the bears would use in going from their resting places to feed, and in these places to shoot them in the evening as they came out to feed, or in the morning as they returned.

Confronted with year round pursuit by determined men, the grizzly bears that once roamed California in abundance were doomed. Their numbers had fallen with terrible swiftness and few people ever saw a wild grizzly bear in California after the turn of this century.

In view of this, the astonishment that registered on Jim Agnew's face that August day in 1922 is understandable. On his Tulare County ranch, Agnew came upon a large bear that looked like a grizzly at a time when all grizzlies were said to be gone. Agnew did exactly as thousands of others had done before him: he raised his gun and brought the bear to earth. What the Spanish Californians, American frontiersmen, and ranchers had worked at so relentlessly, Agnew had apparently finished. He had killed the last grizzly bear in California.

A couple of years after Agnew's bear fell there were vague reports of another grizzly in the vicinity of Sequoia National Park. That was all. The California grizzly bear was no more. Today, only the stories persist. The bear's image as the emblem of California on the state's flag reminds us that the fabled bear is gone forever from the coastal state where it once prospered. The story of the grizzly bear's passing was replayed in state after state, sometimes expedited by men in pursuit of those special bears they had condemned as outlaws.

Chapter 7

The Unforgettable Renegades

The "man with the iron stick" commonly saw the grizzlies, even those that never tasted beef or mutton, as super enemies, out of place in this civilized world of cowboys and sheep herders. In this atmosphere, the occasional grizzly brazen enough to kill a domestic beast was hated with a special passion and the "goddamned grizz" was pursued in a frenzy. If the bear killed, or was believed to have killed, half a dozen animals, it was often given a name of its own, bringing it to the special attention of ranchers for miles around. The longer the bear eluded its pursuers, and the more domestic animals it took, the greater its fame, until it became a legend. Such a bear was Big-Foot Mary.

When she was finally killed south of Grand Junction, Colorado, she had, according to *The Mammals of Colorado* by Edward R. Warren, been known for a quarter century. Big-Foot Mary, notorious consumer of beef, had teeth worn to the gums. Her hide measured eight and a half feet, and she yielded enough fat to render out one hundred and sixty-six pounds of oil.

Most of the named grizzlies were identifiable by the special track left after having a foot mutilated in a trap. There was Old One Toe, Old Two Toes, Old Clubfoot, and old Bloody Paws who was a special case.

Bloody Paws, perhaps the best known grizzly in all of Wyoming, had become a specialist in killing sheep, calves, and colts with a single blow to the head. As the old bear added new depredations to her record, the efforts to terminate her life doubled and redoubled. She was said to be a giant bear, silvery white in color, and was credited with a career total of at least five hundred and seventy-five head of stock.

Her real specialty was killing sheep, and on one memorable night she swatted fifty-two sheep into the next world, while killing another two hundred and eleven by causing them to run over a cliff in sheer panic. After a dozen years of raiding ranches and eluding trappers and hunters, Bloody Paws fell victim to rancher Jack Madden's gun, and Madden collected the reward being offered for her death. Newspapers over a wide area, even in some eastern states, announced the fall of the famous grizzly.

In the early part of this century the best known bear around northwestern Montana was an old male whose troubles began the night he followed his nose directly to a baited trap. As the bear began to eat, it softly placed the broad pad of its right front foot on the pan of the steel-jawed trap and sensed at once that something underfoot was strange and unnatural. His reflex action drew the paw up with lightning speed but still not swiftly enough to allow him a clean escape. The jaws snapped shut on a section of the foot including two toes.

When the trapper returned a few days later, the place looked as if a mini-tornado had touched down. Blood, fur, and broken trees littered the ground and the footprints of the big grizzly told their story. But the bear was nowhere around. The scene was quiet. The trail, however, was easily enough followed and the man found his trap several hundred yards away, still chained to the log. Clamped in its jaws was a piece of bear foot with two toes attached. Those two amputated toes were to give the bear his name as his exploits brought him fame over the next several years.

After he pulled his toes off, according to various sources, including *Notorious Grizzly Bears* by W. P. Hubbard and Seale Harris, the old bear went on a rampage killing many cattle around his territory, and ranchers plotted to terminate his career.

One rancher who suffered heavy losses brought in a noted hunter, a determined man who stuck to the trail like a demon until one day, after several months of tracking, he spotted the bear and began his stalk. He came close enough to get off two fast shots and, judging by the bear's stumbling and bawling, both shots scored.

The bear escaped into a small patch of thick-growing timber, and the hunter, sensing victory at last, foolishly made the error of going after the wounded grizzly. Before the hunter could do much to protect himself, Two Toes rushed him and, with his first swat, sent him sprawling. Mercifully, the man was rendered unconscious by that first blow so he did not yet feel what the bear did to his body in the next few minutes. When the man was found the following day, his left leg had suffered compound fractures as well as multiple puncture wounds.

Furthermore, the angry bear had mutilated the hunter's heavy rifle by breaking the stock and bending the barrel. He had good reason to remember that bear the rest of his life. The attack had shortened one of his legs so drastically that he had difficulty walking in a straight line.

We will never know what drove the old bear to roam those mountains, leaving behind his trail of dead beef animals. Ranchers complained that sometimes he did not even bother to eat the animals he killed. We do know that killing large animals demands the use of energy, and always carries some element of danger, even for a grizzly bear. Some folks speculated that this bear was driven by anger rising from his inability to comprehend the source of the pain from his old bullet wounds. There is no way of knowing precisely how many domestic animals Old Two Toes killed in those years. The losses were believed to be in the thousands of dollars and continued until he was finally killed by an elk hunter who collected the rancher's $575 reward.

Another grizzly, guaranteed his niche in history, was Old Ephraim, a bear that became a legend in his own time in the grazing lands of northern Utah's Wasatch Mountains. The giant bear had one claw missing from its left hind foot. This deformity, plus the size of his massive foot, identified the animal. Few people actually saw the elusive old bear, although many saw his tracks.

He was not an indiscriminate killer, but picked and chose his victims as appetite and opportunity dictated. This was sufficient to bring him to the attention of Frank Clark, a sheep herder who looked upon bear control as one of his primary duties. Beginning in 1911, Clark killed assorted bears as he came upon them, all the while searching in vain for Old Ephraim.

His unrelenting pursuit of the old bear went on for some ten years until Clark wondered if Ephraim might just continue his depredations until old age brought him down. But Clark finally had a lucky break

A Wounded Grizzly *by Charles M. Russell. When the famous western artist painted this scene in 1906, cattlemen and sheepherders were waging war against the grizzlies, and scenes like this one were common.*

when he stumbled on a spring where the old bear came every few days to cool in the water. This gave Clark his idea.

He packed in one of his twenty-seven-pound bear traps, attached to an eleven-foot chain. He spiked the end of the chain to a heavy log, positioned the trap carefully in the center of the pool, then stirred the water so the settling mud would hide the pan. Then he returned to his camp to wait.

When Old Ephraim next came to his favorite bathing hole, he immediately became uneasy. He sniffed around until he found the hidden chain and mud-coated trap. Then he carefully lifted them out and set them on the edge of the pool before settling down to refresh himself in the water. Clark tried his idea several more times but always with identical negative results.

Then, Clark discovered that the bear had a new wallow below the first one and he moved his set to the new location. Again he settled down in his camp a mile downstream to wait.

In the middle of a beautiful moonlit night he suddenly awakened to the roaring of a great bear. Not even bothering to pull on his trousers, he slipped into his boots, grabbed his rifle, and had scarcely started down the trail when he met a giant bear coming toward him with a huge trap clamped to one front paw and the chain wrapped around its arm. The bear was still dragging the section of log to which the chain was spiked.

The sight of the giant bear waddling toward him, in the pale moonlight, as it worried with the trap and bawled with the pain, made Clark's hair stand up on the back of his neck. "It chilled me to the very bone," he later wrote in *The Utah Fish and Game Bulletin.* Clark took command of his emotions and put six shots from his rifle into the great bear, and Old Ephraim fell dead at his feet. He stood over the mighty bear looking down upon it silently, and a feeling of sorrow washed over him.

Grizzly bears, especially giant ones, were already becoming scarce in much of their former range, and as an animal becomes rare the attitudes of people toward it begin to change. In death, Old Ephraim, believed to be the last of Utah's grizzlies, attained a degree of respect. He was buried on the spot. Over the grave, to which many visitors have made their pilgrimage, a simple marker was erected telling the details of the bear's life and death. This sign in northern Utah, is a bleak reminder that this was once the land of the great bear. It reads: "Old Ephraim's Grave (Grizzly Bear) Killed by Frank Clark, Malad, Idaho, August 22, 1923—weight approximately 1100 pounds—height standing, 9 feet 11 inches—Smithsonian Institute has Ephraim's skull."

SHEEP AND GRIZZLIES

Even as the grizzly approaches extinction in much of its range, there remain those who firmly believe that we should eliminate the last of these wilderness giants, reaffirm our role of dominance and feel no remorse. There can be no doubt that some grizzlies sometimes kill livestock. But this is little reason for killing all bears. Many of the domestic animals killed by bears are grazing on public lands in the national forests surrounding Yellowstone and Glacier national parks. Sheepmen with grazing allotments on these forest areas have no love for the grizzlies. Wool growers associations insist that the attitudes of their members are changing, that sheepmen now cooperate fully with government workers who want the grizzly protected on public lands in accordance with the laws.

But many grizzly bear workers believe meanwhile that the poaching continues. "We have in this country what is called the SSS Club," one Forest Service worker explains. "Shoot, shovel, and shut up." The bear killed is quickly buried and the matter silenced. To report it would mean an investigation into killing a threatened animal. It would also mean that the stockman might lose his grazing allotment, because increasingly sheep are being moved off the national forest lands where they conflict with bears.

This loss of the rare bears to herders is well known to the U. S. Fish and Wildlife Service which sometimes sends its undercover agents into sheep country posing as good ole boys and carrying a six-pack. These law enforcement agents have been told by shepherds about bears they shot. "Sheepherders are responsible for protection of the sheep under their care," said one noted grizzly bear biologist in a report to officials, "and routinely kill bears and other predators."

This is emphasized by Larry Roop, Wyoming's widely known grizzly bear biologist. Roop, who spends much of his time working with the bears around Yellowstone, says unequivocally, "You can't have both grizzly bears and sheep in the same place. Putting sheep in grizzly bear range is asking for trouble." Roop, who has worked with the grizzly since 1973, compares this practice with mixing matches and gasoline, or building a house on a flood plain.

The sheep owners rebuttal is that he is protecting a way of life and the property that supports his family. He objects vigorously to suggestions that he move his flock to other grazing allotments in the national forest system and off that part of the public land that his family may have used, and considered its own, since the time of his father and grandfather.

Conservationists argue that sheep should be moved off the public lands within prime grizzly range because the Endangered Species Act officially gives the bear priority in these areas. One study showed that in the five years between 1970 and 1975 twenty bears were killed on sheep allotments around Yellowstone, and two on cattle allotments.

One grizzly bear biologist sums it up: "Grizzly bears and sheep are not compatible." The grizzlies lost to sheepmen may well be a major factor in further reducing the Yellowstone bear population below that point where there is hope for it into the future. Biologists R. R. Knight and S. L. Judd, working with the Yellowstone grizzly population, believe that any sheep allotment within twenty kilometers of the park boundary is a hazard to the Yellowstone grizzly population.

Sheepmen have often inadvertently conditioned bears to the taste of mutton by their management practices. Bringing sheep onto spring range too early when the bears are still feeding in these lower elevations, puts bears and sheep close together. After early July, the bears may be back in the higher country. Flocks are sometimes left without sheepherders to watch over them at night, or moved through grizzly country with less attention than they should be given. "When a herd is on the move," writes Charles Jonkel in *Western Wildlands*, "it is common practice to leave dead, injured, and sick sheep behind. This practice baits bears to the herd. A grizzly that kills a sick or injured sheep learns to kill more sheep. If herders killed dying sheep before moving on, and disposed of sheep carcasses by burying them or treating them with strong chemicals, grizzly attacks would probably decrease."

From the sheepman's view, as he stands on a mountainside surveying his flock, the grizzly bear is a threat to his business and his family. In his worst dreams, he sees Bear Number 38, and recalls the tribulations of Bill Enget in the summer of 1983.

For sixty years the Enget family had moved its sheep every summer to the high country in the Targhee National Forest where it held a grazing allotment on Two Top Mountain. Much of Targhee, which lies in Idaho, west of Yellowstone, is prime grizzly country where, between 1970 and 1974 there were thirty-two known grizzly deaths. Twenty-eight of these bears deaths resulted from conflicts with livestock, mostly sheep. After the grizzly was classified as a threatened species in 1975, the Two Top Mountain area was designated Situation One land under the grizzly bear recovery plan, giving the grizzly priority over all other uses, including livestock grazing.

This was the situation when Number 38, accompanied by her two large cubs, began moving toward Two Top Mountain. Because the old bear wore a radio collar, biologists soon knew what direction she was moving. Word went out to Enget that the bears were coming and as they moved steadily closer to Enget's allotment, the biologists began hazing them with a variety of weapons they hoped would turn them back across the mountains toward Yellowstone.

A crew of Forest Service workers moved in to try to keep sheep and bears separated and spent the nights listening to the signals from the radio worn by Number 38 and responding with flare guns, noise makers, and rifles fired into the air. The Forest Service even tried an electric fence which Number 38 and her offspring walked around.

Enget, meanwhile, was saying that the bears should have been stopped long before they reached his sheep on Two Top. The biologists could tell what direction they were traveling and should have, he felt, trapped them and moved them back into the national park. Finally, the grizzly bear team decided that Enget, in keeping with the law, must move his sheep.

There were several reasons why Enget preferred not to move. Transportation is costly and the sheep business operates on a narrow margin. The lambs would probably fail to gain weight as rapidly as they would on Two Top and this would mean lower prices on the market. Besides, the older ewes in the flock knew the Two Top area and were less likely to get lost there.

On the other hand, Number 38 had managed, in spite of the harassing, to kill several of Enget's sheep. The Forest Service officially placed the number at six, although Enget said that, including those scattered and lost because of the bears, the figure was closer to twenty-five.

In the following days, as the flock was herded slowly out of the Situation One land toward a new area, the bears simply tagged along. The biologists decided there was no choice and brought in culvert traps and captured all three bears and moved them back into the national park.

Later, while Number 38 was being trapped and handled again in the park, her heart stopped beating and did not start again even though she was given an antidote and a lengthy session of cardiopulmonary resuscitation. Sheepmen say she died of the drug administered, others speculate that her breathing was cut off by cramped conditions in the trap, and the official finding was that the exact cause of death was unknown.

Many people had a hand in it, but the underlying cause remains the old problem of competition between man and bear for space. Wayne Arnst, outdoor editor of the *Great Falls* (Montana) *Tribune,* writing about Number 38's passing, is on target when he says, "The only reasonable answer we can come up with is that she was not killed by any one individual or group."

But whatever the cause, or causes, Number 38, once a healthy and productive female grizzly, died. Furthermore, Enget's troubles started a campaign among the sheepmen to get the boundaries for Situation One lands redrawn to better protect the sheep, and the noose tightened a little more around the neck of the troubled grizzly bears.

PREDATOR CONTROL

Historically, the federal government has been a partner in the killing of grizzly bears. As herds of cattle and sheep spread across the western states the ranchers asked for government aid in controlling predators on public land, and in 1915 the federal government eased into the predator control business. That year the Bureau of Biological Survey was handed one hundred and twenty-five thousand dollars and instructed to use it for killing predators.

With this budding effort to rid the West of mountain lions, wolves, bears, and other wild meat eaters, the government had taken a step not easily reversed. Government programs have a tendency to become locked into the structure. Although there have been major attitude changes, and increasing public resistance to killing predators, the federal government still supports, within the U. S. Fish and Wildlife Service, a branch whose technicians make their livings as government hunters.

A growing percentage of American citizens, however, question the need for all-out control efforts aimed at eliminating whole populations of coyotes and other wild meat eaters. Instead, the present official predator control effort is slanted toward concentrating on the trouble causers, while allowing the remainder to go their way.

Among early government trappers this brand of thinking would have been good for a laugh. The government hunter's success depended on how many predators he could take out of circulation. "Almost all you had to do then," as George S. Rost, President of the National Animal Damage Control Association told a symposium on predation recently, "was to give a man a horse, a sack of beans, some traps and strychnine, thirty dollars a month salary, and point him in the direction of the coyote or wolf problem. The only time you saw him was when he had to come in for more beans. He had millions of acres of public land over which to roam unrestricted."

To these early government trappers, as well as ranchers and many others, there simply was no such thing as a mountain lion, bobcat, coyote, wolf, bear, or eagle, along with a lengthy list of lessor predators, that deserved to live. Predator control was a numbers game. For thirty years, ending in 1970, the number of animals killed by federal trappers was a matter of record. The trappers and their supervisors kept score, and their bureau used the kill figures to justify their requests for funding in Washington.

In those three decades, federal employees killed thousands of coyotes, bobcats, wolves, and mountain lions. Their score card shows that they took forty six thousand seven hundred and seventy-two of the small southern red wolves which, significantly, are now considered extinct in the wild.

These were not just convicted livestock killers, but instead were victims of a blanket killing operation. The annual cost to taxpayer of this federal trapping program rose eventually to more than four million dollars. The idea was to eliminate predators and make the West safe for the slow-witted herbivores immediately useful to man.

In pursuit of this policy, government hunters sent a long list of grizzlies, both guilty and innocent, to their final reward. The official records show a total kill of at least twenty-two thousand six hundred and seventeen bears, including both black and grizzly bears. There were years when these government trappers admitted to killing more than a thousand bears. Often the trappers neglected to report the species of the bear killed. This was especially true for such areas as Colorado where the grizzly was "officially" supposed to no longer exist, or where there was known to be public opposition to killing bears. Some estimates put the grizzly bear kill by Animal Damage Control agents at thirty-five thousand.

THE GIEFER GRIZZLY

We think of the renegade grizzlies as history long past, a part of the Old West, legends the likes of which we will never again see in our time. But never sell the grizzly short. Even in recent times, as the great bear grows steadily more rare, the spirit of independence pulses through his shaggy breast. There is always promise that new names may be added to the long list of unforgettable grizzlies that gained fame by living outside the rules prescribed for them by man.

Bears that run amok of man and become famous trouble causers are usually specialists, and perhaps the most recent famous grizzly to maintain the old tradition of outlaw bears was a large male that specialized in house breaking. He kept property owners in the Flathead River country of northwestern Montana frothing for two years as he added new break-ins to his record. This bear, however, happened to be one of the more elusive bears ever to roam these mountains, and he had everything going his way until an April evening in 1977, when he was feeding on an avalanche chute in nearby Canada and came into the sights of a skilled big game hunter from Pennsylvania.

For years, this grizzly wandered through life, attracting no special attention from the people who shared those mountains with him. He ranged the North and Middle Forks of the Flathead, no doubt wandering up the little side creeks and on occasion crossing over into the wilderness of Glacier National Park. Year after year he lived the life of the wild uncorrupted bear, harvesting roots, berries, small rodents, and other bear foods that conditioned his growing body for the long winter sleeps.

Then one day in the valley of the Middle Fork, he came upon a shabby little cabin being used by a developer laying out a new summer-home subdivision. A warden with the Montana Department of Fish, Wildlife, and Parks recalls that, "It was an old cabin that didn't amount to a damn. They had cooked fish and left garbage lying around and this probably attracted the bear." The bear, perhaps coming upon this structure in his territory for the first time, lifted his broad head to the breezes and savored the tempting odors.

Gaining entry to cabins was no problem for a beast of the strength and intelligence of this male grizzly. In the coming months people up and down the valley would learn to board up windows and drive long spikes through doors from the inside to discourage the bear, but on this first cabin job all the old bear had to do was enter at his leisure because the doors and windows had been left open.

In this early effort at breaking and entering, the bear found enough tempting supplies to plant the seed of a new behavior pattern. The numerous cabins, often vacant much of the year, held treasures that sent him checking one cabin after the other. At this stage, his depredations were concentrated in the area where Giefer Creek flows into Bear Creek which soon joins the Middle Fork, so the bear became known as the Giefer Grizzly.

The big bear learned as he went along. As he became more proficient, he was less destructive. Where he found nothing of interest, he sometimes merely opened doors, checked for food, and left a few muddy footprints behind him as he departed.

After his first few cabin jobs, angry owners started calling the Montana Department of Fish, Wildlife, and Parks for assistance. This brought Warden Captain Louis Kis of Kalispell to the scene. Because the department was dealing with a threatened animal for which it was deeply concerned, it planned to move the bear instead of execute it.

The workers wheeled in a culvert trap on a trailer, set and baited it and waited for the Giefer Grizzly to enter. He declined.

Next, the wildlife crew arranged one of the foot snares widely used for bears and put a bait behind it. Three nights later they caught the Giefer Grizzly for the first time. He was a fine big bear and did not display any special bad temper toward his captors. After drugging the grizzly, biologists attached an aluminum tag to one ear. Then, they transported the bear fifty miles away to Sullivan Creek where he was set free to wander off into the bush. This was the final report of the Giefer Grizzly that year.

Among the wildlife workers, there were those who suspected that they had not heard the last of this bear. They were right. The following spring brought a call that a grizzly bear had left its tracks around a newly invaded cabin, and other reports from angry cabin owners soon followed. The bear's fame was spreading.

Once more the wildlife professionals moved in and the bear was eventually recaptured. This time he was tattooed and outfitted with a collar carrying a small radio transmitter, then moved north almost to the border between Montana and British Columbia. As the break-ins continued, the officials knew they had no choice. The Giefer Grizzly was declared incorrigible and condemned. Sometimes the grizzly returned and raided cabins he had already broken into several times, but mostly he seemed to be curious about the contents of cabins new to him. People could now count up a total of fifty or more break-ins credited to this bear. They told new stories all the time about him, and local newspaper editors kept everyone up to date on the latest grizzly developments.

Pick-up truck jockeys declared, on occasion, that they'd take care of this goddamned grizz, legal or not. But they didn't. Old Giefer Grizzly went quietly about his housebreaking business and all anybody saw of him was the mess he left behind. Typically, he would push in the door, enter, check for canned foods on the shelves, perhaps upset a can of flour and roll it around the floor, and tear out any pots and pans carrying remnant odors of bacon or other foods, bring down any hanging meat and help himself, bite into cans of corn, green beans, and peaches and lap part of the juices from the sticky floor. Then sometimes he would tear open bedding and scatter the remnants around the premises until he left behind a thoroughly junked property. Here was a genuine original that merited the respect of all. More than once there were false claims that the Giefer Grizzly had been killed, stories which the old bear soon personally disproved by breaking into another cabin or two. Sometimes he broke into several in the same night. He seemed to be no threat to people. One victim told how the bear had cleaned out the kitchen while his two boys slept in an adjoining room.

One favorite story was the tale of how the bear had rid itself of the collar and miniature radio transmitter with which the biologists had fitted it. Biologists, tracking the grizzly, followed the beeps of their sophisticated little transmitter to an unoccupied cabin and there, in the middle of the floor, among assorted ripped and spilled groceries, lay the state-of-the-art collar that the Giefer Grizzly had personally removed from his furry neck.

Recapturing him became increasingly difficult. The third time, the best trapping crews from government agencies as well as the Border Grizzly Project failed in their efforts to capture him. Meanwhile, he continued to raid trap sites and cabins nightly while easily avoiding the cleverest sets and confounding the official hunters waiting for him in the dark. "Nobody even came close to taking him," recalls one of those working on the project. "He could figure out new sets as fast as they were designed and built."

Winter came before his sentence was carried out. That winter, a couple of thousand miles to the east, Ray S. Koontz, a noted big game hunter, was thinking of adding a new animal to his outstanding trophy collection. Koontz, owner of the supermarket in the county seat town of McConnelsburg, Pennsylvania, already had hunted around the world. There was space in his basement trophy room, along with the heads making up his super grand slam on sheep, a glacier bear from Alaska, and other trophies, for a grizzly bear, which he planned to take during the authorized spring season in British Columbia.

On the evening of April 24, 1977, Koontz and his British Columbia guide were watching over a small snow slide beside a wooded area where bears were known to feed. A large grizzly, the only one Koontz saw on the hunt, came out of the woods and turned broadside to him. Koontz placed the first two shots in the neck, precisely where he aimed, then at the urging of his guide, who wanted to take no chances of having to trail an injured bear into the bush, added what he considers an unnecessary third shot when the bear was already down.

As they began examining the grizzly, both Koontz and his guide realized that they had taken a marked bear. One ear was decorated with a blue aluminum tag the size of a half dollar and carrying the numbers 4037. In the other ear was a smaller red tag numbered 2179. Both carried the identifying mark of the Montana Department of Fish, Wildlife and Parks. One tooth was missing.

Ray Koontz, a Pennsylvania hunter, shown here with his trophies, ended the Giefer Grizzly's string of depradations on April 24, 1977. The Giefer bear is at far left.

The Montana wildlife professionals became excited when they heard the numbers read from the tags. There could be no doubt; the Pennsylvania hunter, to the relief of many, had taken Montana's most famous modern bear. The story of the Giefer Grizzly had ended. A headline in the *Montana Standard* said, "The Giefer Is Dead", and other newspapers, even in distant states, reported the death of the grizzly that had left his indelible imprint on the land where he was born.

He proved that a grizzly bear, even one wearing a radio transmitter designed to make it easy for people to locate him, can still out-wit dozens of people, at least for a while. Charles Jonkel says that he learned more respect for grizzlies from this one bear than from all the thousands of other bears he has studied combined.

In the end, however, even the most elusive grizzly with the maximum capacity for survival loses. The Giefer Grizzly, estimated by officials to have weighed six hundred pounds, and taken by a skilled hunter in a legal hunt, stands as a full mount now in a trophy room in Pennsylvania. If he had not been taken in a natural setting in this early spring season, the condemned grizzly would doubtless have gone on matching wits with the finest trappers. "And probably won," says one of them.

Chapter 8

A Grizzly Pushed Too Far

When James W. Anthony, out of breath after eight miles of running and trying to catch up with his hounds, approached the grove of aspens in the mountains of southern Colorado on April 30, 1904, he was about to make local history. Suddenly he was face to face with the most feared grizzly bear in all the West. Most of the famous renegade grizzlies earned their name by killing livestock, but Anthony must have felt some inner tremblings in that moment because the bear that rose to its hind feet in front of him was known to have tasted human flesh.

This outlaw bear, even after death, was to be memorialized as his life story was repeated and embroidered in ranch homes, saloons, and newspaper offices for years.

This special attention is understandable because the true renegade bear is not the normal run-of-the-woods grizzly. Instead of making a profession of keeping away from people, these aberrant individuals boldly satisfy their newfound taste for domestic livestock wherever the opportunity coincides with hunger.

This bear's long string of transgressions could probably be traced to his earliest meetings with people and their property, and we can imagine the possible sequence of events. Early one autumn evening the grizzly might have arisen from his resting place and headed down the wooded slope, searching for foods to quiet his rumbling belly.

His world was no longer the wilderness known to his ancestors. The mountains were still there, as steep and high as ever, and so were the forest and the alpine meadows. But there were differences. The old bear saw the new signs often when he came across footprints in the trails, the grass trampled by sheep, the little herds of cattle, the fences in the foothills, and the timber cuttings in the highlands. And more often each year, he saw the men themselves.

He followed no special plan in his search for food. He may have come upon the remains of a stillborn calf, and fed. Another time, still driven by hunger, he came upon a herd of cattle in the night, and there was historic precedent for what he did next. To this bear, how much different were the man-kept cattle from the buffalo of earlier times?

The bear was upon the cattle before they sensed the danger, and his victim was denied even time enough to issue a final sound before its neck snapped. The following morning, the rancher whose property the bear had destroyed, mounted his horse and followed the tracks but lost the trail in the hills. He studied the tracks carefully, swearing that he would know them the next time he saw them.

This was the beginning of big trouble for the bear, but trouble also for those wanting to see his hide stretched on the wall. Many an animal would grease this old bear's chin before he departed this mortal coil and, as it turned out, man would be listed among his victims. Already condemned for killing numerous cattle—some people placed the total at an unlikely eight hundred head—this bear finally committed the unforgivable.

His home territory saddled the continental divide and spread over an area of perhaps seventy-five miles in diameter. The big grizzly first came to the attention of rancher Wharton H. Pigg when Pigg began losing more head of stock than he considered either normal or acceptable. Pigg, who named the giant bear "Old Mose," tried his best to intercept the big grizzly in the hills, but only rarely did he even see him.

Word of the bear's raids spread among surrounding ranchers, while none of them had any more success in taking the beast than Pigg had. Old Mose was even developing a reputation for breaking up hunters' camps. The first of these episodes occurred late one night as a small party of bear hunters sat around their dying campfire, spinning yarns. The camp was quiet and peaceful beneath the starry Rocky Mountain sky as the whisp of gray smoke from the glowing embers drifted up into the yellowing aspen. The chilly evening air had carried the odors of human food over the slopes to be picked up by the sniffing grizzly, fresh out of his day bed. The results are easily enough visualized.

The bear eventually followed the tantalizing odors of frying food to the edge of the little camp and stood silently in the bushes, studying the scene.

The horses were the first to raise the alarm. They grew nervous and, because they failed to settle, their owners began wondering what was lurking out there in the shadows. At this juncture a cautious bear might melt into the dark recesses well back out of the danger zone. But Old Mose was not the average bear.

One of the hunters rose to check the horses, and as he moved off, a giant grizzly bear lurched into the circle of light, causing hunters to tumble over backwards in a scramble for safety, then begin reaching wildly for their guns. The bear rushed straight through the camp, scattering people, pans, whisky bottles, and saddle blankets in all directions, and was headed for his exit around the tent when one of his broad feet became entangled in a corner guy rope.

Now, added to the crashing of runaway horses, the yelling and cursing of men, one of whom ran right through the campfire in his stocking feet, and the clattering of kitchen ware, were the grunting and chuffing of a furious grizzly bear entangled in a canvas tent in which he had gift-wrapped himself. Old Mose was equal to the challenge and, within a minute or less, escaped the now-demolished tent and dashed off into the night, leaving behind a thoroughly destroyed camp.

This story spread around the countryside, adding to Old Mose's growing reputation. If wrecking camps, however, had been the worst of his sins, Old Mose might have been taken less seriously.

The more infamous Old Mose became for his livestock depredations, the more tenaciously he was hunted. So many claimed to have wounded him that, if true, Old Mose would have carried souvenir lead from most of the hunters in his territory and a respectable number from outside the region as well. An unknown percentage of these hunters probably told the truth, and each new scrape with people made the elusive old bear more wiley than ever. But the angry and frustrated ranchers still found Old Mose's footprint around their dead cattle.

Some reports say they placed rewards on the head of Old Mose in those years, but he would have been hunted anyhow because those pursuing him understood that taking this bear would bring them instant fame.

OLD MOSE BECOMES A MAN-KILLER

Occasionally there were reports that Old Mose had attacked and mutilated some ranch hand, and the story would pass around until nobody could any longer recall the unfortunate's name or even the ranch on which he had labored. Evidence that the old bear, for all the trouble he had caused, was really a man-killer was too flimsy to stand up. But this was before that autumn day when Old Mose encountered a lanky bewhiskered hunter named Jake Radcliff.

Radcliff and two hunting buddies had camped in the mountains, planning to ambush the crafty bear. Old Mose had been killing cattle again, and rancher Pigg needed help. Early in the morning the hunting companions split up, each intending to explore separate areas.

Radcliff worked his way down a ravine until he saw a pile of freshly dug earth which he went to investigate, thinking that the bear might be excavating his winter den. Whatever the reason for the digging, and it was probably to cache food, Old Mose was nearby watching the invasion of his territory and, as Radcliff poked around, he heard a threatening growl and chomping of teeth that made his pulse pick up speed.

Although Radcliff was an experienced hunter, and must have speculated often about how calm he would remain if he ever came face to face with Old Mose, he was startled by the fact that the giant bear was only a few yards distant. Quickly, Radcliff swung his gun to his shoulder and sent a bullet into the bear. But the shot hit Old Mose in the shoulder and the giant bear was scarcely shaken by it. Before Radcliff could take any other action, the bear was upon him.

Old Mose slammed Radcliff to the ground, pounced upon him, grabbed him in those powerful jaws, and threw him into the air. Radcliff landed hard and was already in bad shape. He lay there motionless while the giant bear stood over him sniffing and chomping. Then Old Mose, apparently harboring no special grudge, turned and began wandering off.

But he stopped and waited. Radcliff could no longer hear the bear, but he waited a while longer, then gingerly lifted his bleeding head to see if Old Mose was gone. He wasn't.

This was all the bear needed and now he charged down on the hapless Radcliff again, his fury renewed, and began shaking and chewing the man. Radcliff maintained his consciousness and the next time the bear departed the hunter did not risk raising his head, if indeed he was able.

Radcliff's friends found him in due time and, although the injured hunter was near death, he managed to tell them his version of the encounter with the famous bear. The two companions fashioned a stretcher from a blanket and two aspen poles and carried Radcliff down the mountain to the nearest ranch. From there he was loaded into a wagon for the trip to town and medical help. Jake Radcliff died on the way and in that instant Old Mose became more famous than ever. Now he was a man-killer.

Efforts to take the old bear intensified. Hunting parties scoured the mountains throughout the bear's territory, but the elusive grizzly was seldom spotted. His tracks were seen occasionally, often near a freshly killed steer, but he seemed to understand that he was hunted, and he was exceedingly skilled at avoiding his pursuers.

Some of those who pursued Old Mose tried to take him in traps. One trapper set out a beer keg with a ring of spikes driven through it so the sharp ends pointed inward at an angle. The bear is said to have put his head into the barrel, eaten the bait, then smashed the barrel to escape.

Another trapper baited a log pen with part of a steer near which was set a powerful bear trap with spring jaws. Old Mose was extremely thorough in examining such situations, however, and according to old newspaper accounts, could even tell which traps were still set and which sprung. If the trap was still set, he never touched the bait.

Eventually, the old bear's habits were well understood. From the tracks he left on the trail and the occasional brief sightings, his pursuers knew that he sometimes took a dip in a small lake on Black Mountain. This caused one of the trappers to set his trap in the shallows where he had seen tracks of the big bear. The trick almost worked.

The rancher who set the underwater trap dispatched a boy one morning to the crest of the hill from which he could look down upon the lake and see if there was a bear in the trap. The boy lifted his head above the ridge and there, to his delight, thrashing around in the shallow water trying to pull free from the trap, was the biggest bear he had ever seen.

The excited boy raced back to the ranch and reported that Old Mose, the famous grizzly, was caught at last. In minutes, a fully armed posse was riding off in a cloud of dust to bring the outlaw bear to what they considered his rightful end. The cowboys topped the ridge, reined to a skidding halt, and looked down upon the lake. All was quiet and serene. No bear. They did find the trap sprung and fastened in its steel jaws were two big bear toes.

Whether or not Old Mose killed more than one man has never been proved, but on flimsy circumstantial evidence he was often credited with the death of at least two others. The mutilated body of James Asher was discovered in the old bear's territory, and this was enough to pin it on the grizzly. Another time, a group of prospectors came upon the old bones and boots of a cowboy where the agent of death could have been any of various causes including old age, Old Mose, Old Monongahela, gunshot, or snakebite. But there was no doubt in many minds where the real blame lay—that renegade old bear had struck again.

OLD MOSE MEETS HIS MATCH

In those years when Old Mose's reputation was growing, bear hunters from distant places took a keen interest. One of these hunters was Anthony, who had become so intense in his pursuit of the old bear that he loaded up a couple of dozen of his best bear hounds and brought them down to Colorado from Idaho. Anthony was no new-comer to grizzly bear hunting. He had already taken more than forty of the big bears, none of them, however, famous outlaws.

Anthony became a good friend of Pigg on whose Stirrup Ranch Old Mose seemed most at home. In the spring of 1904 these two hunters decided to go after Old Mose and stay until the job was done. Part of the story of that famous hunt is to be found in the *Denver Republican* for May 3, 1904, which reported that the two men and a pack of twenty dogs swept back and forth over the Black Mountain country for many days searching for clues to the location of the great bear.

Anthony and Pigg continued their hunt for nearly a month, scouring the hills each day, waiting for Anthony's dogs to pick up old Mose's trail. No matter which direction they went, or what mountain they climbed, they failed to cross the famous bear's track. Then one day the pack opened up, announcing its discovery, while Anthony, within hearing distance, realized that the hounds had put the bear into motion. For eight miles, the hunters followed the dogs across the mountains.

Finally, the dogs brought the grizzly to bay. When he caught up with them in a grove of quaking aspen, Anthony saw the dogs, now crazy with excitement, had surrounded the biggest bear he ever saw. The bear walked along paying scant attention to the dogs that were harassing him, and took little notice of Anthony either.

The hunter first fired when about seventy yards from Old Mose. He scored three more hits in quick succession, but none brought the bear down. Said Anthony, "He stood on his haunches and looked at me, dropped down and started for me."

Anthony held his fire until the bear closed the distance to three yards, then took careful aim and, as he reported, "Got him between the eyes." Old Mose fell and never moved again under his own power.

The old bear's weight is not known for certain. One report says that he weighed almost nine hundred pounds, hog-dressed, when taken shortly after his emergence from his long winter sleep. A photograph of Old Mose taken at the time of his death shows him to have been a very large grizzly. Newspapers of the day said that, from nose to tail, the hide measured ten feet, four inches and its width when stretched out was nine and a half feet.

The hide hung on public display in Canon City and numerous hunters came to view what remained of the old grizzly and sometimes point out holes they claimed were put there by bullets from their guns. Some may have been right because the old bear carried a handful of bullets by the time he was finally taken, at least one of them believed to have been put there by Jake Radcliff.

The *Denver Republican* reported that Pigg and Anthony, "last Saturday afternoon succeeded in killing 'Old Mose' the largest and most famous grizzly bear ever known in southern Colorado.

"Old Mose has figured in the annals of Fremont and Park counties for many years, and hunters have made special efforts to bag this splendid specimen of his tribe, but invariably returned disappointed."

Whatever the old grizzly's crimes against people, he was not a man-killer by choice. There is no evidence that he ever attacked a person unprovoked. He eluded people whenever possible, but they had made it increasingly difficult for man and bear to avoid each other as ranchers moved their herds of tempting cattle into his native territory, and hunters and their hounds pursued him for years into every hidden corner of his wild mountain domain.

Chapter 9

How Smart Is the Grizzly?

Those who know the grizzly bear well generally credit it with being intelligent and resourceful, quick to learn and slow to forget. There was a time, in scientific circles, when wild animals were thought to lack the ability to reason and all their actions were credited to instinct and nothing more. This belief supported man's sense of superiority, flattered him, and left him convinced that he was unique in the world where no other creature possessed the ability to figure anything out for itself. Charles Darwin's theories began to turn this around, and we have come to understand that other animals, while they may lack the highly developed brain of the human, do possess intelligence. The bears seem to rank well up the ladder in intelligence and sometimes demonstrate what appears to be a remarkable capacity to reason.

This has been noted by many who knew bears from first-hand experience. Harold McCracken, naturalist, explorer, and long-time student of the grizzly bear in its natural haunts, wrote in his notable book *The Beast That Walks Like Man,* "The better acquainted I have become with grizzlies, the higher opinion I have of them; and this applies to their intelligence as well as their dispositions."

"I would give the grizzly first place in the animal world for brain-power," Enos Mills adds.

Naturalist David Star Jordan classed the grizzly bear as mentally superior to the dog, horse, and gray wolf, and said that the grizzly has, not only instinct, but also the power to reason. Seldom does anyone call the animal dumb. Theodore Roosevelt, who knew both his share of grizzlies and the men who spent much of their lives chasing them, said, "The grizzly is a shrewd beast that shows the usual bear-like capacity for adapting himself to changed conditions."

The evidence is found in accounts of the great bear's skill at avoiding trouble and outwitting people. William H. Wright, who tracked grizzlies for many years wherever he could find them, recorded the story of the most remarkable grizzly he ever encountered.

"The grizzly bear," said Wright, "far excels in cunning any other animal found throughout the Rocky Mountains, and indeed for that matter, he far excels them all combined." Wright's candidate for the head of the class was a grizzly living in the Bitterroots at the time the naturalist accompanied a hunting party into those mountains.

The party camped on a tributary of the Clearwater where one of the hunters had spotted a giant silvertip bear. He killed an elk, and after the elk was dressed, the scraps were carried to a gully a mile or so from camp. Here the group built a log pen, tossed the remains of the elk into it as bait, and set their trap where the grizzly, if he came, should step right into trouble.

When Wright returned to the site, it looked as if a tornado had touched down. The pen was torn down and the logs heaped up over the trap which had not been touched. The bait, however, had been deftly removed.

Wright looked around. "Fifty feet away," he wrote, "I saw a large pile of moss and leaves scraped together and beside it a bed where the bear had been lying." Wright found that the moss covered what was left of the bait and this gave them an idea. They rescued the trap from beneath the heap of logs and made a new set in the bear's pile of leaves and moss, then tossed pieces of the elk meat around the set, congratulated themselves, and left to await the bear's return.

"That night," according to Wright, "the bear came again, picked up all the loose meat, but touched nothing under the moss."

The audacity of this elusive grizzly became almost a personal affront to members of the hunting party. About the time the grizzly frustrated the trappers in their second attempt, three members of the party shot three elk, a cow, calf, and bull. They decided to divide the meat between themselves and the local monarch that was making fools of them. They would use the bull, plus the remnants of the other two elk, as bait for the bear.

Some distance upriver from camp, they found the perfect place for their next attempt on the grizzly bear's life. An almost vertical gully reached from the top of the bank to the water's edge a hundred feet below. If the bear were to claim the meat he would have to negotiate a constricted passage between a log jam and a rock outcropping. It was here that the hunters rolled the excess elk meat down the slope.

The first night they set no trap but were content to allow the grizzly to find the meat and claim it. The following morning they were encouraged because they could read in the bear's tracks the story of what he had done. After eating all he wanted, he had dragged the remnants of the bait together in one place and covered them with dirt and leaves. He would be back. They promptly set bear traps around the bait, taking full precautions to hide evidence of their work. Again, the bear easily avoided the traps.

Members of the party, after again measuring the animal's giant track, wanted more than ever to take this smart old bear. By now, they were down to the final days of their hunt, and some of the group decided to rig a set gun, or spring gun, for the bear.

SET GUNS AND BEAR TRAPS

This brand of guerrilla warfare, using an untended gun with a string attached to the trigger against grizzlies, was not an uncommom practice in those times. There was apparently little question about whether or not a set gun was fair to the game or even to some wandering human it might unintentionally kill. There were no early laws to protect either bears or people against such booby traps, and some considered any tactic fair against bears. Not only set guns, but also the massive bear traps so commonly used, posed an ever-present threat to human life. Theodore Roosevelt often discussed this danger with western outdoorsmen and once wrote about it.

"There is, however", said Roosevelt, "one very real danger to which the solitary bear-trapper is exposed, the danger of being caught in his own trap. The huge jaws of the gin are easy to spring and most hard to open. If an unwary passerby should tread between them and be caught by the leg, his fate would be doubtful, though he would probably die under the steady growing torment of the merciless iron jaws, as they pressed ever deeper into the sore flesh and broken bones. But if caught by the arms, while setting or fixing the trap, his fate would be in no doubt at all, for it would be impossible for the stoutest man to free himself by any means. Terrible stories are told of solitary mountain hunters who disappeared, and were found years later in the lonely wilderness, as mouldering skeletons, the shattered bones of the forearms still held in the rusty jaws of the gin."

As the members of Wright's hunting party prepared their set gun reception for the big bear, Wright, himself an outspoken admirer of the grizzly, may have had reservations. Nonetheless, he joined in the plan. The gun was set with the butt against a rock and the muzzle pointing at the trail the bear must follow, or at least the trail they thought he would follow. A silk fishing line, tied to the trigger, stretched across the bear's trail.

Then a second gun was rigged with a line a dozen feet from the first and parallel to it, leaving the bear a narrow pathway between the log jam and the rock outcropping which would help guide him to his fate. As the hunters viewed it, the big grizzly had only two choices. He could either give up his idea of elk for supper, or he could stumble across the strings and shoot himself in the side.

No one heard the gun fire during the night, so the hunters went the following morning to see what had happened. The tracks showed plainly that the grizzly had approached the silk string and stopped. When he tried to reach the bait from another direction, he again came to the string and suddenly stopped. Finally, instead of leaving hungry and frustrated, he climbed over the rock and worked his way from ledge to ledge until he could come down to the bait and eat in safety. Then he backtracked and departed by the safe path he had worked out. The hunter never saw him. Wright called this, "as wonderful a record of animal sagacity as I have ever seen."

This bear's achievement becomes more believable when compared with the case reported by Enos Mills for about the same period. Mills wrote, "Formerly it was not difficult to trap a grizzly. But he quickly learned to avoid the menace of traps. The bear sees through all the camouflage of the trapper. Deodorized and concealed traps, traps near the bait and far from it, traps placed singly and in clusters —these, and even the slender concealed string of a spring gun he usually detects and avoids."

Mills once had the opportunity to accompany a trapper who set out to take a big grizzly that ranchers had identified as an outlaw cattle stealer. The ranchers brought their cattle in early from the summer range and pledged a thousand dollar reward to the person who killed the bear.

One of them donated an old cow as grizzly bait, and the trapper led the creature into a gulch which he considered suited to his purposes because its banks would help guide the bear to the bait. There he picketed the cow and began rigging his surprise for the bear. When all was in readiness, the old cow stood tethered on a short rope, and surrounding her were three spring guns, each pointing down a potential bear approach route. "The strings to these guns," Mills recorded, "were silk line stretched over bushes and tall grass so as to be inconspicuous." In addition, the trapper set four heavy bear traps around the bait in case the bear should slip past the artillery.

The first night, as Mills and the trapper set up their camp and waited, a light snow fell. When morning came they went to the gulch, and there stood the gaunt old cow. Waiting. There was no bear track anywhere around.

When the trapper returned the next night, however, a line of tracks showed that the grizzly had picked up the scent from a mile distant and come in a straight line to the tethered cow. What he did next was written in the snow for Mills and the trapper to read. The bear halted within two feet of the silk line. He would not touch it. Instead, he followed it around the cow without finding the end to the string.

If the record of what the bear then did had not been written in the snow, Mills might not have believed it. "He then leaped the line," Mills said, "something I had never before heard of a bear doing." In approaching the cow the bear managed to avoid each of the traps as if he carried a map of their locations. Moving in between a trap in front of the cow's head and one at her side, he killed the cow, then fed on her where she fell.

When finished with his meal, the grizzly dragged the carcass across two of the traps, springing them, turned and leaped back across the line and departed down the booby-trapped gulch without suffering a scratch.

The trapper, knowledgeable about bears, sensed victory. Now the pattern was set. The bear had claimed his kill and when hunger awakened within him again, the location would be fresh in his memory and the trip from his day bed would be a short one. In the precise spot where the bear landed as he jumped over the silk line, the trapper set still another heavy metal trap. Then he added a fourth spring-gun set to the arsenal, installing this one somewhat below the bait, and stretched the string across the bear's path.

That night, just as the trapper predicted, the bear returned. But instead of coming up the gulch as he had the first night, he approached from above. He retraced his earlier steps around the lines. Something alerted him at the site of his first crossing where the new trap now waited, so he crossed instead at another point where there was no trap.

Still avoiding all the traps, the grizzly ate his fill, covered the remaining meat with some dead logs, and leaped back over the set lines, and vanished into the night, well fed. Instead of going out by the way he entered, he started down the gulch, a route that would bring him into contact with the new spring-gun set. But he stopped while still a dozen feet from the line, and one can imagine the erect form of the great bear standing there, head up, sniffing the night air for clues.

Instead of advancing, the bear turned and followed the string until he came to the cocked gun waiting at the side of the gulch. Then he simply walked around the rifle and plodded on into the night.

A gigantic trap used for grizzlies in the West around the turn of the century. The one danger of the trap was that the trapper himself, or a passerby, might get caught in its merciless jaws and perish in the wilderness.

To be outwitted by a bear was more than the trapper could stand, and he renewed his vow to take this animal and claim the reward. Convinced that the grizzly would return, he spent a good part of the next day building a log pen around the remaining bait. The back of the pen was a giant boulder. At the entrance of the pen he set two traps, one inside and one outside. The spring guns remained in position.

The trapper was correct; the grizzly did come back. By this time he knew the drill. He returned with his usual caution, and leaped the string with his usual agility. But at this point he was frustrated. At the single entrance of the pen he apparently once more detected the presence of the hidden traps that guarded the door. His response was to climb to the top of the boulder and, reaching down into the pen, drag up the bait so he could eat.

In doing this, he brushed off one of the pen's top poles. The pole rolled sideways, then fell, crossing a string and firing a rifle. The shot was a complete miss. Who would have thought to aim the rifle at the top of the boulder?

As nearly as Mills and the trapper could reconstruct the bear's reaction to the shot, the animal paused in its feeding and, leaving the meat, climbed down from the boulder. He went to the smoking gun and inspected it.

He then returned to his meal, dragged the bait from the boulder to the ground and cleaned the remaining bones of all their meat. No longer was there food here for him to protect, and the bear made no effort to cover the bones. He crossed the line leading to the gun that had fired by his stepping over it where the fallen log held it down. He then went up the gully, instead of down, and left the trapper with nothing but the story to show for his days of work.

To what extent the bear actually reasoned as he eluded the trapper and his spring guns is open to question. The possibilities that he saw the strings in the middle of the night are slim. Experience had surely taught him to beware of human odors, but the threatening odors conflicted with the promise of food. Nobody can know how much either of these bears used its sense of smell to discover the slender strings that were tied to the rifle triggers, but there is the probability that even the silk strings carried lingering odors from hands that touched them, giving the alert bear all the clues necessary.

These cases were both reported by reliable observers who witnessed the events personally and can therefore be trusted more than can some of the bear stories that circulated from person to person and suffered embellishment in the retelling. Regardless of how the traps and strings were located by the grizzly, the interesting question is how

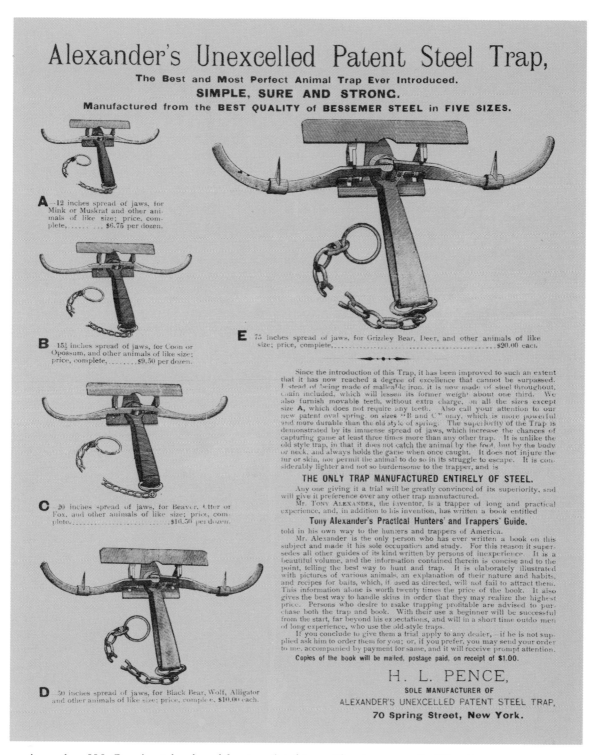

A page from H.L. Pence's catalog showed five sizes of steel traps. These traps were of a different design than the grizzly trap shown in the preceding photo. The largest, shown at "E," was used for grizzlies.

the animal worked out a path around the disturbing barriers. Although they might never before have encountered spring-gun sets, the bears were able to transfer the lessons from other experiences to this situation, and react to the warning clues in a manner that allowed them to eat the bait and escape the booby traps that were set to kill them.

Faced with today's long-range rifles and widespread human odors, the grizzly may have less chance to develop survival skills that will protect it from man, but the Giefer Creek Grizzly demonstrated again that the great bear retains its incredible capacity to adapt to complex situations. One of the trapsites prepared for this bear included a bag of bait suspended from a branch with five snares set below. The theory was that, in acquiring the food, the bear would forget where his hind feet were. The theory was wrong.

The grizzly's capacity to adapt to new situations may be a measure of its intelligence and this, plus its wide range of suitable foods, has prolonged the bear's survival in this world of people.

Chapter 10

The Man Who Lived With Grizzlies

Uncounted thousands of people who pursued bears over the ages found it sufficient to kill the bear and take possession of the dead body. There were some, however, who delighted in keeping live bears as pets. In one sense, we all keep live bears for our own needs when we hold them in zoos. Until recent years hundreds of bears lived in shabby little roadside cages beneath signs encouraging tourists to buy gasoline. The captive bear, docile and demeaned, becomes conditioned, eats, sleeps, breeds, and defecates displaying little recollection of its lost wild heritage.

Probably there have been far more bears held as private pets than we realize. We hear of only a few, including an occasional Gentle Ben that gets on television, alternately playing black bear or grizzly bear roles, depending on the script.

Men have kept bears captive since ancient times. In the fourth century, Roman Emperor Valentinian I owned a pair of huge brown bears, the European equivalent of the grizzly. Furthermore, the Emperor used these giant animals as his body guards and had them chained in front of his chamber every night. His son, Valentinian II, later adopted the practice. According to German author Hermann Dembeck, the Valentinians were good to their pet bears; they fed them people as a special treat.

Perhaps best known of all North Americans who have attempted to domesticate bears was a singular man that newspaper reporter Henry Hittell met one afternoon in 1856. After finishing his daily chores at the newspaper office, Hittell was walking along Clay Street, in San Francisco, when he saw a placard posted on a basement door.

"It announced the exhibition there," Hittell later wrote, "of The Mountaineer Museum—a collection of wild animals of the Pacific Coast."

This was enough to arouse the reporter's curiosity and take him down the stairway to the entrance. Here, in the long, dark and dingy basement with its low ceiling, he met the most unusual man he ever knew. Hittell found the proprietor in the middle of the large room and recalled that he was "quite as strange as any of his animals. He was a man a little over medium size, muscular and wiry, with sharp features and penetrating eyes. He was apparently about fifty years of age, but his hair was very gray and his beard white. He was dressed in coat and trousers of buckskin, fringed at the edges and along the seams of the arms and legs. On his head he wore a cap of deerskin, ornamented with a fox tail, and on his feet buckskin moccasins."

Hittell was, at first, somewhat taken aback by the animals the mountaineer had assembled. Among them were three immense California grizzly bears, two of them wandering around like pet dogs. The reporter was so intrigued by the man and his bears, however, that during the following days he returned repeatedly to talk with the man who said his name was James Capen Adams.

Those conversations continued for the next year and a half, until Hittell knew the full details of this strange man's life and perhaps understood his compulsion to bring giant bears under his absolute domination. The reporter cross-questioned Adams about his adventures and tried to catch him up in tall tales. He told Adams that he wanted nothing but the truth, and the bear man said this was what he would get. The reporter later told Adam's story in his book *Adventures of James Capen Adams.* What Hittell heard and recorded is one of the more remarkable cases ever found in the association of man and the great bears.

Adams was born in Massachusetts in 1807, of practical hardworking parents who believed a young man should grow up prepared to earn his way in a trade. They chose shoemaking for James, and day after day, he bent over his cobbler's bench, learning his trade and hating it. Although he became good at making shoes and boots, he was depressed by the monotony and drudgery, and this caused his mind to skip often from the dingy little shop to the wide open spaces. He was prepared to leave as soon as he was old enough, and change his line of work to something more to his liking.

He met the owner of a traveling show and explained that he possessed great skill in capturing and bringing back alive all manner of wild beasts. His story must have been good because he was hired and promptly dispatched to the wilds of New Hampshire, Vermont, and Maine where he captured a long list of wild animals, including bobcats, cougars, and foxes. He had found his life's work and there was no room left for shoemaking, or so he thought.

All went smoothly with Adams and his wild animals until one day his employer began talking about the troubles they were having with their Bengal tiger. The big cat simply refused to do the bidding of those who had tried so far to educate it, and the owner wondered if Adams would mind giving it a try.

Adams felt that his experience with other animals made him a natural for the tiger training job, and with sufficient youthful self-confidence to match his inexperience, he entered the tiger's cage. For some time, Adams remained the tiger trainer in residence, continuing to enter the cage and work with the beast. The tiger eventually got enough of this hazing, or simply had a bad day, and swatted Adams to the floor then leaped upon him and clawed and bit him severely before he could be rescued.

Once Adams found that he would survive, he had to face the fact that the big cat had rendered him physically unfit, at least for a while, for the rugged animal work he enjoyed. It was back to the cobbler's bench for him, and for the next fifteen years he made shoes and boots, always longing for the exotic life he had tasted.

Eventually, Adam's spinal injuries healed and he gained strength. He had also managed to save money from his business until he decided that he had enough to make a bold step. He converted his six thousand dollars in savings into shoes and boots and set out for St. Louis where business was booming, fully expecting to double his money. Maybe triple it. Instead, the St. Louis building where his wares were stored caught fire and Adams' fortune was wiped out in a single night.

This was late in the 1840's and the talk was all of California and gold being scooped from the ground there. The mass migration was in full force; thousands of souls were setting off for the West Coast following the trails the mountain men had blazed. Adams, who soon joined the other westering souls, arrived in California in 1849.

There he tried various ways to make a living. He farmed, raised stock, did some mining, and attempted different businesses. "Sometimes I was rich," he said, "other times poor." His ill-fortune with the burning shoes, however, seemed to establish a pattern he could not shake. After he built up a herd of cattle worth several thousand dollars, rustlers cleaned him out in a single night. His own speculation, as well as his gullibility when dealing with others, led to defeats that began to sour him on the world and the people in it. Adams displeasure with the world around him festered in his mind until he decided to shuck it all and go live in the hills as a hermit.

ADAMS AND BEN FRANKLIN.

THE FRIGHTENED GRIZZLY.

Two illustrations from Adventures of James Capen Adams *by Henry Hinkel, a newspaper reporter who met Adams in 1856 and subsequently wrote his biography.*

THE MOUNTAIN MAN

When Adams took stock of his chances for becoming a successful mountain man, he had several things going for him. He was strong and healthy enough to go all day on the trails with little need to eat. He was an excellent shot and had been since boyhood. "I was in the prime of life," he told Hittell, "and could bear almost any degree of exposure, privation, or fatigue."

He started into the Sierras with an ox team attached to a creaking old wagon, taking along three guns, lead and powder, blankets, some clothing, and several knives, but not much else. His intention was to live off the land. He felt good. "The mountain air was in my nostrils," he said, "the evergreens above, and the eternal rocks around."

Adams quickly established himself as a mountain man. Deer were plentiful and he shot extra meat for his Indian neighbors who then lived in the high country in summer and moved down the mountains for the winters. In return, the Indians built him a lodge and helped him stack wild hay to winter his oxen. They also taught him to tan skins, and the women made him several buckskin outfits which he continued to wear even after he left the mountains. When these people departed for the season, Adams stayed behind, locked into the snowy landscape through what he claimed was the happiest time of his life. He learned to live on natural foods and studied the wild animals he encountered. The old urge to capture and keep some of these beasts was rekindled.

During his first year in the high country, Adams frequently met the grizzly bear for which he had a healthy respect. There were still vigorous populations of grizzlies across California. Adams, who looked upon the great bear as the superior of the lion or tiger in strength, said, "He stands ready to face any enemy and turns not from the sight of man. I paid him the respect to keep out of his way."

But like nearly everyone else who encountered the great bear in those times, Adams could not resist the temptation to send an occasional shot after the retreating grizzly. Increasingly, he yielded to this overwhelming temptation and pursued the bears even though he had gone to the hills to live in peace. "I considered it a point of honor to give battle in every case," he said.

Adams strange life in the remote hills might have gone on for years except for a visit he had in the spring of 1853. He was puttering around his camp one day when he looked up to see a man approaching. According to Hittel's account, the man was Adams's brother, William, who had come to California at the height of the human migration but, unlike James, had now made good and was headed back for Massachusetts a rich man. The brothers had not seen each other in years, and when William learned where James was living, he had come into the hills to find him.

William made his brother two offers of aid, one of which was accepted and the other rejected. James was not interested in returning to Massachusetts and having his brother set him up in business. He was, however, willing to have William stake him in a new business capturing and exhibiting wild animals. They drew up a partnership arrangement, and William went back east while James set forth on what he called his "first great hunting expedition."

This was his opportunity to explore the Oregon and Washington country which he had long wanted to see. He found three other men who wanted to accompany him, including one who had been to Washington and Oregon. The other two were young Indians. All were good shots and excellent woodsmen.

Two weeks later they were in the Klamath region, and they pushed on and crossed the Columbia to come, at last, to a splendid valley where they made their camp for the summer. When they arrived here, they already carried baskets on their mules, and in them rode two small black bear cubs they had captured along the way.

One day Adams noticed the tracks of a large grizzly in the valley near his camp. He tracked the bear and, as he said later, "discovered on the mountainside the den of an old grizzly with two yearling cubs. The animals were in the habit of descending into the valley every night, and had worn a trail, along which they almost invariably passed in their excursions. I immediately determined to slay this dam, and make myself master of her offspring, which were two of the finest looking young beasts I had ever seen."

Capturing the two cubs was going to involve more difficulty than Adams had thought. Step one was to hide along the trail and be there ready when the bears came up from the valley in the early morning. He had both of his rifles well primed and lying beside him as the bear family plodded up the slope. "As the oldest approached," he recalled, "I drew Kentucky and planted a half ounce ball in her breast." The impact brought the great bear down, but in an instant she was on her feet bawling in her madness and coming down on Adam's position at full speed. "I fired a second shot through her open mouth into her brain," said Adams. He was fully aware of the fact that a grizzly, even when fatally shot, may go for some time and attack while dying, but in this case the old female did not move, and after waiting a few minutes to be certain that she was gone, Adams set off in pursuit of the cubs.

"I seized a lasso which lay at my side," Adams recalled, "and rushed towards the cubs." Adams had expected this to be the easy part of the adventure, but the husky cubs were not making it a simple matter. The three creatures, two grizzly bear cubs and a bewhiskered mountain man clad in fringed buckskins, raced in and out of the brush for the next half hour until all were exhausted.

At this point the cubs turned on Adams and attacked with such vigor that he went scampering up a tree to safety and from his perch studied the formidable teeth and claws of the young bears while pounding their paws with his gun butt to discourage them in their efforts to climb up and get him.

Gradually, Adams realized that these two cubs were not going to be taken with the lasso, and he began thinking about other ways to capture them. He attempted to drive them down into the open valley with horses borrowed from the nearby Indians, believing that he could then rope them more easily, but this also failed. Next, he located the spring where he believed the bears must drink and hid among the ferns to waylay them. During the middle of the night, however, he fell asleep and was awakened just as the cubs, having drunk their fill, were departing. Adams scrambled to his feet and again rushed after them but the cubs escaped easily into the chaparral.

Later he tried again and this time the two cubs, taken by surprise, split and ran in opposite directions with Adams pursuing one and his three companions the other. He chased the bear into the open country and put a loop over her head only to have her push it off and start running again. This was repeated numerous times until Adams eventually secured the rope. He leaped from his horse and hog-tied the young bear for transport back to camp where he found that the other cub had also been taken.

LADY WASHINGTON

The cub he had taken was described by Adams as being so beautiful that he had to stand and admire her. In the years ahead she would become one of the best known grizzly bears that ever lived. For some reason, he named her "Lady Washington."

Training Lady Washington seemed in the beginning to be an impossible task and the more kindly Adams treated her, the more surly and uncooperative she became. So much for the kindness approach. Adams called his companions to witness the next phase and come to his rescue if need be. No free-spirited grizzly bear should have to suffer the indignity he then inflicted.

He cut a stout whip, walked up to where the bear was chained and began whipping her on the back. This made her furious and she struck out, fought the chain, snarled and tried her best to attack

Adams who only kept up his punishment until at last the exhausted bear lay down, body beaten and spirit broken. "It is a cruel spectacle," Adams admitted, but he considered it essential in the case of Lady Washington to "lay the foundation of an education."

Within a few weeks Adams was able to lead the now submissive young grizzly around camp on a rope. Gradually he was convincing her that she was his slave and that obedience was the price of comfort. Normal grizzly bear traits were to be sacrificed for this new way of life.

Her brother, whose name was Jackson, was even more truculent and difficult to train. To get him to lead, Adams had to mount a mule and pull him along with a rope attached to the pommel of the saddle. When the young bear lunged at the mule's legs, he was kicked into the grass and, being a fast learner, did not attack the mule again. Adams soon also had this bear conditioned to the life of a captive, and so uncharacteristically docile for a grizzly that Adams could walk up and pat him on the back. What the trainer had done, was begin to mold two spirited, healthy young bears into creatures that were grizzlies in form only.

Soon Lady Washington was following Adams around camp without a leash. The bear became so attached to Adams that she accompanied him on longer trips. He went four miles from camp one day to build a new trap and the bear tagged along, never leaving his sight. At noon Lady Washington sat beside him and shared his lunch.

When Adams broke camp at the end of summer, he delivered his captured animals to Portland where they were taken aboard a ship bound for Boston. But one animal did not sail. He could not, he explained, bring himself to part with Lady Washington. He started back for his California mountain camp with the great bear padding along behind him.

Adams had long wanted to train the female grizzly to help him carry burdens in his travels, but she had torn from her back the sacks of sand he placed there. Then, one day, after he killed a fine buck and the meat was too heavy for him to carry back by himself, he finally succeeded in getting the bear to help pack out the meat. Lady Washington, who now always accompanied him on his hunting trips, stood still enough while he lashed half of the deer on her back. Then, however, she tried to pull it off, and several times rolled with the weight, attempting to free herself of the burden. Each of these efforts earned her added whacks from Adams until finally she gave up and carried her share of the load, and the great grizzly had now become a pack animal as well as a pet.

Adams even learned that, on cold nights, he could cuddle up with the grizzly on one side and a fire on the other and sleep snugly until morning without a blanket. If Lady Washington had to get up during the night, she soon returned, licked his hands, and lay down against him.

BEN FRANKLIN

Adams captured two other grizzlies of note, one of them a bear that was to rise even higher in his affections than Lady Washington. He looked upon this capture as "the most fortunate of my career." It was also among the most dangerous encounters he ever managed.

Adams and his companions, drawn by the wealth of wild animals to be captured and killed, had moved into the strikingly beautiful Yosemite country. The old grizzly hunter's eyes never rested, the pursuit of animals was always at the front of his mind. On his first hunt in the headwaters of the Merced, he spotted a grizzly bear den on a steep slope and sensed at once that this was a special circumstance. More than anything else in the world in that moment he wanted to dispatch the old she bear who commanded the den and thereby come into possession of her cubs. "I thought and dreamed of nothing else but how to take it," he said. "This at once, became all my ambition." Deer, mountain lions, wolves, and other bears for once in his life went unheeded, even if they crossed his path.

Adams decided to handle this one on his own and sent his companions off to hunt in other places. "I cleaned my rifle and pistol, sharpened my knives, prepared muzzle and strings, furnished myself with provisions, and, packing my blankets upon a mule, started off for the scene of my labors."

Adams eased down into the steep-walled brushy ravine and took cover in the thick-growing chaparral above the den on the opposite slope. The den looked much like that of other California grizzlies he had seen, except for the huge amount of earth the old female had pushed out onto the hillside.

For three nights Adams waited opposite the den for the old bear to emerge and give him the opportunity for a shot. Then, as daylight filtered into the ravine, he decided to bring the encounter to a head. He stuck some green branches in his cap for camouflage, cocked his rifle and began yelling at the bear.

His yelling echoed up the canyon and the old bear responded. She came rushing from the den, growling and chomping, then stood on her hind feet to search for the source of the disturbance. Adams, amazed at the size of this bear, remained rock still and waited. The bear turned to face the other direction, then sat down on her haunches in front of her den.

The old hunter, afraid that the bear would return to her young, gave a low sharp whistle. The female wheeled about and bounced to her feet again, exposing her broad breast. "It was then, having my rifle already drawn, that I fired; and in an instant, dropping the rifle, I drew my pistol in one hand and my knife in the other. The bear, as the ball slapped loudly into the fat of her breast, staggered and fell backwards, a sure sign of deadly hurt. Copious streams of crimson blood also gushed from her breast, and I knew that they came from the fountain-head. The work was, indeed, nearly done; but so anxious was I to complete it at once, that I commenced leaping over the bushes to plunge my knife in her dying heart; when, gathering her savage strength, and, with one last desperate effort, she sprang towards me. The distance between us was only thirty feet but, fortunately, full of brush and she soon weakened with the prodigious energy requisite to tear her way through it. I discharged the six shots of my revolver, the last of which struck under the left ear, and laid her still in a moment; then, leaping forwards, I plunged my knife in her vitals. Again she endeavored to rise, but was so choked with blood that she could not. I drew my knife across her throat and after a few convulsive struggles she expired."

By this time in his life, Adams had lost count of the number of grizzly bears and other animals he had slain, and one wonders what, if anything, he felt as he stood over the mighty dead bear which, until that morning, probably had never before seen a human, or any creature it could not kill. We do not have to wonder long because Adams recalled his emotions when talking with Ted Hittell, and the reporter wrote them down. "I was alone in the gorge, and, as I looked upon the dead monster, felt like Alexander sated with victory and wishing another foe to engage, worthy of my prowess." In that moment, Adams epitomized the insatiable compulsion of the human to over-power the greatest of the world's carnivores. Adams, of course, went a step further; the bears he did not kill outright, he reduced to a condition of servitude.

With the great bear dead, he now advanced on the cubs. The danger was past. Hidden in the leaves and grass at the back of the den, he discovered two small cubs, so young their eyes were still closed. Both were males. Adams gave one of the cubs away and kept the other as a companion for Lady Washington. This one he named Ben Franklin. Both of the tiny new cubs were nursed by Adam's greyhound bitch, which had recently whelped.

Ben Franklin grew to be the constant companion of Lady Washington and of the man who became known as "Grizzly Adams." The three of them, the shaggy man in buckskins, followed by two huge grizzly bears, later walked the streets of San Francisco together.

SAMSON

Although the taking of cubs pleased Adams, he nurtured a latent desire to capture a giant adult grizzly and haul it out of the mountains alive. His opportunity arrived one day when he chanced upon a monstrous track. He stood silently beside the track, spellbound by what he was seeing. "I determined to capture him at all hazards," said Adams. He waited by the trail until he caught a glimpse of the animal, fat now in November with the stored energy that would see him through the winter. Adams had seen many bears, but this was the largest he had ever met.

He and his companions began building the strongest bear trap they could imagine. They spent days cutting and hauling logs. Then, they used them to erect a log-cabin-like structure which could be baited and equipped with a locking door.

In due time the the huge bear found the bait, sniffed the air, entered the trap and was locked into the strange log prison. The great bear shook and battered the trap with such savage fury that Adams stayed near it day and night, poking the bear back with iron rods and firebrands to keep it from tearing the trap apart.

For four weeks the giant bear, named Samson by Adams, was held in the trap until he quieted enough to be crated and hauled away. Samson, king of the mountain, never became the subservient, hand-licking pet that Adams had made of Lady Washington and Ben Franklin. But the mighty Samson did play his role eventually in Adams Mountaineer's Museum in San Francisco. Ted Hittell saw the huge bear there for the first time that day he met Adams in the basement zoo. The two milder tempered grizzlies were roaming the room in freedom, demonstrating their docility and their willingness to carry packs for their owner, but Samson, the monarch, surly and growling, was secured behind heavy iron bars.

Adams strange menagerie eventually arrived in New York where the old man with the long gray beard and fringed buckskin clothing made a popular display for several weeks. Adams never again returned to the western mountains and the wild grizzly bears. It is believed that one of his animals administered a head injury to him during the boat trip from the West Coast and he never fully recovered. He died of the injury near Boston where his remaining relatives lived.

Regardless of all his years of experiences with bears, and his own love for the wide open spaces, Adams apparently never truly felt called upon to leave the grizzly bears free to roam the wild places in which he found them. If the story we have of the man is to be believed, he was a crack shot, tireless outdoorsman, and possessed of steel nerves.

He once killed three grizzly bears, a female and two large cubs, while his companion took refuge on a high rock.

Adams even used his pet grizzlies to help him capture and kill other grizzly bears. Grizzly Adams's true nature was not the gentle and syrupy character with which the usual television version misinforms it viewers. To him, a bear located in its native setting was a personal challenge, a creature to be killed or subdued.

This comes through plainly enough in what James Capen Adams once said to Hittell. The statement reveals a strangely corrupted idea of what a wild animal should be, and in a sad way reflects on all people who might have given the grizzly a better chance. Adams told the reporter, "The grizzly bear possesses the nature which taken in time, and carefully improved, may be made the perfection of animal goodness." To him Lady Washington was the "good" grizzly, and he seemed not to understand that a grizzly robbed of its wild free spirit is not really a grizzly at all.

Chapter 11

Parks That Saved Bears

An office worker in Cheyenne, Wyoming, returned from Yellowstone telling her fellow workers that her September, 1984, vacation was the most exciting ever to the national park. She had gone to hear the haunting autumn call of the bull elk during the rutting season. "And would you believe," she said, "a grizzly bear came right into the Old Faithful area? It stayed around there most of the day. Thousands of people saw it. Rangers were everywhere. On horses, on foot, in vehicles. Nobody got hurt and only one person got chased. He got too close and the bear charged him. And the bear was gaining on him! The guy ran right past trees trying to get away. The bear finally stopped. This was my first grizzly."

Did she hear any elk bugle? "Oh, yeah, but who cares?"

Most of us privileged to see a wild bear have encountered the animal in a national park, if not Yellowstone, then Great Smokies, Glacier, Yosemite, or a handful of others. These parks have introduced millions of visitors to genuine wild bears, usually black but sometimes grizzlies as well. Grizzly and brown bears live in five American national parks and monuments including Yellowstone, Glacier, Grand Teton, Denali, and Katmai, and in seven national parks in Canada. Yellowstone and Glacier have the distinction of offering the best hope of preserving the grizzly in the Lower 48.

Almost certainly, if Yellowstone's two million or so acres had not been declared a national park the grizzly bears living there would have vanished by now.

But scenery, more than wildlife, drew the attention of early visitors to this region. Mountain man John Colter, discharged early by

Lewis and Clark during their return trip, was the earliest known white man to explore the Upper Yellowstone Valley and his reports were widely believed to be a fantasy because he told of unbelievable wonders and beauty. Legendary mountain man Jim Bridger, "Old Gabe," teller of tall tales, returned from an early visit to this enchanted land at the headwaters of the Yellowstone River telling of giant waterfalls, mud bubbling from the earth, and rivers that give off smoke. Years later these stories were found to be true, except perhaps when, in typical Bridger fashion, Old Gabe, or perhaps it was Joe Meek, added petrified birds sitting in petrified trees singing petrified songs.

Early white travelers followed the river to its spectacular canyon, of which Rudyard Kipling later wrote, "I looked into a gulf seventeen hundred feet deep with eagles and fish hawks circling below, and the sides of that gulf were one wild welter of color—crimson, emerald, cobalt, ochre, amber, honey splashed with port wine, vermilion, lemon, and silver-grey in wide washes. So far below us that no sound of its strife could reach us, the Yellowstone River ran—a finger-wide strip of jade green".

These natural wonders—the canyon, geysers, mud pots, fumeroles, steaming rivers—convinced men of vision that Yellowstone should be set aside for the pleasure of people for all time. But even after the park idea was born, Yellowstone bears were treated the same as bears elsewhere. In 1871 Dr. F. V. Hayden led the first scientific party into the Upper Yellowstone accompanied by the pioneering photographer William Henry Jackson, and their descriptions and pictures influenced Congress to create the national park. They saw nothing wrong with shooting grizzlies during their exploratory visit, and a famous story tells how Jackson killed a huge silvertip by shooting it through the left nostril.

The earliest superintendents of Yellowstone, who were military commanders, were not friends of the predators, but we should view their policies in the context of their time. They came to the job before wildlife management was a profession in itself. The concept of ecosystems, with each organism playing its role as part of the whole, was not yet widely understood. Wildlife management was a mixture of horse sense, political manipulation, and sheepherder style prejudice. Most people were insensitive to the role of wildlife and did not yet understand that a healthy ecosystem includes both predators and prey. Deer, elk, antelope, and bison were the "good" animals that everyone wanted in abundance. Killing the predators seemed an easy way to save the herbivores, so wolves, mountain lions, and coyotes were eliminated whenever possible. The park was eleven years old before hunting was prohibited within its boundaries, but the new rule against

Mountain man Jim Bridger was one of the earliest explorers of the Yellowstone region. He told of giant waterfalls, mud bubbling from the earth, and rivers that gave off smoke.

hunting still did not protect the predators, including the bears which went unprotected for another three years.

By 1935, the predator control people had killed off more than four thousand coyotes within the park. During the same period they eliminated wolves so methodically that, to this day, they have not recovered.

FEEDING THE BEARS

The bears were finally given protection because the park managers grasped the practical significance of these animals. They saw that the happiest Yellowstone visitors were those who could go home and report the antics of the bears to wide-eyed neighbors and friends who then also wanted to travel to Yellowstone to see them. For the fifty million visitors coming to Yellowstone National Park in its first century, perhaps no other feature of the park was a bigger attraction than the bears. The bears were Yellowstone's ambassadors, and enchanted visitors influenced their congressmen to provide funds for the park. In their eagerness to entertain the tourists, early park administrators did their best to bring the bears within easy view of the visitors by offering human foods to the bears, and the highly responsive bears quickly adapted to this new source of food.

Naturalist Edward R. Warren, of Colorado, once described the early bear watching in Yellowstone, following his trip there in 1904. "I went to the dump," he wrote in *The Mammals of Colorado*, "to see what could be seen, being very anxious to know if what we had heard about the tameness of the bears was true." A large grizzly came to the edge of the dump and a small black bear that had been feeding scampered away. Another grizzly arrived and he too was chased off, with the two bears "stirring up as much dust as a four-horse team."

On the return to their camp, they passed the boarding house where the stable hands and stage drivers lived. "It was then about dusk, but seeing a bear or two about the kitchen door we stopped to watch, and presently there seemed to be so many bears moving around that I thought it wise to leave, fearing one of us might bump up against a bear in the dark and get into trouble."

At night the grizzlies, already indoctrinated to breaking into tourists' vehicles, ripped the canvas covers of the two horse-drawn wagons in which Warren's party rode and carried supplies.

An early student of Yellowstone's bears was M. P. Skinner, who spent years observing them. In 1925, in his book *Bears of the Yellowstone*, Skinner mentioned that "practically all the bears" were seen around kitchen scrap piles and gathering food from the campgrounds. He

A massive Yellowstone grizzly peers from behind an evergreen bough. Realizing that bears were a park attraction, managers gave them protection early on, and the bears began to feed in garbage dumps and took up panhandling.

added, "Of course, it is fortunate for us all that bruin does like these man-made foods, otherwise most of us would not see so much of him as we do." Thinking about that, Skinner added, "On the other hand, we would not have so much trouble with camp foraging bears and we would not have to guard our supplies so closely . . . it has become an established custom to pour out these supplies for them at certain well-known places."

Skinner's observations make it clear that people corrupted the bears of Yellowstone and turned them away from foraging in the wilds as they had done for countless centuries. "These bears did not take to garbage suddenly and at once," Skinner wrote. "They had to learn that they would be safe, and even had to learn to like man-made food. When they started to show themselves way back in the early nineties, they came at dusk and only one or two at a time. As they learned they were safe, and the food rich and easy to get, they came oftener, earlier in the day, and in increased numbers." Although some bears still preferred the wild foods and did not come regularly to this cafeteria style lunch, Skinner believed they all knew of its availability and that most of the bears, at some time, took advantage of it. Once they were given official protection, the Yellowstone bears, according to Yellowstone historian and former ranger-naturalist Paul Schullery's excellent book *Bears of Yellowstone,* the bears soon lost their shyness. They were first noticed assembling more freely at park garbage dumps around concessionaire-operated hotels and campgrounds. These were bears that would indoctrinate their cubs. At one period, park administrators constructed bleachers from which tourists watched the bear shows.

These evening concentrations of garbage fed bears taught park visitors to carry cookies and other choice bear bait to entice the animals even closer. Not until 1941, did the bear feeding shows stop. By the early 1900s, bears, conditioned to feeding at garbage dumps around hotels and campgrounds, learned that, when they appeared along the roadsides, vehicles slowed down and still more human foods landed in front of their noses.

As surely as the Crow, Cheyenne, and Blackfoot had counted coups on the bears, the modern tourist would develop his own way of displaying his personal daring. "Maud, look at this picture I brought back from Yellowstone. I tell you I was close enough to smell that bear's breath."

Such wholesale intermingling of bears and people made thoughtful park officials nervous, and park superintendents began posting rules against feeding the bears. People went right on feeding them anyhow while rangers looked the other way.

Concessionaires in the park loved the bears for attracting people,

Having lost their fear of people, some Yellowstone grizzlies wander into camps in search of food. The huge grizzly above came right into a tent area and went for the food strung high in a tree (right). He almost reached the meat.

and encouraged feeding the roadside bears long after the practice was outlawed. A retired Yellowstone ranger recalls, ''When the store's cookies became too stale to sell for human consumption, the concessionaire would put up a sign saying these cookies were the bears' favorite, and sell out quickly—unless we saw the sign and went in and had them take it down.''

As each new generation of cubs grew up hand-fed on human

snacks, roadside panhandling became the standard lifestyle for a percentage of Yellowstone's bears, especially the black bears. The same thing was happening with the black bears of the Great Smoky Mountains National Park and a few other parks. The bears were highly adaptable opportunists, yielding quickly to the lure of easy living, and they were degraded and demeaned in the process.

Even those bears converted to dump feeding and panhandling retained some of their age-old wariness. Each spring, when they came from their winter dens and began feeding again, they approached the garbage centers cautiously and reluctantly. Gradually, their natural shyness disappeared and the show was once more ready for the big summer influx of tourists. Skinner recalled that the bears even seemed to know when the truck was due with the daily garbage offering, and that tourists at Lake and Canyon could frequently see twenty or thirty black bears and a dozen or so grizzlies assembled around the garbage.

But the time of reckoning was coming. The experienced park workers, more than the visitors, respected the fragile relationship between people and bears in Yellowstone. They lived with the bears and knew they were unpredictable and potentially dangerous. Retired ranger supervisor Dale Nuss, who worked as a Yellowstone ranger for thirty-four years, recalls the evening he mounted his young daughter's bicycle and rode down the lane behind his Park Service home to inspect the waste treatment plant.

Nuss had remounted the bike and started back up the lane when he heard a loud *woof,* which he recognized immediately. "I knew I had trouble," said Nuss. He saw the female grizzly with two cubs, mumbled "oh hell," stopped the bike and stood straddling it, motionless with both feet on the ground. "She charged," Nuss recalls, "and I figured she was going to take me." The cubs were running off. On the strange bike and rough terrain there was no possibility Nuss could out-distance the old she-bear which he now saw was quartering to cut him off.

She came to a stop twenty-seven feet from where Nuss waited, and after a moment of staring in his direction, turned and followed her cubs.

When it seemed that she was at a safe distance, Nuss mounted his bike and pushed down on the pedal. Hard. This was all the watchful mother grizzly needed to bring her back on a renewed attack. Once again Nuss slid to a halt and stood motionless over his bike. This time the bear came to within eighteen feet of him before stopping. Nuss thought she was going to repeat the attack a third time, but instead she chose to follow her disappearing cubs. Nuss waited until absolutely sure the bears were gone before riding back home somewhat shaken by the closest call he ever had with a Yellowstone bear. "It was one of those times you know you can be in serious trouble," he said.

PEOPLE-BEAR ENCOUNTERS

In recent years, visitor traffic in the national parks has grown tremendously, and with it has also come a steady increase in foot traffic into the back country. The outcome was predictable: an increase in people-bear conflicts.

The wonder is that there have been so few people killed and injured by the grizzly bears. Biologist Dr. Stephen Herrero, a bear authority on the faculty of the University of Calgary in Alberta, writing in *BioScience,* calculates the human fatalities from grizzlies in national parks that have the great bears at about one in thirty million visitors. In the first ninety-seven years, following establishment of Yellowstone, according to Herrero's research, only five people, about one every twenty years, were killed by grizzlies in all North American national parks.

At least some of these tragedies were the result of stupidity. In 1907, while bear watching at a Yellowstone dump near one of the hotels, a tourist chased a family of grizzly bear cubs up a tree and for good measure began poking the mother with his umbrella. We will never know his motivation, but the outcome is a matter of record. The enraged bear partially eviscerated him and gave him the distinction of becoming the first tourist killed by a grizzly bear in Yellowstone National Park.

The increase in human traffic in the parks has been accompanied by a substantial increase in injuries and deaths caused by national park grizzlies. Even the most trusted bear can go astray when corrupted by people.

On a June night in 1983, Bear 15, numbered and marked by grizzly bear research biologists, surprised everyone who knew him. He was first captured as a yearling cub in 1971, and biologists believe that he was already thoroughly conditioned by his mother's leadership to feeding on bread, cookies, potato chips, cantaloupe rinds, meat scraps, and assorted other human treats. Although the sources of garbage inside the park had been largely cut off for the Yellowstone bears, park bears often range beyond the park borders, especially if human foods are available in nearby towns where tourist oriented communities were reluctant to stop feeding grizzlies.

Bear 15's habits became well known to the biologists who tracked him. He was a good subject for their study and they retrapped him many times. He even served as the subject of a graduate student's research. One year he was captured three times, always near sources of garbage. The biologists conferred and made their decision: Bear 15 would have to be moved far enough away that he should not return. The drugged grizzly was suspended from a helicopter and airborne more than ninety miles into the heart of the Shoshone National Forest where there is good grizzly bear habitat and a population of the big bears.

In due time, Bear 15 made his way west again to the town of West Yellowstone and resumed his garbage-eating ways. He was relocated several more times. He became expert in killing elk from the flourishing Yellowstone herd, but never forgot the people foods to be gleaned from dumps and dumpsters around West Yellowstone.

By the time he had been trapped nineteen times and weighed some six hundred pounds, the huge bear was perhaps the grizzly bear biologists' best known, and best liked, subject. He was a tractable beast that had never threatened anyone, and he was easy for the biologists to handle. He became so accustomed to entering traps that he went into them as a trade-off, just one more way to obtain food.

As nearly as officials can reconstruct the events of the night of June 25, 1983, Bear 15 was wandering around West Yellowstone searching for human foods. He investigated the dump, then garbage cans, and finally wandered into the National Forest Service's nearby Rainbow Point campground. In the dead of night, he moved from one camp to the next until he came to a small tent in which William May, from Wisconsin, was sleeping. The bear poked along the edge of the canvas until his sensitive nose touched a living creature separated from him by only a thin sheet of canvas. Bear 15 bit into the neck of William May, severing the carotid artery, then dragged May into the woods and ate part of him.

The following evening Bear 15 was recaptured for the last time. Laboratory tests left little doubt that this was the animal responsible for May's death, and Bear 15 was given a massive drug overdose.

Bear 15 had firmly established habit patterns before the biologists began working with him. His mother, who probably learned about human foods from her mother, led the cub to feeding places where experience told her that people made foods available for bears. Once introduced to garbage, the bear, with its long memory, is a life-long junkie and can hardly be blamed for consuming the edibles that people provide. "That first feeding experience takes the bear across the fine line," says Sandi Fowler, Yellowstone bear management specialist. "There is no going back."

One outgrowth of the Bear 15 tragedy was a move by the Montana Stockgrowers Association to have more grizzlies eliminated from the national forest lands adjacent to Yellowstone. According to *The Billings Gazette,* an officer of the association, expressing concern for "the lives of our families and our employees," was asking for a hunting season to kill twenty-five grizzlies annually in the area. The Yellowstone grizzlies could not long survive this added drain. Besides, Montana's Department of Fish, Wildlife, and Parks would lack authority to set such a season in the unlikely event that it agreed with the idea. The *Gazette* came down on the side of the bears. "Man is pushing into the bear's limited range with increasing frequency," it said editorially. "But bears will more likely be the victims of those clashes than man will".

The following summer twenty-five year old Brigitta Fredenhagen, of Basel, Switzerland, came to America with her brother and sister-in-law to visit Yellowstone National Park. From the beginning, Brigitta Fredenhagen wanted to hike into the Yellowstone backcountry and camp there far from the highways and campgrounds. When her companions decided not to make the hike, she set off alone.

That night she prepared her camp according to the directions issued by the rangers when she registered for her backcountry permit. She was traveling light, but what food she had she hung from a rope stretched twelve feet above the ground between two lodgepole pines. Then, she set up her tent and spread out her sleeping bag eighty-five feet from the food cache. That night, using low limbs, a bear managed to climb high enough to drag down the little bag of oatmeal cookies, sliced ham, and fruit that had drawn it to Fredenhagen's camp. The food was apparently only enough to whet the bear's appetite. It dragged the camper from her sleeping bag, killed her, and ate a substantial part of her body.

There were other grizzly bear attacks that year. A middle-aged man and wife were mauled by a female grizzly and her two cubs when the bears were interrupted as they fed on a buffalo carcass. In another incident, a grizzly attacked two people who were gathering huckleberries in Glacier National Park.

Glacier National Park lies two hundred and fifty miles or so to the northwest of Yellowstone, in northwestern Montana. This park and the adjacent Waterton Lakes National Park in Alberta lie in the heart of spectacular Rocky Mountain scenery astride the Continental Divide. In these "Shining Mountains," where active glaciers hang on the distant alpine slopes far above hidden blue lakes and rushing streams, live the golden eagle, mule deer, and elk. Here the grizzly bear survives in part of what the bear biologists refer to as the Northern Continental Divide Grizzly Bear Ecosystem.

Standing in a misty field, a Yellowstone grizzly (left) presents an easy target for a park ranger equipped with a drug rifle. Rifleman and cameraman approach the downed bear (above). It takes five men to carry the grizzly from the field (below). Rangers will examine the bear and probably tag it for future study.

For forty-five years after Glacier National Park was created in 1910, only one person was injured in the park by a grizzly bear. Then came a decade, beginning in 1956, when bears attacked ten people. Still the bears had caused no fatalities, and this brings the story of Glacier's grizzlies up to the tragedies of 1967.

Park officials had worried increasingly about the bears, but concessionaires still fed them as a tourist attraction, even around the backcountry chateaus. There had been behavioral changes. Some of the grizzlies were no longer so skittish around people as the bears once had been. They seemed more inclined to hang around lodges and campgrounds.

Nineteen-year-old Julie Helgeson, from Minnesota, was a seasonal worker in Glacier that summer. Another seasonal worker was Michele Koons, also nineteen and a university student from California.

On one of her days off, Julie Helgeson and a friend hiked deep into the park and prepared to stay the night near a designated campground. They knew that there had been grizzly bears visiting the area and feeding on whatever human foods could be found, but the campers discounted the possibility of trouble. Seasonal workers were often less wary of the grizzlies than fulltime Park Service employees were.

Meanwhile, a small group of hikers arrived at Trout Lakes twenty miles away. Among them was Michele Koons. They were also accompanied by a small dog whose presence in itself could trigger an attack by a bear. They too had heard that bears were in the area where they intended to camp. Late in the day, a scrawny grizzly arrived in their camp and the hikers moved off some distance, watched while the bear ransacked their camp, then debated whether or not to stay. Darkness came, and they stayed.

Late that night one of them awakened to see the dim form of a large bear moving around their camp. The campers came awake, scrambled from their sleeping bags, and took refuge in nearby trees. They watched in horror as Michele Koons tried in vain to move the stuck zipper on her sleeping bag. While Michele screamed, the bear dragged the sleeping bag and its occupant for several hundred yards into thick cover. Michele Koons died from her injuries.

That same night, another bear came to the camp of Julie Helgeson and her companion, and killed Julie. Incredibly, Glacier National Park, after so many years without a bear-caused human fatality, suffered two on the same night. Two of the bears killed in the following days showed evidence of being the individuals responsible for the deaths of the two girl campers. In both cases, the bears had been conditioned to human foods as well as to being around people.

The Glacier National Park tragedy, in 1967, fulfilled a long-time prophecy of biologists and some national park administrators. As the numbers of visitors increased in the parks, the chances of serious conflicts grew. The Park Service, stunned by the events of this summer night, soon instituted a new program aimed at reducing bear-people contacts.

The word went out. Wherever bears were part of the park scene, steps were taken to cut off their sources of human food. Garbage dumps were closed precipitously. Garbage cans were equipped with bear-proof lids, campers were instructed repeatedly about the dangers the bears presented, and campgrounds were more heavily patrolled by rangers to keep the areas free of foods that might draw in the bears.

There is evidence that the abrupt closing of Yellowstone's dumps led to grizzly bears moving into camp areas and this action brought on an increased destruction of bears that the Park Service feared were a threat to people. As long as the grizzlies fed at backcountry dumps, they apparently did not associate food with people. In campgrounds, however, where food and people are closely associated, bears lose their natural fear of humans. Park Service management of the grizzlies in Yellowstone and Glacier has been a matter of much heated debate and sometimes bitter disagreement. The arguments centered around the manner in which the dumps were closed, not whether or not they should have been closed. Tragically, all research ceased with closure of the dumps. Scientists were denied the opportunity to learn what the massive changes in lifestyle meant to the grizzlies.

Other attacks continued at Glacier. In the fall of 1967, a hunter was attacked by a grizzly bear just outside the Glacier National Park boundary. This bear was killed by the man's companions, who shot it eight times. A study of some of the cases the Park Service has recorded since then begins to reveal patterns. Some biologists believe that bear attacks on people cannot be traced to garbage, but others point to incidents such as the following which do indicate a relationship.

In September, 1976, a bear killed a woman camper at Many Glacier Campground. "The bear had previously obtained food from fishermen and illegal campers," said the Park Service report.

In July, 1980, a grizzly killed a man and woman camped at St. Mary. "The bear had been observed on several occasions feeding at a refuse pile outside the park."

In September, 1980, a grizzly killed a man camped alone at Elizabeth Lake. He camped in a closed area after being warned about the bear danger. The blame, however, was placed on a six-year old male bear that "had been observed in the Many Glacier area on several occasions and exhibited habituated behavior toward people."

At Glacier National Park, a helicopter is used to remove a drugged bear from a settled area. The bear is transported in a live-trap to headquarters where its paws are measured, its teeth checked, and its ears tagged. It will then be released.

BEAR SAFETY

This does not mean that only grizzly bears accustomed to eating human foods can be dangerous. Their actions can be triggered by a variety of circumstances created by the mixing of bears and people.

Bears do not like surprises. Given notice of the approach of people, the bear will usually slip away. The one that attacks is the bear that suddenly discovers a person uncomfortably close to it. This puts the person in a hazardous position, especially if the bear happens to be guarding a food cache, or is a female with cubs.

The acceptable distance varies with the bear and the circumstances. The smaller black bear, at the moment of contact, might order her cubs up a tree then make her own exit. The grizzly, for which the treetops offer scant refuge, chases the cubs off, then typically proceeds to chase the enemy off. She is an extremely powerful and protective animal, with an innate sense of dominance and a low kindling point.

In one analysis of national park hikers injured by grizzly bears, seventy-one percent of the bears involved were females taken by surprise as they protected cubs. The hiker can avoid surprising a bear by making noise along the trail. Bear bells, whistling, and talking may accomplish this. In a study reported by Katherine L. Jope in *The Wildlife Society Bulletin,* twenty-two of twenty-three hikers injured by grizzlies in Glacier National Park were not wearing bear bells. Said Jope, "Assuming an equal proportion of hikers with bells throughout Glacier National Park, hikers with bells are injured less frequently than hikers without bells."

The National Park Service passes out bear circulars by the thousands to everyone coming to parks where bears live. Unfortunately, these leaflets are often not read until people arrive back home when their vacations are over. The pointers listed in these leaflets give sound advice, however, much of it having to do with food. Always keep a clean camp and store food out of the reach of bears. This can be accomplished by sealing food in tight containers, then hanging it on a line between two trees, providing it is at least four feet from either tree supporting it and no less than twelve feet above the ground. The car trunk is better yet if you camp close to your vehicle.

Take along foods that are not greasy or rich in odors that will draw the bears in. If you are hunting in grizzly country, store your game where the bears cannot reach it. Do the same with the horse pellets which also attract hungry bears.

Burying garbage is a mistake. The bears can quickly find and dig it out. Pack it out of the backcountry instead, after burning whatever will burn. If you catch fish, clean them beside the water and dispose of the viscera in the water because the odor of decaying fish will draw bears in from surprising distances.

Some people get closer to bears than they need to and consequently get into trouble. Sandi Fowler says of Yellowstone visitors, "I've seen people come within ten feet of a grizzly, even closer, and say things like, 'This is neat,' and all the time that bear is considering whether or not to charge."

A wiser procedure is to give the bears distance. If you spot a bear in the distance, say the guidelines distributed to backcountry hikers by the Park Service, make an upwind detour around it so the bear knows from your scent that you are there and is not taken by surprise. "Better yet," says Jonkel, "turn around and go back until another day. The bear may decide to move into the wind just as you do. You would cancel your trip if baseball-sized hailstones started to fall—do as much for the grizz."

Do not hike alone, and if there are bear sign in the area, move on and don't camp there. Leave your dog and your cosmetics at home because either may draw the bear's attention. Research reveals that menstruating women definitely attract bears, and once close, the bears could feel threatened and attack.

If you suddenly find yourself in the presence of a charging bear, pick a tree that is strong, high, and growing limbs within your reach. Then get up as fast as you can. Sometimes an escapee has been pulled back down from the tree into which he was climbing, but the bear generally accepts your climbing a tree as evidence that you are no longer a threat. A large bear may reach twelve feet above the ground. Attempting to out-run a grizzly bear, or any bear, is a loser's game but, because of a bear's short front legs, you probably stand a better chance running downhill than up.

Every bear may have his own rules. You may outwait him by standing your ground and perhaps talking softly to him until he gives up, and instead of charging, turns and departs. One national park ranger at Katmai National Monument in southeast Alaska rounded a bend in the trail and met a female brown bear with a cub. The ranger began backing away very slowly and the bear charged. When she was within a few feet of him, the ranger threw up both hands and shouted "no," and the bear turned and departed. He considered himself fortunate; the next one might keep coming.

If actually attacked by a bear, play dead. Get down with knees up under your chin and your hands clasped behind your neck and stay there, immobile. The bear may give up and depart because you no longer appear to be a threat. If so, stay where you are. There's no hurry even if ants are crawling over you and vultures circle overhead. Looking up too soon may bring the watchful bear back to the job. One hiker, who prefers not to be identified, suffered the humiliation of having the bear defecate on him as he played dead.

In one study of bear attacks in the national parks, Stephen Herrero, author of the book *Bear Attacks,* took a careful look at the conditions surrounding numerous bear-person encounters. His data showed that playing dead seemed to work in many instances, especially where a female with cubs was disturbed by the closeness of a person. He also pointed out that the idea might be less effective when a bear in search of food attacks campers.

Guns, of course, are forbidden in national parks, and might not help at any rate, unless the person is skilled in the use of the gun, and is fortunate too. The gun makes one overconfident and tempts one to shoot when he might more easily escape. An injured bear is more dangerous than one that doesn't hurt. One experienced Arctic biologist, setting off on a seven mile hike over the tundra to an airplane accident site, picked up his shotgun and slugs, which are considered highly effective at close range. Asked if he would use the gun if he saw a grizzly, he replied, "Only if he comes for me, and not then until he is within ten feet."

Getting along with bears is often a matter of respecting the bear and knowing what might trigger an attack. During their eleven-year bear study in Yellowstone, the Craigheads handled five hundred and twenty-four grizzlies, made more than thirteen thousand observations of marked bears, and hiked a hundred and sixty-two thousand miles in grizzly country, and no member of the team suffered a single injury by a bear.

Whenever a national park grizzly kills someone there are those who ask if parks are for bears or people, and suggests that the parks be cleared of their grizzlies. Gairdner B. Moment, of the Department of Biological Sciences, Goucher College, writing in *BioScience,* advocated elimination of the park grizzlies.

Most people seem to disagree. If the grizzlies were gone the experience of visiting the parks would be less stimulating. There is something satisfying about knowing that you are sharing the land with the world's largest carnivore. In an attitude survey, The *Christian Science Monitor* asked several thousand subscribers if the grizzlies should be eliminated from the national parks and, even though this survey was conducted only two years after the two fatalities in Glacier in 1967, only three percent of the respondents wanted to sacrifice the great bears to make the wilderness more city-park-like for people. The grizzly belongs to the wild scene.

Robert Hahn understood this. Hahn, a school teacher, was camping and hiking in Glacier National Park when he spotted a female grizzly with a cub along the Going-to-the-Sun Highway. Hahn began making pictures, the female looked up, saw him, and immediately rushed him. Hahn had already picked out a tree into which to retreat if necessary. But he could not get high enough soon enough, and the bear reached up and dragged him back to ground level where she bit and clawed his hands and legs.

Hahn and the grizzly then rolled down a snow-covered bank together for one hundred feet and bounced into a tree where Hahn managed to get the tree between them. The bear kept on rolling, but was soon rushing back up the bank toward the teacher, who was by this time climbing the second tree. Again she reached him and had him by the foot when he kicked her off. She came back again and once more Hahn managed to kick her away. This time she gave up and departed.

From his hospital bed, Hahn said, "I don't want anything done to the bear. She was only protecting her young and her territory." He insisted that the attack would not keep him from hiking in the wilderness again. "When anyone advocates the destruction of grizzlies," he added, "they are in essence advocating the destruction of true wilderness".

The trail a hiker chooses may be a factor in the risk of a grizzly bear encounter. Jope's study in Glacier National Park indicates that grizzlies may be less inclined to attack hikers on trails frequently used than they are on remote wilderness trails. "Although bears were seen as often on heavily used trails as on trails with little human use," wrote Jope, "full charges occurred primarily on trails with little human use."

Chambers of Commerce worry that the tourist trade may suffer from publicity growing out of attacks by bears. Perhaps some travelers stay home for this reason. But those who study statistics and bear behavior explain that the risk of being attacked by a bear in a national park is slight compared with the possibilities of injury from automobile accidents.

There is something about the way we feel towards bears that gives conflict between bears and people instant news value. These stories are frequently exploited in more lurid detail than facts justify. Typically, the fate of the fisherman who drowns on the Firehole when his waders fill with water merits six inches of copy on page eighteen. But the park visitor hospitalized after tangling with an angry grizzly has his story spread over the top of page one, and the disparity goes unnoticed by all except a handful of bear biologists.

This fascination with the great bears may have its roots deep in our ingrained fear of predators big enough to attack us. Steve Mealey, supervisor of the Shoshone National Forest, and the instructor of a short course on grizzly bears every summer in Yellowstone, has often thought about the way we feel toward bears. He thought of it at length following the death of Briggita Fredenhagen. "I was a member of the team that investigated the attack," he said. "I saw what the bear did to her, how it ate part of her, and I felt a deep hatred for that bear. I really hated that son-of-a-bitch. Not just that bear, but in that instant all grizzly bears. I thought a lot about that and the reason for it and came to the conclusion that my hate grew out of the knowledge that this animal could kill one of ours.

"I think this stems from a deep, primal fear that may reach all the way back to the Plains of the Serengetti. The grizzly bear lets us know what it is like to be the prey species. I have come to grips with this. It has given me a better understanding of the grizzly and why the bear adds so much to our outdoor experience."

Viewed in relation to the number of visitors to the parks, the problems from bear-human confrontations are minimal. Park Service biologist C. J. Martinka, who studies the bears of Glacier National Park, points out that statistically your chances of being injured or killed by a grizzly in a national park are about one in a million.

We hear about the bears until we imagine a killer grizzly lurking behind every bush, but the fact is that most people, vacationing in grizzly bear range, never see a grizzly bear. The presence of the great bears need not discourage travelers. Knowing that the bears are out there sharpens the senses and adds an element of adventure. It also motivates the traveler to play by the rules and follow the prescribed guidelines for traveling in grizzly country and avoiding close encounters. The average tourist, wed to his automobile, is the least likely of all to see a grizzly in most years, while the hiker in the backcountry assumes some added risk, especially if the plan includes overnight camping.

Whether or not we can go on sharing the parks depends on our willingness to give space to the bear. We must crowd the grizzly less and understand its wilderness nature better. The grizzly bear is not programmed to become anyone's puppy dog, and cannot change what it is. If we can overcome our drive to dominate the wilderness and its creatures, we can share these lands with the great bears.

Chapter 12

Saving the Grizzly

Following World War II, bears, especially grizzlies, were caught in a squeeze play. Human use of the national parks was multiplying dramatically, and this brought intense pressure on the bears. Meanwhile, little was being done toward understanding their needs. A handful of biologists, most of them connected with state agencies and universities, were especially concerned about the bears. They knew that there were voids in our knowledge of how the grizzly lived, and what it needed as seasonal feeding areas, denning habitat, travel corridors, and solitude.

Beyond the professional interests of these few biologists, there was little concern for the welfare of the grizzly, and essentially zero funding for grizzly bear research. One biologist recalls, "Most people simply did not give a damn for the bears. Bears were still seen as garbage dump animals and a threat to property."

Growing pressures on the grizzly and its habitat, combined with invention of a dart gun and fast-acting drugs that could quickly immobilize bears for study, prompted a few independent wildlife research scientists to set up their own pioneering bear studies.

The Craigheads put their research project in motion in Yellowstone in 1959, with approval of the National Park Service and the financial support of private individuals and organizations. By the time their project terminated eleven years later, they had accumulated an impressive store of basic information on the grizzly's way of life in the Yellowstone ecosystem and set the stage for other scientific studies that would follow.

A few other independent scientists have worked with bears. At the University of Montana, Charles Jonkel organized The Border Grizzly Project in cooperation with the Montana Fish and Game Department. This study group has not only carried out field investigations on grizzlies in a number of areas, but also trained many of the biologists now working with bears.

When the Craigheads began working with the Yellowstone grizzlies, the federal government displayed little interest in carrying out its own grizzly bear research, and this reflected the low level of public concern for the great bear. In the opinion of many, the grizzly bear had not outlived its historic status as a varmint, along with the wolves, coyotes, mountain lions, and assorted other predators.

This view of the bears was to undergo a major change. In recent years public support for the grizzly bear has flourished, as word spread that the big bear was in trouble. We have a way of waiting until a situation is critical, then rushing to the rescue. New research projects were put in motion and many who watched the events closely say the change started with the 1967 incident when grizzly bears killed Michele Koons and Julie Helgeson in Glacier National Park. The Park Service had just hired biologist C. J. Martinka to work with the bears of Glacier. By 1973, it also began increasing the tempo of its bear research in Yellowstone to fill the four-year data gap left by the departure of the Craigheads, who were forced out following a disagreement over the sudden and complete closing of backcountry garbage dumps where Yellowstone bears had long fed.

A PROTECTED SPECIES

The biggest boost for the grizzly came in 1973, when Congress passed the Endangered Species Act. Under this act the Fish and Wildlife Service could, after investigations and public hearings, declare certain wild species worthy of special protection because of their rarity.

Two years later the federal government brought the troubled grizzly bear into the family of wild creatures protected under this federal legislation. Some insisted that the grizzly be classified as endangered, but the U. S. Fish and Wildlife Service compromised and designated it a threatened species throughout the forty-eight states south of Canada. Under the Endangered Species Act, this status, threatened, is granted to species approaching endangered population levels, or living in habitat conditions where they might become endangered. This made the grizzly an instant candidate for federal and state funds for research and management, which quickly focused added attention on the great bears.

The grizzly's new classification as a threatened species brought problems to a number of government agencies that administer public lands where grizzlies live. The real purpose for classifying an animal as threatened or endangered is to bring it back to a secure population level so its name can be removed from the list. The U.S. Fish and Wildlife Service, Forest Service, Bureau of Land Management, and National Park Service, as well as the state governments of Idaho, Montana, Washington, and Wyoming all had new responsibilities under federal regulations to protect the bear and improve its chances of survival.

As a result, agencies began developing their own grizzly bear programs and assigning biologists to work with the bears. The Director of the U.S. Fish and Wildlife Service, which has overall authority for administering the Endangered Species Act, watched the various groups start off, each in its own direction, and suggested that they come together in a unified research approach to the bear's problems. These agencies then organized in the Interagency Grizzly Bear Committee. Members of this team are the decision makers, high government officials at the regional levels. Included are the directors of state wildlife agencies from Montana, Wyoming, Idaho, and Washington, as well as officials from the Forest Service, National Park Service, Bureau of Land Management, and Fish and Wildlife Service.

In addition, there are subcommittees for research and management, and these include the working bear biologists from federal agencies as well as the state governments involved. These workers, along with the remaining independent workers and university people, constitute a corps of perhaps sixty specialists, giving the grizzly bears south of Canada at least part of their professional time and attention. The entire effort toward the federal government's grizzly bear recovery program is supervised and coordinated out of Missoula, Montana, by bear biologist Dr. Chris Servheen.

One of the earliest tasks faced by this team was writing a plan that could turn the affairs of the grizzly around and set the bear on the road to recovery. After uncounted meetings, under the leadership of Don Brown of the Montana Department of Fish, Wildlife, and Parks, the comprehensive Grizzly Bear Recovery Plan was completed in 1982, and it remains the blueprint by which state and federal workers, are attempting to rescue the great bear and secure a few of its populations in the face of all the mounting human pressure.

The cost of our commitment to the grizzly now comes to about two million dollars a year. According to Servheen, "This is more than we spend on any other animal on the official list of threatened and endangered species." This is a remarkable turnaround. The beast that we tried for so many decades to erase from the face of the continent has become, within a relatively short time, a national concern meriting our close attention and our tax dollars. We may, after all, be maturing in our understanding of the world around us and our attitudes toward wildlife communities.

Listing the grizzly under the Endangered Species Act also brings it added protection against poachers. The illegal killing of a grizzly is a federal offense that can now bring the convicted poacher a year in jail and fines up to twenty thousand dollars. Furthermore, an informant may be paid up to twenty-five hundred dollars for information leading to the arrest and conviction.

In the backcountry, where grizzly bears live, U.S. Fish and Wildlife Service law enforcement agents, in the company of state conservation officers, travel unannounced, by foot and horseback, visiting sheep camps and outfitters. Poachers never know when a federal agent, working under cover, may be drinking beside them in the village saloon or chatting with them around a campfire. The illegal killing still goes on, however. The conservation officers and federal agents are too few in number to be everywhere at the right time to make arrests. Furthermore, the policy too often calls for taking bear cases into state instead of federal courts, and state courts are more lenient with wildlife law breakers. One Montana court fined a grizzly bear killer fifty dollars—about the price of a speeding ticket—for an offense that could have brought a year in jail and thousands of dollars in fines.

Although the federal and state governments have the big stakes in grizzly bear research, the bear still benefits by the work of independent research scientists, environmental organizations, and plain concerned citizens. Many of the people living in grizzly bear country are deeply troubled about the bear's future.

In 1982, a group of such citizens organized The Great Bear Foundation, an association of ranchers, teachers, loggers, scientists, and others. Most of them live in western states where the bear lives. They "watchdog" government agencies, particularly the Forest Service, whose projects effect bear habitat, and monitor the decisions of the Interagency Grizzly Bear Committee. The Foundation, which can be reached at Box 2699, Missoula, Montana 59806, publishes *Bear News,* a scientifically sound news letter that follows the affairs of the beleaguered grizzlies. This group has also established a plan for a kind of insurance program to compensate those who suffer property losses because of grizzly bears.

Meanwhile, the National Audubon Society established a fifteen thousand dollar "grizzly bear fund" for paying rewards to informants who supply information leading to the arrest and conviction of grizzly bear poachers. The Society then distributed ten thousand posters through grizzly bear country announcing this reward program. In less than a year, the Audubon Society granted one informant an award of twenty-five hundred dollars, and another one forty-five hundred dollars in successful cases against grizzly bear poachers.

Management of the national forests where the grizzlies live, plays a critical role in the grizzly's future. Where there must be development, the bear biologists believe there is a right and wrong way to go about it. "Rugged land, small trees, and closed roads all provide cover or isolation from people," says Jonkel, "and the bears can find these areas." The National Forest Service is making progress in managing the grizzlies on its holdings, but the level of commitment to the bears varies from one forest supervisor to the next, while political pressures in behalf of private interests whittle away at habitat.

Roads are among the big enemies of bears. New roads lead to virgin forests or to new mines, or enable technicians to explore the backcountry. A road can be rushed straight through to its destination, or it can be planned in consultation with grizzly bear experts, then be closed again once the immediate need is served.

A grizzly bear does not have to be hit by a car or truck to die because of a road. When the roads are left open, they permit the invasion by crowds of people into the wild lands, bringing stress to the bears, and increasing the potential for poaching and other bear and people conflicts.

Some areas are closed to people to reduce pressure on the bears. In surveying ways to keep grizzlies and people separated, the bear biologists and park administrators even considered locking campers up at night behind bear-proof fences, an idea that never flew.

One part of the official Grizzly Bear Recovery Plan, the U.S. Fish and Wildlife Service's book length blueprint for rescuing the grizzly bear, has tried to identify areas where today's grizzlies live, in the Lower Forty-eight, and figure out what, if anything, can be done for each of these populations. Today the grizzly, south of Canada, probably lives in only four states at most: Wyoming, Montana, Idaho, and Washington. Furthermore, the grizzly occupies only half a dozen pockets of bear habitat in these states. Bear workers refer to these habitats as ecosystems, but as Chris Servheen explains, several are "population islands", surrounded by human developments. Together, the bears of all six groups may total nine hundred or fewer.

THE GRIZZLY-POPULATED ECOSYSTEMS

In at least half of these six grizzly populations, the number of bears has fallen so low that there is little hope of saving them. The official recovery plan, finally approved in 1982, concentrates the available money and work on three areas that biologists feel have the best chance to turn the trend in the grizzly's status around. These are the Yellowstone, the Northern Continental Divide Grizzly Bear Ecosystem, which includes Glacier National Park, and the Cabinet-Yaak population in the Cabinet Mountains of northwestern Montana.

YELLOWSTONE GRIZZLY BEAR ECOSYSTEM. The best known grizzly bears, and those most frequently written and spoken of, live in the mountains and valleys of Yellowstone National Park and the surrounding federal and private lands. This is an island of bear habitat where grizzlies are cut off from other grizzly populations by at least a hundred and fifty airline miles of people country. The Yellowstone ecosystem covers an area about twice the size of Yellowstone National Park, and includes Grand Teton National Park, the John D. Rockefeller, Jr. Memorial Parkway, and five surrounding national forests, a total of some four million acres of beautiful and remote mountain country.

There are varying opinions about what is happening to the Yellowstone bears. Some experienced bear research scientists, pointing to the fact that bears have been showing up in areas where they had not been for years, think the numbers may even have increased slightly in recent times. Others believe the number of Yellowstone bears is still sliding.

In the summer of 1982, Dr. Roland Wauer, then chairman of the Interagency Study Steering Committee, which draws up guidelines for the Interagency Grizzly Bear Study Team, wrote a memorandum that shook up the grizzly bear workers as well as conservationists nationwide. "Unless some change occurs to reduce the grizzly bear's mortality rate soon," he wrote, "the probability of retaining this wildland species in Yellowstone National Park is minimal."

Dr. Richard Knight, the highly respected bear biologist employed by the National Park Service to study Yellowstone's grizzlies, appears to share this pessimism. At one point, he told a reporter that he gave the Yellowstone grizzly another twenty to thirty years.

Several authorities on the grizzly bear, including John Craighead, Charles Jonkel, Steve Mealey, and Chris Servheen appear somewhat more optimistic. Jonkel says that, "Yellowstone has plenty of habitat to support the bears and, with proper management, we could have grizzly bears there indefinitely." The key words are proper management and this translates into people, money, and habitat management. Larry Roop, Wyoming's veteran bear biologist who has been studying grizzlies in and around Yellowstone since 1973, believes the bears have increased there in recent years.

All agree, however, that these are critical times and the great bear is far from safe.

The bear population of the Yellowstone Ecosystem is not known precisely because bears are notoriously difficult, if not impossible, to count. There simply has never been a satisfactory census method worked out for bears. The figure handed out for the Yellowstone Ecosystem is usually around two hundred grizzlies, and estimates range up to three hundred and fifty. The number of productive females, however, may be as low as thirty, and they are the key to this population's survival.

Furthermore, the age structure of this bear community seems to have slid in recent years, leaving a younger population which may, at least temporarily, reduce the reproductive efficiency and the potential for building the numbers. In summary, the hard fact is that the Yellowstone grizzlies, especially adult females, remain dangerously low in numbers, while more habitat is lost each year. The weakest link is that part of the grizzly's range in private ownership. Federal and state governments are limited on what they can do for bears on these lands. Besides, local governments and private property owners are often development oriented.

In behalf of the troubled bears, the administrators may have to make decisions unpopular in some circles. Yellowstone National Park, according to the Grizzly Bear Recovery Plan, is classified as Situation One land, giving the grizzly top priority. Certain areas important to the bear's feeding and denning may have to be closed seasonally to hiking and other human uses.

Furthermore, everyone who goes to the park is going to have to help in the everlasting effort to keep the bears separated from people and their foods. Otherwise, the bears will continue to be sacrificed as they become conditioned to people and become a threat to human safety. The person who leaves food where bears can find it is a menace to both bears and people. According to the Grizzly Bear Recovery Plan, people who provide unnatural food, ". . . whether it be accidentally, foolishly, or intentionally, share moral responsibility for any future acts of damage or violence committed by these grizzly bears."

Protecting the grizzly will call for added curtailment of sheep grazing allotments in surrounding national forests, while thermal energy, oil exploration leases, timbering, and recreational development around the park must be managed with more emphasis on saving the great bear. New tourist-oriented developments inside the park boundaries can threaten the grizzly's future, especially when campgrounds and other developments are located in areas known to be important to the bears.

NORTHERN CONTINENTAL DIVIDE GRIZZLY BEAR ECO-SYSTEM. The grizzlies of this region, which includes Glacier National Park, are estimated at between four hundred and forty and six hundred and eighty bears. Of these an estimated two hundred live within the park. This population of grizzlies reaches across the border into Canada's Waterton National Park and beyond in Alberta as well as onto crown forest lands in adjacent British Columbia. This piece of grizzly bear country includes the Bob Marshall Wilderness, the Great Bear Wilderness, and the adjacent Scapegoat Wilderness, all in northwestern Montana, and the only remaining place in the Lower Forty-eight states where the grizzly can still be legally hunted.

Montana's regulations aim to hold the annual kill of grizzlies in this wilderness area, from all causes, to twenty-five animals, usually leaving from ten to twelve bears to be taken each year by hunters who draw lots for the privilege. If twenty-five bears are known to be lost to poachers and other causes, there are no hunting permits issued. There is considerable belief that no state should any longer permit the legal killing of grizzly bears south of Canada, but Montana officials believe that limited hunting in this area is good for the bears. "There is a different kind of bear in that area than you find in Yellowstone," says one high ranking Montana wildlife official. "They are not the threat to people that the grizzlies are in the parks, because they are hunted and they still recognize that people mean danger." The bears that do become conditioned to people and come closest to the hunting camps are the ones most readily taken by hunters with permits. Others get educated by wounds and near misses. Officials believe that without the hunts, more bears would lose their wildness, get into trouble with people, and end up being killed and not reported.

Most of the same measures needed to secure the Yellowstone grizzlies are essential to the future of this population of bears in and around Glacier National Park. These two ecosystems are the most secure grizzly populations and are generally believed to be the places where the big bears stand the best chance of hanging on into the future. Of the two populations, the grizzlies of Glacier National Park and surrounding areas are believed to be more secure than those caught in the Yellowstone habitat squeeze play.

CABINET-YAAK GRIZZLY BEAR ECOSYSTEM. The Cabinet Mountains and the Yaak River drainage in northwestern Montana are linked by secure bear habitat, but U.S. Highway 2, the Kootenai River, and private property limit the area through which bears can pass from one area to the other. The two areas are considered a single grizzly bear ecosystem, and nobody knows how many bears live in the Cabinet-Yaak area. The numbers, however, are low, perhaps as few as a couple of dozen, roaming over eighteen hundred square miles of habitat.

Wherever the great bears have slipped to numbers this low, there is talk among the biologists of what they call the MVP or minimum viable population. This is the level below which a population cannot be expected to survive indefinitely, and it could be that the grizzlies of the Cabinet-Yaak have fallen below this point of no return. According to computer models, the minimum viable population for grizzlies could be between thirty and seventy bears, depending on the quality of the habitat. The brown bears of Europe seem able to survive in smaller populations, but because they have not faced the precipitous changes that are coming to the grizzlies of the Rocky Mountains, they have had longer to adapt to their altering habitat.

After the Yellowstone and Glacier national park areas, however, the Cabinet-Yaak region is believed to offer the next best possibility of saving a remnant grizzly population. But the wilderness of this area, too, is being chipped away by large industry and road building programs, encouraged by the political atmosphere. According to *Bear News*, "The area has faced increasing levels of development in recent years, and more development is either proposed or being planned.

"The Cabinet Mountains hold reserves of silver and copper ore. Two multinational mining firms have been drilling for these minerals under special permit in the Congressionally designated wilderness portion of the mountains."

Following their exploratory drilling, these corporate giants met the requirements for going ahead with full scale operations with their attendant buildings, power lines, and roads. In addition, the Forest Service has plans for many miles of new roads to open up to people the Kootenai National Forest, the main national forest in which these grizzlies live.

SELKIRK MOUNTAIN ECOSYSTEM. This remnant population of grizzlies in the very northwest corner of Idaho and adjacent lands in Washington may be too small to save. One bear biologist who knows the situation in the Selkirks says, "A wild estimate would be between thirty and forty bears". Others believe this figure too high. In two years of searching in this area, a biologist believes he saw only half a dozen different grizzlies.

The U.S. Forest Service, which administers most of this area is inclined to think conservatively and works with a figure of thirteen grizzlies in the Selkirks. Whatever the number of bears in these mountains, the number of breeding age females is critically low. If there are as many as twenty grizzlies in the ecosystem, it is probable, using what the biologists know of how a grizzly bear population breaks down by age and sex, that only three or four of them would be females of breeding age. How long that number of females could continue to replace the population losses is questionable. There is the possibility, however, that recruits move in from Canada, reinforcing this population of bears.

In the Selkirks, the best efforts of the Forest Service are hampered by local prejudices against the great bear. Ranchers, as well as those who do not want forest roads closed to their recreational vehicles, and private land owners trying to establish new summer home developments and other "improvements", are remarkably vocal against the grizzly where the bear interferes with their own special interests.

SELWAY-BITTERROOT ECOSYSTEM. Nobody knows the number of bears in this northern Idaho region, but it is part of the country's largest mountainous wilderness area south of Alaska. There have been recent grizzly bears sightings in several parts of the region and, granted swift action by research people and managers, there is some slight possibility that the Selway-Bitterroot might be important in preserving the great bear.

NORTH CASCADES ECOSYSTEM. This high alpine country in north-central Washington, with its jagged scenic peaks, hidden lakes, glaciers, and mile on mile of remote wilderness, would seem the right place for grizzlies. There is little question that the grizzly could once more find here the habitat it needs. But grizzly bear sightings in the North Cascades are rare, if at all, any more. Paul Sullivan, of the Washington Department of Game, has compiled a long-time list of such reports. He learned of one grizzly that became a cattle killer in the Winthrop area until a government hunter tracked and killed it.

A year after this bear was killed, W. O. Burgess saw a grizzly on the Chiwawa River road, climbed from his car, and tried to give it one from his Luger. This took the bear's mind off whatever else it was doing at the moment and sent it charging down on Burgess, who won the dash to his car, while ineffectively emptying his pistol over his shoulder in the bear's general direction.

In 1965, William Soren spotted a bear with a shoulder hump "a foot high," at Cascade Pass. He waved his hat at the bear, and shouted down at it, which prompted the grizzly to charge uphill. The bear gave up when Soren jumped off a cliff.

One research paper, prepared for the North Cascades National Park, lists the last confirmed grizzly bear sighting in the area as 1967. "The North Cascades almost certainly lack a breeding population at the present time," says the paper, "although transients may move in on rare occasions."

Hope for a seventh population hangs on by a thread in the San Juan Mountains of southern Colorado. Colorado officials had long considered the great bear gone completely from their state when, in 1979, a hunting guide killed a sixteen-year-old female grizzly. The guide explained, from his hospital bed, that the bear attacked him and that he had to kill it by stabbing it with a hand-held arrow.

This prompted the Colorado Division of Wildlife to dispatch to the San Juans, a search team, which for two years, with the cooperation of the U. S. Forest Service, and the U.S. Fish and Wildlife Service, tramped the mountains and trapped black bears, always looking for a sign of grizzly bears. Although grizzlies once lived here in abundance, the biologists found no grizzlies, tracks, scats, or scratching. Colorado officials now doubt that the grizzly any longer lives in their state although the tantalizing possibility lingers yet. Some believe that the search ended too soon.

Protecting the grizzly bear in the modern world is not easy. The pressures mount. People continue to find new reasons to take over the wild places. There is good work being done in behalf of the great bear, but whether it is enough, or came soon enough, remains to be seen.

With the mighty grizzly reduced to these pockets of its former range, it is natural to ask if the Canadian and Alaskan grizzlies, in the lands to the north, face a better future.

Chapter 13

Great Bears of the North Country

The home of the grizzly extends to the Far North and, on occasion, the modern fisherman, flying low across the arctic barrenlands, will spot the tawny form of this king of bears. In this wilderness realm where caribou roam and jaegers scream, the great bears plod the tundra of the Arctic Plains much as they did the Great Plains far to the south in the time of Lewis and Clark.

These northern grizzlies feed on grasses, search out the the marmot and the arctic ground squirrel and, in late summer, fatten on roots, blueberries, and crowberries. Occasionally they feast on moose calves and try to dig the Arctic foxes from their dens. In season, they may also invade the nesting colonies of snow geese and black brant as they have from time beyond our knowing.

At the northern edge of the continent, grizzlies are not abundant. They wander widely in their endless search for food to fuel their ponderous bodies, and although the Arctic traveler may seldom meet a grizzly, he remains aware that the big bear can surprise him by the river bank, or rise before him from any patch of dwarf willows. They are so thinly scattered over the tundra of western Canada that A. H. MacPherson of the Canadian Wildlife Service once wrote, ''We don't know how many barrenground grizzlies survive in the Northwest Territories, but it is unlikely that more than one thousand remain, and five hundred could be a closer estimate.''

These north-of-the-border grizzlies now live in only two western provinces of Canada, Alberta and British Columbia, plus the Yukon Territory, the Northwest Territories, and northern Alaska. Estimates of the total number of grizzlies in all of Canada most often range between eleven thousand and eighteen thousand. Most of these grizzlies, perhaps ninety percent of them, live in the sprawling wilderness of British Columbia and the Yukon Territory, while Alberta, and the Northwest Territories, may have as many as a thousand grizzly bears each.

As for the grizzlies of Alaska, no one can know how many they number, but in one report they were estimated at thirty to forty thousand. Dr. Albert W. Erickson, formerly with the Alaska Department of Fish and Game, said that the Alaska population of brown-grizzly bears was greater than all the other grizzly bears on the North American continent together. Furthermore, Alaska's grizzlies overall seem to be thriving. In Juneau, a representative of the Alaska Department of Fish and Game said in the mid-1980s, "We have had a dozen mild years in a row, and probably have more browns and grizzlies now than any time since statehood." Few people, however, expect that Alaska will manage to retain a grizzly bear population at these high levels indefinitely.

THE McNEIL RIVER BEARS

Each summer, as the salmon swim upstream toward their spawning areas, a short section of the McNeil River, two hundred miles southwest of Anchorage, becomes the scene of the most impressive assembly of bears on the continent. After entering the river, the salmon swim a mile and half before arriving at the McNeil River Falls. Here, amidst the boulders, all five species of Pacific salmon thrash about in the tumbling white water, but the big attraction for the bears is the dog or chum salmon. The bears wander in from miles around and wade into the water to fish until visitors may see twenty or more bears at one time.

As photographers discovered this concentration of bears, the fame of the McNeil River spread, and the visitor pressure increased. The Alaska Legislature established the McNeil River State Game Sanctuary here in 1965. So many photographers crowded in that the

Dwarfed by Alaska's soaring peaks, three grizzly bears feed on the sparce tundra vegetation. One report estimated there are between thirty and forty thousand grizzlies in the state. →

attendance of the bears began to fall off. They either stayed away or switched to night fishing. As a result, the Alaska Board of Fish and Game wisely established a permit system that limits the number of photographers that can come on any one day and restricts them to assigned areas.

Permits are limited to ten a day, and if you want to see and photograph the McNeil River bears, the first step is to write the Alaska Department of Fish and Game. But those who come should be prepared. There are no special facilities or concessions of any kind for visitors, and following a hundred-mile fly-in from King Salmon or Homer, the photographer walks a bear path to the falls. There, the whole event is carefully managed by biologists concerned with the welfare of the fishing brown bears and determined to keep bears and people apart.

The great bears begin to arrive in the area early and are there waiting when the salmon arrive. The show ends in August, as the blue berries ripen and the bears depart to fatten on the fresh fruit. Katmai National Monument is another famous bear watching location when the salmon are running, and other populations of the giant brown bears live on Admiralty, Baranof, and Chicagof islands, as well as the Alaska Peninsula.

For the bears, the McNeil River has changed. The people are a recent addition. Visitors without limits were altering the feeding pattern when management brought some order to the McNeil River Sanctuary.

ANTI-BEAR CAMPAIGNS

In some parts of the North, bears suffer pressures from too many people just as their cousins have to the south.

Through much of the North, moose and caribou are important sources of human food. Downward fluctuations in the populations of these animals are customarily accompanied by demands to kill wolves and bears which are blamed for taking the game animals. In one such instance, the Yukon government, pointing out that there had been a decline in the southern Yukon moose population, announced its intention to kill wolves and as many as sixty grizzlies.

Word spread and the Yukon government heard not only from grizzly bear biologists, who said that the bear population might not recover from such destruction, but also from angry conservation

Brown and grizzly bears gather along Alaska's McNeil River for the summer run of salmon (overleaf). The bears capture the fish with their jaws and eat voraciously.

groups urging tourists to cancel their plans for traveling to the Yukon. An official said maybe they would kill only fifteen bears. The problem grew from a man-caused imbalance in the moose-wolf-grizzly relationships, and similar proposals will crop up again as surely as populations of game animals fall and people seek an easy cure.

A variation of this anti-bear campaign has been underway for years on Kodiak Island, home of the giant Kodiak brown bears. Of all the brown bears anywhere, none is more impressive than the bears found on this area, thirty miles off the southwest coast of Alaska. The Kodiak bears, the world's largest carnivores, may leave a footprint fourteen inches long and eight inches wide. A large male bear may weigh fourteen hundred pounds, twice the weight of a large inland grizzly. In 1941, more than two-thirds of Kodiak Island was declared a national wildlife refuge to protect the giant bears and other wildlife.

Kodiak was one of the scenes of early research on the great bears. As early as the 1960s, government biologists were drugging some of these bears, marking them, and gathering facts on them, including their weights, which were determined by hoisting them in a net beneath a hovering helicopter. "As the chopper gets close to a sow with yearlings," one of the biologists told a gathering of Canadian and American bear scientists, assembled in the Yukon Territory, in 1968, "they scatter. The sow leaves them on their own, and almost without exception, the yearlings head straight up the hill. They find refuge in rough rock just as high as they can go." What does the female do then? "She will actually turn and threaten the helicopter."

By conservative estimate, there are some two thousand bears roaming this island, and guided legal trophy hunts are big business. On Kodiak, the bears live in a splendid world rich in vegetation and wildlife. Their island home is surrounded by the dark cold waters of the Pacific while, in the center of the Island, mountains rise four thousand feet high. An annual rainfall of sixty inches and a moderate temperature produce abundant food for the bears and other creatures. In addition, a small group of ranchers operate on the island, and this has brought the native bears into conflict with cattlemen, sometimes in nasty campaigns that have even used airborne shooters.

The aerial attack on Kodiak began when one of the ranchers flew with a gunner in his single-engine aircraft. In their running battle against the island's bears the ranchers had the help of state and federal predator hunters.

After a decade of this brand of bear management, the attack took a new turn, as reported in an investigative article carried by *Outdoor Life.* The magazine's Alaska-based reporter learned that the small plane had been converted into a regular fighter type aircraft by mounting an M-1 rifle on it. In 1963, combined air and ground attacks accounted for the deaths of at least thirty-five of the giant bears by Kodiak ranchers. Furthermore, the bears killed were not limited to individuals known to be taking cattle, but included brown bears sometimes miles from the nearest herd.

As this bear slaughter became known, the lid came off and people rallied to the bear's defense. But the conflict between bears and ranchers continues and probably will go on in some form as long as bears and cattle share Kodiak Island.

The fact that cattle are on the island at all can be traced to a branch of the United States Government. While the U.S. Fish and Wildlife Service manages much of the island as a national wildlife refuge, a handful of cattlemen operate there because the U.S. Bureau of Land Management granted them leases, thereby encouraging the raising of cattle. Some of these cattlemen are said to want all the bears eliminated and the island left to livestock, a repeat play of the fate that grizzlies suffered across cattle country in the southwestern states. On the other side, conservationists have suggested that the cattle operations be bought out, leaving Kodiak a refuge for the bears.

Refuge staff people believe that the population of brown bears on the island is stable at the moment, but they worry about the future. The tide here, as elsewhere, seems to be moving against the bears. Recent events have demonstrated the vulnerability of the refuges. In 1971, the Alaska Native Claims Settlement Act transferred nearly one-fifth of the refuge's three hundred thousand acres to private ownership. Says one refuge biologist, "This land was the best bear habitat on the island." He adds that any development could work against the bears and that almost certainly, the owners will have to develop some of the land to cover tax costs.

Another chunk of the refuge's best bear habitat was taken for construction of the Terror Lake hydroelectric project.

In addition, the refuge staff people see the growing invasion of human visitors as bringing increases in the number of bears that have to be killed in defense of life and property. These pressures for more recreational and commercial use of Kodiak are still growing and cutting into the habitat available for bears.

Moose hunters have also called for the killing of bears on another Alaska refuge, the famous Kenai National Wildlife Refuge, which sprawls over three thousand square miles two or three hours drive south of Anchorage. Most of the wild species that live in Alaska are found here, along with a remarkable variety of habitats, including twelve hundred lakes and a thousand miles of rivers where salmon swim, bears feed, and the world's largest moose wade.

Most of the bears on the Kenai National Wildlife Refuge are black bears. The refuge staff estimates their numbers at somewhere between one thousand and fifteen hundred. There are also an estimated one hundred adult brown bears scattered thinly over this broad range.

The giant moose for which this refuge is famous first began to filter into the area following devastating fires that swept the Kenai peninsula, beginning in 1871. The second growth vegetation was an invitation to the moose, and their numbers increased steadily until they peaked about 1925. Then, for several years the moose numbers gradually declined, and as their numbers fell, the moose hunters began pointing their fingers at the black bear and accusing the bear of eating moose calves which, admittedly, it does savor.

As far back as 1950, Edward F. Chatelain of the U.S. Fish and Wildlife Service office in Anchorage reviewed this series of developments for the professional wildlife workers attending the North American Wildlife Conference. He explained that bear predation on moose calves was a long-standing controversy on the Kenai Peninsula. He added, "Local residents and guides have attributed a great decline in Kenai moose numbers to bear predation. Sportsmen's groups have agitated for some sort of black bear control, and have even gone so far as to suggest a bear derby with prizes to those who killed the most black bears." The case against the bear was strengthened by occasional reports from local people who watched while bears killed or chased moose calves.

There is no question that the Kenai bears include moose calves in their summer diets. But this is natural, and the moose are abundant and flourishing regardless of the calves the bears take. Besides, the land is a national wildlife refuge for all native creatures.

A staff member of the Kenai National Wildlife Refuge says, "While black bears do take a large number of moose calves each spring, the moose population has been steadily increasing, despite the high calf loss." The mid-winter moose population on the Kenai stands at about fifty-five hundred. This may result from habitat management rendering the area more productive for moose, and this could hold a lesson: if the habitat can be managed for maximum production for a wide variety of wildlife, there might well be enough moose calves to satisfy the seasonal hunger of the bears and still provide a satisfactory harvest for the hunters.

But, given our history of intolerance for the bears, the documented loss of a single moose calf might be sufficient evidence to condemn the entire bear population and bring forth more suggestions for "bear derbies". Some observers insist that people, not bears, are over-harvesting the moose.

By all measures, our spectacular northern state still has vigorous populations of bears, but the competition between bears and people mounts. *Bear News,* published by the Great Bear Foundation has said, "Alaska brown bears are beginning to feel the pressure felt by brown bears in the forty-eight adjacent states." Pressures are brought on the bears by oil exploration, timber cutting, and people moving into grizzly habitat.

Bear biologists in Alaska's Department of Fish and Game realize that their two big tools in keeping the bear population healthy are control of shooting, both legal and illegal, and preservation of habitat. The department has carried out bear studies since the early days of statehood, and it recognizes the conflicts inherent in the state's rush to build its economic strength. An Alaska publication sums up the challenge this way, "As Alaska develops, it will be necessary for land-controlling agencies to recognize that, in order to maintain wildlife habitat, restrictions will be required in some areas of agriculture, logging, and oil development."

Alaska is North America's most important remaining stronghold of the great bears. But, as human pressures move northward, there appear disturbing parallels between Alaska and states to the south. In competition with people, the black bears can adapt, within limits, while their large grizzly and brown bears cousins simply dwindle away.

The Alaskan bears, however, have some big advantages. The major ones are that attitudes toward bears may be changing as we gain understanding of these animals. Besides, we know the needs of the giant bear better today than ever before. Maybe, just maybe, we are prepared to keep the bears of the last frontier from following those of the lower forty-eight down the sunset trail.

PART TWO

The
Black Bear

Chapter 14

Would a Black Bear Kill You?

By the time we reach grade school we already have a twisted idea of the character and behavior of the black bear. We are conditioned by children's books and television. Gentle Ben, Teddy Bears, Smokey Bear, we know and love them all and are sometimes shocked to learn that this roly-poly clown, or his mother, would do us bodily harm.

This innocence is based on our inexperience because most of us have never even seen a wild bear, by nature a shy, elusive, solitary, mind-your-own-business animal that avoids people. One hunting guide in Maine shot a bear out of a tree with his handgun, and when the wounded bear fell to the ground and then tried to run away, shot it four more times. Only then did the crippled bear, pushed too far, turn on the man and maul him while the guide pistol-whipped it about the head with his .32. Finally, the bear lay down and put its head between its paws while the man ran away. His friends later tracked the bear down, with the help of hounds, and killed it.

But like the grizzly, the black bear can never be trusted, or its reactions to a situation predicted. Park visitors are becoming increasingly wise to the black bear's potential for causing injury. One should never assume that the black bear simply can't or won't attack. They can be individualists and, now and then, a bear pushed too far by people, hunger, or its protective instincts, goes a step beyond the usual bluff charge and attacks. Black bears, under stress, have killed their share of people. Furthermore, just enough black bear attacks seem to be unprovoked to assure us that this aberrant behavior, although extremely rare, could occur again. The truth probably is that even the "unprovoked" attacks are triggered by our presence, rather than a case of bears seeking out victims.

UNPROVOKED ATTACKS

A California deer hunter was attacked by a black bear that rushed him for no reason that anyone was ever able to determine. The man told his story from a hospital wheel chair. While the bear held the man down and chewed on his left hand, the hunter worked his rifle with one hand and put five bullets into the bear's chest, neck, and head. The bear died, but not before injuring the hunter severely. Who knows, however, whether the bear might have been assaulted earlier by another hunter, or surprised in its bed by the hunter it attacked?

One of the best known cases of a black bear's apparently unprovoked attack on a human occurred in the middle of a summer afternoon, some years ago in Michigan's Upper Peninsula. Arthur Pomranky was at work as a fire tower lookout. His wife was at home in their cabin on the edge of the forest. Their son was playing in the basement, while their three-year-old daughter, Carrol Ann, played in the yard. Mrs. Pomranky was in the kitchen talking with a neighbor.

Suddenly she heard Carrol Ann cry out in alarm. Mrs. Pomranky wheeled toward the back door and saw her daughter scrambling halfway up the short flight of steps and reaching for the screen door while right behind her came a lean, shaggy black bear. Even as Mrs. Pomranky screamed at the bear, the animal grabbed the little girl by the arm and dragged her off toward the woods.

The neighbor lady held Mrs. Pomranky back, preventing her from rushing through the door at the bear. The frantic mother raced to the bedroom and returned with her husband's revolver, but she was so distraught that she could not load the gun. By this time, it did not matter; the bear and its victim had both vanished into the forest.

Mrs. Pomranky frantically called the forest ranger station and told ranger Bruce Elliott what was happening, and he called ex-state trapper Alex Van Luven. By 3:10 Van Luven arrived at the Pomranky home, accompanied by his three-year-old Labrador retriever. The Pomranky child had now been gone for forty minutes.

People were arriving steadily. Van Luven had them stay back, to avoid confusing the dog with strange scents, and followed the Lab into the forest, accompanied by four local hunters he selected for the task. Soon the dog picked up a scent, and shortly the party came upon one of Carroll Ann's shoes and a blood trail.

Another hundred and fifty yards brought them to the badly mutilated and party eaten body. Van Luven left one man guarding the body as he pushed on with his dogs.

He may have passed the bear and not known it. Wayne Weston, meanwhile, standing near the body, was straining to hear every sound. He did not have long to wait because, regardless of all the strange noises and odors in the woods at the time, the bear was returning to its kill.

Weston saw the animal slipping through the forest toward the body of the girl. He stood motionless, waiting. The bear did not detect the man's presence until it was too late, and as the animal came within range, Weston took careful aim and fired, then fired again and kept it up until he had shot the bear five times.

Van Luven raced back to the scene and found Weston standing over the dead bear. There was no doubt in their minds that they had the animal responsible for the tragedy, but the carcass was shipped off to be checked. The bear's stomach was practically empty except for some human flesh.

Investigators could find no explanation for the bear's unusual behavior. There was no dump nearby and the Pomrankys had not put out food for animals. Pathologists could find no abnormalities in the brain or other organs. The bear was a very thin male weighing one hundred and twenty-five pounds. No one knows why he was so thin at a time when there was abundant wild food, but there was speculation that he had been released by people who took him as a cub and no longer wanted him, in which case, he would be conditioned to people and know nothing about how to hunt for wild foods.

The Pomranky incident was widely reported and, in 1950, was included in a paper in the highly respected *Journal of Mammalogy.* This prompted another report in the same journal of an attack by a black bear in southeastern Manitoba, late on an August evening in 1929.

In this case, Mrs. Fred Gregorchuck decided to take supper to her husband who was working late in the fields. Her three children, ages seven to two, were left in their bedroom with the door securely shut. Mrs. Gregorchuck returned from the field at seven thirty to find that the bedroom door was broken in and her children all missing. The two younger ones, who escaped to the neighbors, reported that a huge bear broke into their room and caught Olga, the oldest girl. The partly eaten body of the girl was found at the edge of the forest, nearby.

The following day, three constables, armed with pistols and a machinegun, went into the woods, and as they approached the site where the body was found, they were charged from behind by a large bear. They riddled the bear with machine gun bullets, and it fell a few feet from the men who had come for him. It weighed four hundred and twenty pounds.

This was listed as one more example of an apparently unprovoked attack on a human by a black bear. Both cases were considered so unusual that the prestigious Society of Mammalogists felt they should be recorded in the scientific literature.

A more recent incident occurred on a trout stream in northern

Saskatchewan where three fishermen ran afoul of a large black bear. Saskatchewan wildlife authorities report a growing bear population in recent years. "We're finding bears expanding into areas where they haven't been for a long time," says one biologist. There has been a growing number of complaints from bee keepers having bear troubles, and stockmen have reported increasing losses to bears. This province claims some thirty thousand black bears, and this, along with the steadily increasing number of people finding their way into the back country for recreation and other purposes, may be related to the strange case on McDougal Creek in May, 1983.

That day two fishing buddies drove out to Nipawin Provincial Park for brookies. As evening came on, they were fishing a hundred yards or so apart. One of them, Larry Reimer, later wrote about the events of that evening in an *Outdoor Life* article.

Reimer heard his partner shout that there was a bear on the prowl. Then Reimer realized, from the tone of the calls, that the bear was attacking his partner and he ran full speed toward the trouble spot. The bear, after being kicked in the nose by the first fisherman, crossed the stream to the other side where he now charged Reimer. He drew his filleting knife and dived into a deep hole where he floundered, as his waders quickly filled with water.

The bear caught up with him in midstream and grabbed one of his legs. This gave Reimer one chance to run his filleting knife up to the hilt in the bear's throat. The bear, perhaps because of the throat injury, gave up and swam to shore where it died of its wound. Reimer also managed to make shore.

Saskatchewan wildlife workers found no evidence that this bear, a male weighing perhaps three hundred pounds, suffered from any abnormalities. They also believe that this was probably not a bear that had been held in captivity or been otherwise corrupted by people. One possible explanation, advanced by Wayne Pepper of the Saskatchewan Wildlife Division for the attack, was that the bear may have been guarding its kill when the two fishermen approached closer than the bear could tolerate. The nature of the bear's kill brings the story to its gruesome end.

Melvin Rudd was also a local fisherman fond of fishing McDougal Creek for brook trout. When he failed to return home on time, his family began phoning around the neighborhood. His pickup truck was located near the stream where Rudd had parked it.

That evening the police brought in a tracking dog and soon discovered Rudd's remains not far from the creek where the bear apparently had killed him and fed on his body. "Maybe he had caught some fish," says Wayne Pepper, "and the bear was attracted by the fish odor. We'll never know."

Of the thousands of confrontations between Saskatchewan bears and people, this was the first record in the province of a bear killing a human for food. One contributing factor might have been the cold spring and the shortage of natural bear foods. Furthermore, the previous fall's blueberry crop had been a failure, and bears may have come out of the dens with a lower fat reserve than usual.

Officials in Saskatchewan heard of one other bear fatality the year Melvin Rudd died. A trapper, living far back in the boonies, died of a broken neck from a single swat by a large black bear. There is a belief, however, that this was a provoked attack, that the man had been feeding the bear and had been caught by the bear in one of its sour moods. The Saskatchewan officials believe that more hunting of bears might exert greater control over them and reduce the danger of attacks.

Low supplies of natural foods may also help explain the rash of black bear attacks on Alaskans in the summer of 1963. Biologists there reported a short crop of blueberries that year, at a time the bears normally rely heavily on the fruit. A sleeping fisherman was dragged off, sleeping bag and all, but saved by a companion who shot the bear. About the same time another Alaska black bear attacked four hunters in their tent, and it was also killed on the scene. A third victim was treed by a black bear that then climbed up after him and bit him severely before being chased off by another person. Finally, a black bear killed a miner. All of these Alaskan attacks occurred in a matter of a few weeks.

Some years later on the night of July 25, 1971, in a private campground not far from Rocky Mountain National Park, John Henri Richardson, a thirty-one year old Denver, Colorado, man was pulled from the tent where he, a companion, and a Siamese kitten were sleeping. Richardson was dragged a hundred and fifty feet into the woods and the bear only dropped him there because Richardson's father, who was camping nearby in a motor home, banged the animal on the head repeatedly with an iron skillet. The victim was loaded into the motor home and rushed to the hospital where the staff verified what the relatives already feared. The death of Richardson became the first recorded instance of a black bear killing a human in Colorado.

The following day, the bear believed to be responsible was tracked and killed two miles up the mountain from the scene of the attack. The animal was a three-hundred-and-five-pound male. Its teeth were worn to the gums. The bear had been foraging in garbage, and the stomach was empty except for pieces of plastic, egg shells, coffee grounds, and other refuse. More than a dozen years later, this still stood as the only known case of its kind in Colorado history.

In Pennsylvania, where there are thousands of meetings between bears and people every year, biologists say, "there is no known case of a serious mauling by a black bear." These bears have been hunted since the earliest days of the country's settlement, and hunters have continuously culled the bears, eliminating those that display signs of antagonism toward people. "The more aggressive ones," explains one biologist, "are the first to go."

PROVOCATIONS AND CORRUPTION

Many, but not all, of the black bear attacks on people, as with most grizzly attacks, can be traced to people who provoke or corrupt the animal. Bears of any kind that have had close contact with people can be dangerous. This contact might take the form of feeding at dumps or eating foods spread especially to attract bears, a hobby still practiced in some places, including the Pocono Mountains in Pennsylvania, where some predict serious human injury from bears if the feeding continues. It is also true that wilderness bears who have rarely if ever seen a human, or eaten people foods, have attacked those who invaded their space.

Black bear cubs have often been kept as pets, legally or otherwise, then released as they grow larger and less cuddly. These bears are denied the learning experience other bears have when their mothers teach them how to obtain food in the wild. Until recent years, many black bears were commonly kept in small roadside cages, especially in the Great Smoky Mountains, to attract tourists to gasoline pumps, souvenir displays, and lunch counters. Writer Lew Dietz told in *Field and Stream* of the Maine garage owner who was killed by a black bear. The man kept the bear in a cage to draw business, apparently abused the animal and fed it poorly, until one day it escaped. The first matter of business the bear took care of after gaining its freedom was to kill the man who imprisoned it, scarcely an "unprovoked" attack. The behavior of captive bears is no guideline to the nature of a wild bear. In recent times, laws have been tightened against the keeping of bears.

In some areas bears simply encounter hikers and others so often, and escape safely, that they gradually lose their natural fear of people. This is especially true in parks where people are not a threat because hunting is forbidden. Instead of permitting hunting in parks, there must be other management methods to keep bears and people apart. Studies at the University of Montana are exploring the ways of conditioning bears to stay away from people and become wild and wary again.

Many of the black bears that have attacked people have done so under the stress of defending themselves from men and dogs. Theodore Roosevelt, writing in his classic *The Wilderness Hunter* tells of a raftsman who came upon a bear while dogs held it at bay beside the river. The angry bear broke through the dogs and rushed the man who, soon after, bled to death from a bite in a femoral artery.

Attacks on humans are unusual cases; they are atypical, not the common daily habits of the standard run-of-the-mill black bear. Bear biologist Lynn Rogers, after handling hundreds of black bears, finds them generally "timid" by nature. Teddy Roosevelt summed up the nature of the black bear, even when it is feeling antagonistic. "But a black bear", he wrote, "is not usually a formidable opponent, and though he will sometimes charge home, he is much more apt to bluster and bully than actually to come to close quarters." Roosevelt said that, in all his bear hunts, he had only once seen a person injured by a black bear. The hunter came upon the bear suddenly in a thickly wooded area, mortally wounded the animal, then moved right in to finish the job. Not surprisingly, the injured bear rushed the man, knocked the gun from his hands, and left him to use only his knife. Both bear and hunter suffered severe injuries, but the bear died and the man recovered.

DEALING WITH THE BLACK BEAR

Wherever the black bear is encountered, it should be granted the respect due any wild creature. It is well equipped to inflict heavy damage whether using teeth, claws, or both.

The best rule for avoiding bear trouble is to keep distance between you and the bear. That color slide you want of a close-up park bear, or the story you bring home, is not worth the risk you take. Forcing an encounter on the bear is unfair to the bear. The human will ordinarily escape, but the bear that makes threatening movements toward a person may be killed by rangers, stockmen, or outfitters to protect people and property.

Studies in national parks reveal that by far most of the aggressive acts of black bears toward people are little more than warnings. Of six hundred and twenty-four aggressive acts investigated in the Great Smoky Mountains National Park, the bears were judged to show remarkable restraint. Fewer than six percent of the instances ended in physical contact between bear and human. What the person needs to remember in such a case is that no one can ever be entirely sure what manner of bear he has met, or what its mood or level of stress might be at the moment. For example, a furious fight with another bear might have left it in a nasty mood.

Some rangers familiar with black bears believe that these animals can size up a person, and that they learn to judge which people are submissive and which are a threat to bears. "They work the crowd," says one Great Smoky Mountains National Park ranger. "They can tell which people might give them food. If you see the ears laid back, and there is growling and jaw popping, the bear is ready for a bluff charge and this, coupled with food denial, or submissive behavior, may become a real charge."

Bears accustomed to being around people can be aggravated until they charge, and the person responsible never knows, at first, whether it is a bluff charge or the real thing. Park rangers, identifying some of the actions that have aroused the animosity of bears, mention crowding, feeding the bears film wrappers, teasing bears by withholding food, trying to lasso bears, and throwing sticks and stones at them.

Remember not to kneel in front of a bear, searching for a low camera angle, because this is seen as submissive behavior and may trigger a charge. In dealing with a charging black bear, it is generally better to be aggressive and threaten the bear than it is to play dead.

Boiled down, getting along with bears, except perhaps for those taken by surprise, is largely a matter of attitude. The opportunities for conflicts are growing, and unless people can adapt to the bear's needs, black bears as well as grizzlies may be in serious trouble throughout much of their range.

Where the black bear still hangs on, we can share this land with him, and usually without serious risk of bodily harm, providing we understand both the bear's strength and swiftness and its need for space.

Chapter 15

Understanding the Black Bear

One autumn day some years ago, Washington State bear biologist Douglas J. Pierson encountered a bear that reconfirmed his faith in the animal's adaptability and intelligence. Pierson had captured and anesthetized several black bears, outfitting them with collars and small radio transmitters that enabled him to follow them in their wanderings. He was especially interested in learning how the bears reacted to the opening days of the hunting season.

One of his bears gave him a most difficult time. After the first two days of the open season, Pierson knew the bear was still in the field. He could pinpoint its location with his radio equipment. But he still could not find the bear. Furthermore, although the reception told him that he must be very close to the animal, the bear was stationary, and Pierson wondered if it might be injured, or perhaps already dead.

When Pierson climbed onto a large log for a better view, the signals came in louder than ever, so the biologist climbed down again and walked around to the hollow end of the log. Bending over in front of the dark interior, he was greeted by an explosive "woof!" Even then, the bear stayed in its sanctuary. Pierson, saying nothing about his discovery, backed away and left the animal hiding in the log.

The following morning he returned and approached the log quietly to check. The signals had grown faint on his receiver. The bear, after being discovered, had vacated its hiding place, and Pierson located it three miles away, in the heart of a wildlife refuge where there was no hunting. Furthermore, the bear stayed there for the remainder of the hunting season.

This gift of adaptability manifests itself in numerous ways, some of which endanger the bear's own welfare. The black bear has learned to gather honey at the hives of the commercial apiarist, sweet corn in the farmer's fields, pigs in the barnyard, apples in the orchard, dog food from the back porch, and tidbits from the garbage can. It sometimes tolerates the presence of man better than man adapts to the presence of the bear.

But it has other attributes going for it, and one of these is its uncanny ability to hide. Although it is a large animal, the black bear can stay so well hidden that most people, even if they live in bear country, go for years without seeing a bear. One reason is that the black bear has adapted to the threats from people by learning to sleep through the day and confine its feeding to the hours of darkness. Black bear, black night. Many a bear has watched from the roadside shadows as unsuspecting people passed either on foot or in vehicles. Certainly, the black bear sees us more often than we see it. The Craigheads found this to be true of grizzly bears, as well. Tracking grizzlies in Yellowstone's backcountry, and knowing the locations of both their crew members and the bears, they frequently found that the instrumented bears slipped out of their day beds ahead of the people and departed without ever being seen by the field workers actively looking for a bear and sometimes being within a hundred yards of them. Said the Craigheads, "This occurred in spite of our knowing the approximate location of the animals from our directional radio receivers."

Black bears have been known to den in culverts within a few feet of passing vehicles, under occupied houses, and one bedded down thirty feet from the centerline of U.S. Highway 2, east of Libby, Montana. Most biologists who have studied bears closely agree that the black bear is intelligent, elusive, and secretive, characteristics that help make it a survivor.

Until recent times we have known surprisingly little about the black bear. The animal's elusive nature makes it difficult to study, and consequently misconceptions about it have flourished.

SIZE AND WEIGHT

Even the size of the bear is deceiving. It is often smaller than the observer thinks. The *Pennsylvania Game News* once reported on a project in which the Old Town Sportsmen's Club of Clearfield County asked people to guess the weight of a black bear held in a cage there. The actual weight was three hundred twenty and a half pounds, but estimates went as high as sixteen hundred and fifty pounds, while many guessed the bear at more than seven hundred pounds.

The average adult male, depending on the season and the habitat in which he lives, can be in the two-hundred-and-fifty-pound range. The females are considerably smaller. One study in New York State revealed that the average weight of fifty-four bears trapped was two hundred and twenty pounds, with males weighing in at two hundred and forty pounds and females one hundred and eighty-nine pounds.

Now and then, a truly giant black bear is weighed. In 1916, on Avery Island, Louisiana, a male was weighed at six hundred and seventy-seven pounds. A bear taken some years ago near Tupper Lake in New York weighed six hundred and five pounds. The old male was tagged and released, unharmed. Another huge black bear, taken in New York in 1975, weighed an estimated seven hundred and fifty-nine pounds, computed on a field-dressed weight of six hundred and

2'–3'

4½'–6'

The black bear has a straight profile and hardly any shoulder hump, small eyes and well-rounded ears. Average males weigh from 200 to 300 pounds, but many specimens have been recorded that measured up to 9 feet in length and weighed over 600 pounds.

As these two photos reveal, the black bear varies in weight. The husky specimen above, clothed in its late-summer coat, is an unusually large bear.

sixty pounds. Perhaps the record is held by a bear taken in Wisconsin in 1885, a monstrous bear said to weigh eight hundred and two and one-half pounds. Any black bear weighing more than three hundred pounds, however, is unusually large.

The adult black bear stands as high as three feet at the shoulders and may reach a length of five feet or more from the tip of his pointed nose to the end of his ridiculously short tail. Like all bears, the black bear has a heavy, powerful build and relatively short legs, but he lacks the shoulder hump by which the grizzly is known.

Whatever its size, the bear is exceedingly swift when speed is called for. One bear biologist, young and in top condition, was once chased by a female, and three cubs just out of the den, and weighing maybe a dozen pounds each. "Even the cubs were gaining on me," he said. Jonkel once clocked a black bear running ahead of his pick-up truck at thirty-eight miles an hour.

In Wisconsin, another bear researcher once ran after a one hundred pound bear for nearly five miles through dense alder thickets without catching it, even though the bear was dragging a trap and chain weighing twenty-six pounds.

Biologist Bill Cook, of Great Smoky Mountains National Park, has watched adult black bears, in Cade's Cove, overtake and kill adult whitetail deer. "I wouldn't believe it, if I hadn't seen it," says Cook.

The speed with which the black bear can move its front paws is astounding. Lou Izzo of Jeannette, Pennsylvania, describes it as instantaneous! "I once volunteered to wrestle a six-hundred-and-fifty-pound tame bear for a muscular distrophy benefit." says the burly Izzo. The bear, in spite of the fact that it was muzzled and had no claws, knocked Izzo down repeatedly, fell on him, and cuffed him. Izzo tried to hold the bear off with his fist. That's when the bear swatted him on the side of the head. Izzo swears that nobody could see the bear's paw move. One moment the bear was standing there with his arm down at his side and the next moment the human wrestler was flying across the ring, after which he spent several days in bed and couldn't talk for two weeks. Says Izzo, "Never again."

A bear's tracks are easily enough recognized because he walks on the bottom of his plantigrade feet and the marks of the five curved, nonretractable, inch-and-a-quarter-long claws show with the footprint.

COLORS

Black bears are not always black. In some areas brown and cinnamon color phases are common. This is true of the black bear population in Yellowstone National Park and elsewhere in the northwestern section of the country, and all three colors sometimes occur in the same litter. There is a record of an albino female black bear that lived along the Assiniboine River in Manitoba. She once gave birth to a litter of four cubs that were a mixed bag. One, like its mother, was pure white with red eyes and nails, while a second one was brown, and the other two black.

Even the bear that comes in the predominantly black color phase may have slight variations. It normally has a cinnamon-colored patch across the muzzle. It may also carry a spot of white on the throat or chest.

There are two other rare and unusual color phases. In the coastal area of the Gulf of Alaska lives an estimated five hundred black bears of the beautiful blue-gray color known as glacier bears. The rarest of all may be the Kermode's bear, first recorded in 1905, from the coastal mountains and nearby islands of central British Columbia and named for Francis Kermode, a museum curator. Prior to that, this bear was only known from having been seen on fur markets where it was consistently misidentified as a young polar bear. The Kermode "black" bear is snow white.

These variations in colors within the black bear clan may be more than quirks of nature and may give the animals added survival value. Idaho bear biologist John Beecham has looked into the significance of the color phases and, if asked what accounts for the different colors, says that while he has no proof, he has "some ideas." He studied the growth rates of the black color phase and compared them with the growth rates of the bears with brown fur and found that the brownish bears grow faster and reach sexual maturity earlier than the black ones.

He also explains that the lighter colors tend to show up more frequently in northern latitudes. In Idaho, as you travel north, the percentages of browns and blacks approach fifty-five, and in the northern part of the state as many as sixty-five percent of the black bears may be the brown phase. Biologists Jonkel and Ian McTaggart Cowan, in an earlier study, demonstrated that the black bears feed longer on grassy south-facing slopes without overheating, and this may contribute to their more rapid growth rates and earlier sexual maturity, giving them a survival edge over their black relatives in semi-desert areas.

FEEDING

The bear roams its range searching for food, then beds down wherever caught out. The home area of the male is larger than that

Black bears are not always black. Above, two black bears, one cinnamon-colored and the other black, engage in a sparring match. The bear below is an example of the brown phase. All three phases may occur in the same litter.

covered by the female, but in any instance depends largely on the quality of the habitat in which the animal lives. Studies in Idaho show that male black bears, in that state, range over an average of thirty square miles while the females make their homes in an area covering five to seven square miles. They possess a strong affinity for this home range, as biologists often learned after they move problem bears to new areas, only to have them return. Bears finding themselves in strange country apparently feel compelled to move, and furthermore, they have an uncanny ability to move in a direction that takes them back toward their old haunts. In a study in Michigan's Upper Peninsula, one displaced black bear traveled one hundred and forty-two and a half miles to get home.

Bears are not territorial in the sense that wolves or cats are. They do not mark off territories, then defend them against others of their kind. The bears, especially adult males, sometimes bite or scratch trees, presumably as high as they can reach. They have even left their marks on porch posts and sign posts, as well as creosoted telephone poles. One study disclosed that the marking reached a peak just ahead of the breeding season and that the bears marked a wide variety of trees. This is believed to be their way of announcing their presence to other breeding-age males. If bear ranges overlap, they ordinarily pay little attention to each other, except that females and young avoid the old males which might kill the sub-adults and sometimes consume them.

Bears tolerate each other enough to congregate where there is abundant food. When brought this close together, however, the bears spat and quarrel, with the big bears disciplining the smaller ones or making bluff charges. Rarely in these concentrations of bears does one animal injure another. Instead they communicate and are guided in their social structure by their own system of facial expressions and body language. Living off a garbage dump, however, is an unnatural way of life for the bear. Under natural conditions, they are solitary creatures, avoiding other bears, except for the brief mating periods and the family associations of females and young.

Acceptable black bear foods come in many forms, both animal and vegetable, and what the bear eats depends on what is available at the moment. In spring the wandering bears feed on a wide variety of

A black bear stands on its hind legs to make long scratches in a tree. Although bears are not territorial, they do mark trees, especially during the breeding season. This is believed to be a way of signaling their presence to other males.

This aspen tree in New Mexico's San Mateo Mountains wears the scars of many bear scratches. If bear ranges overlap, the animals pay little attention to each other.

grasses, sedges, roots, and leaves. In summer the diet extends to berries and fruit, which are always favorites, and blackberry pickers may have to share the harvest with the bears. A farm wife in Wisconsin once reported that she left the berry patch to go home for more containers, leaving behind a three-gallon bucket of blackberries to be picked up later. She returned to find the berries claimed by a large black bear sitting on his haunches, gripping the bucket with his front paws, and eating greedily. The lady said she felt lucky to get her pail back. The farmer may also share his ripening apples with the hungry bear. The fruit-picking bear climbs a tree, pulls the branches toward himself, and breaks them until he sometimes makes a shambles of the tree.

In late summer and fall the bear's feeding tempo picks up as it harvests fruits, nuts, and acorns adding weight at a remarkable rate, sometimes several pounds a day.

In the early part of this century, black bears and other forest wildlife suffered a disaster that demonstrated the unpredictable nature of the human impact on bears. The earliest settlers, coming through the eastern forests, encountered broad stands of giant chestnut trees, a favorite with people as well as wild animals. The wood was tough enough to use for ax handles and wagon tongues, but could also be fashioned into fine furniture. From cradle to coffin, the chestnut tree

In spring the black bear feeds on grasses, leaves, sedges, and roots; as summer comes, it consumes berries and fruit.

served people well. In autumn, children and adults alike gathered the rich chestnuts that showered from the heavy branches, sharing them with squirrels, deer, and bears that had harvested the nut crop for uncounted centuries. Hunters knew where the bears liked to feed on the chestnuts, and they also knew that bears that had fed on chestnuts and wild grapes provided meat with a fine, sweet flavor.

The chestnut was the dominant tree in the eastern forests, making up forty percent or more of the forest through much of the Appalachians. Its natural range spread over two hundred million acres of North America until the imported oriental chestnut fungus destroyed the native tree which had no natural resistance to the disease. By the late 1920's, sixty percent of the Great Smokies had been logged and the bears were relegated to the highest country. The tragedy of the chestnut blight, first seen in the Smokies in 1925, struck them another blow. Nobody knows the full impact on the native bears of this single introduction of the fungus, but the last good crop of chestnuts in the Smokies came in 1938, and thereafter the bears were said to increase their raids on livestock outside the park, which meant more bears killed to protect property.

Although half of the bear's food, and as much as ninety-two percent in one study, is plant material, the foraging bear consumes animal matter when given the opportunity. Most of the bear's prey are small creatures: grubs, worms, ants, mice, snakes, and nestling birds.

The black bear, like the grizzly, tears up logs and turns over rocks, uncovering whatever foods hide beneath them. The bear may slap the scurrying prey with a front paw, then slap it again with the other paw, and hold it until it can take it into the mouth. In some areas, bears are also fond of fish and will wade into the shallows to catch them with their mouths.

Although not a highly efficient predator, it may, on occasion, kill a fawn, pig, calf, or other larger animal. Perhaps more often it becomes a consumer of carrion, with little regard for the state of decomposition. Terry S. Chilcoat and Dr. Michael R. Pelton who, with their associates, have studied the black bear extensively in the Great Smoky Mountains, finds that less than one percent of the bear's food may be freshly killed prey, and this means that healthy large animals are rarely in danger from black bears unless, of course, the occasional renegade bear becomes a specialist in killing sheep or calves.

In its everlasting search for food the bear is aided primarily by three of its senses. Writers have often claimed that the black bear has poor vision, but recent research credits it with more effective eyes than we have previously believed. Studies reveal that not only does the bear possess pretty good visual acuity, but it also distinguishes colors,

SOME FAVORITE FOODS OF THE BLACK BEAR

Persimmons

Ground Squirrels

Fawns

The black bear uses its claws like the grizzly to tear open logs for whatever food it can find within—grubs, worms, mice, snakes, and nestling birds.

which is not too surprising when one considers the extent to which it depends on ripe fruit for its food.

In addition, the bear has an acute sense of hearing which may be more useful in helping it to avoid danger than in locating food.

Most of all, the black bear, like the grizzly, has a keen sense of smell which both warns it of danger and leads it to available food, sometimes from remarkable distances.

MATING, HIBERNATION AND BIRTH

The mating season for black bears comes in late June and early July, and during the few weeks that the female is receptive she may mate with two or three males in a few days. The male approaches the receptive female and engages in rubbing, caressing, and biting, followed by copulation that may last for half an hour or so with the male frequently biting the female's neck. During the act she may wander about as if nothing memorable is happening, and continues to wander about afterwards while her mate lies down to rest or cools himself in a nearby stream. Minnesota research demonstrated that bears travel remarkable distances after the mating season with males wandering as far as one hundred and twenty-five miles before returning to den near the area of mating.

The fertilized egg does not develop steadily right up to the time of birth as it does in most mammals. Instead, it divides several times, then ceases to grow. In the following November, the free-floating blastocyst becomes implanted in the uterine wall, and growth resumes and continues until the time of birth.

In this manner, the bear delays the burdens of pregnancy, helping the female through those demanding months of late summer and autumn when she must feed heavily to store fat for the coming winter. One Wisconsin bear, killed and autopsied during hibernation, was thirty-six percent fat by weight.

During the winter months, usually from November to April, the bears become inactive and go into a deep sleep. The first to go to their winter dens are the females and young, followed within a few weeks by the adult males. The time of denning is believed by some scientists to be triggered by a combination of satiation, food shortages or the coming of shorter days. In northern latitudes especially, those bears still out often taken to their winter beds during the season's first heavy snowstorm. As the time approaches for the bear to go to its den, it undergoes a remarkable change in behavior. It becomes lethargic and insensitive to danger.

When the time comes to den up for winter, the bear moves to a hiding place beneath the roots of a tree or beneath a rock shelter. A wintering bear may make its den in a hollow tree, taking advantage of this shelter's thermal efficiency as well as the protection the tree offers from dogs and people. The hollow tree den also offers the cubs protection from death by flooding.

The entrance to one bear's den in a hollow bald cypress tree in Louisiana was ninety-six feet above ground level. The bear may descend inside the tree as far as the hollowed space permits, sometimes all the way to ground level. Preserving old growth forests is important to tree denning bears especially in the Southeast.

The bear going to winter quarters often collects and carries leaves and grass into the den. The female is more likely to provide a soft bed for her winter sleep than the male is. The den need only be large enough to accommodate the body of the bear.

In the den the bear rolls into a ball, moves little, and minimizes heat loss by covering its head. In its torpor it neither eats nor regularly casts off body wastes. Although the breathing rate, rate of metabolism, and heart beat are slowed in a form of hibernation, it does not undergo the dramatic temperature changes recorded for deeply hibernating animals such as the woodchuck.

The bear awakens frequently and adjusts the den entrance and its bed. But it does not seek more food. It has eaten its last meal until spring comes. Even in the South, bears go into their deep winter sleep although they may be somewhat more active than in colder northern latitudes. The bears lose weight in their winter dens. Lactating females sacrifice the most weight and may emerge in spring weighing only two-thirds what they weighed at the beginning of their winter sleep.

The bears often awaken if a person looks into the den and may allow him to approach to within a few feet. But no one should make the mistake of thinking that the black bear is always harmless if rudely disturbed during its winter torpor. It may awaken enough to come charging out at the intruder. More often, it will watch you for a few moments, then drift off to sleep again if the intruder sits quietly.

In the very heart of winter, usually in January, the pregnant female gives birth to her cubs, which have also drawn on the mother's fat during their development. The new cubs weigh about half a pound each and there may be from one to five of them. Most often there are twins, or triplets. The first-time mother usually has a single cub. Thereafter, she will breed every second or third year and give birth to the usual two or three cubs.

When first born, the young bear's eyes are closed and they remain that way for the next twenty-five days. The tiny cub, covered with fine hair, snuggles into the heavy fur of its mother for warmth and begins growing on the milk she provides.

Two examples of rock dens used by the black bear during the winter. The bear may also den in a hollow tree, which has the advantage of protecting the cubs from flooding.

A black bear pokes its head out of its den in midwinter. On pleasant days the bear may even leave the den and wander around for a spell, then go back to sleep. But it does not seek food until spring.

When these infant bears leave the den in the spring, they may weigh ten pounds or so, but in many areas weigh considerably less. Biologists found that Minnesota cubs, at this stage, weigh four to seven pounds. After that they gain at a remarkable speed if they live in good habitat, and should weigh forty to fifty pounds by mid-September, and perhaps sixty-five pounds or more when they go into hibernation. During the winter of 1951, Pennsylvania naturalist Harold O. Guiher discovered a rare opportunity to make a close-up study of the early life of new black bear cubs in the den. Tramping through the snow of Clearfield County, Guiher discovered the lair of a female black bear beneath a giant fallen log.

He could not dismiss the bear from his thoughts, and the following day he returned, determined to get a better look at the animal sleeping beneath the log. He continued to go back to the bear den frequently and kept detailed notes on what he observed. His account was later published in the *Journal of Mammalogy,* adding considerably to what was then known of this early phase of the bear's existence.

Reading the signs when he visited the area in January 3, Guiher found that the old bear had come out of the den, walked a short distance, then returned. She may have been restless due to the approaching birth of her cubs because Guiher, visiting the den the following day, could hear the squeaks of new cubs. He thought they sounded "like little pigs."

Five days later, he managed to see the cubs and reported that they looked like "little tan colored pigs about the size of a rat." When they were two weeks old, the cubs were already covered with shiny brown fur. They were cradled against their mother, lying between her front and rear legs and covered by her head and neck.

Then, Guiher made a disturbing discovery: he was not the only person who had found the bears. Perhaps others had followed his footprints, but there were trails left by four other people. Knowing that although most hunters are citizens of honor, there is always an outlaw element ready to dispatch any bear without reason or regard for the law, Guiher called the Pennsylvania Game Commission and arrangements were soon made with the landowner to declare the den site a game sanctuary. Then, the game commission assigned officers to patrol the site and protect the old bear and her cubs. The protected female stayed until March 23rd.

By April or early May, most cubs are ready to leave the den. The young ones soon learn that a grunt from the mother means to scoot up the nearest tree, while mother either runs off or hides in the nearby bushes. She may attack or bluff charge whatever she views as a threat to her cubs.

A female bear with her cubs at the entrance of her den. Cubs are born in January; they weigh about a half-pound each at birth but grow to weigh ten pounds or so by spring.

Throughout the summer, she guides her cubs through the woods, introducing them to bear foods, and in the process, putting up with considerable play as the cubs roll, tumble, slide, wrestle, and fight each other.

During their first winter the cubs stay with their mother and leave the den with her in their second spring. Now, they are about to depart and wander off on their own as the female once more approaches the time of breeding. The young ones may stay together through the summer, or even into the following winter, and they occasionally stay

Propped against a log, a mother bear nurses two of her cubs (right), then reclines as two more of them pounce on her in a nursing spree (below).

When the mother and her cubs leave the den in spring, she guides them through the woods, introducing them to bear foods and all the tricks of survival in the wilderness.

with the female a second summer. If they survive to enter the breeding population, the young female settles near her birthplace while the male moves on to an entirely new, and perhaps distant, area.

The black bear's maximum life expectancy in the wild is about fifteen years, although there are records of wild females living up to twenty-four years.

Their greatest enemies remain the people with whom they share this altered world, but modern game laws and, we hope, changing attitudes, give them an element of protection they never had when settlers came to their frontier world.

One of the survival tactics the cubs learn is to scoot up a tree at a grunt from the mother. This they do with great alacrity. Sometimes the mother demonstrates tree climbing by example. The bear at right looks comfortable enough to fall asleep.

Chapter 16

Bears on the Frontier

Old records make it plain that grandpa was a bear hunting man. On the American frontier, killing bears added spice to the daily chores and necessities to the family larder. The bear that poked its snout into a farm clearing made a monumental mistake. The average pioneer was a fine shot; he had to be. He carried a single-shot, muzzleloading smoothbore that seldom gave him a second chance. Lead and powder were costly, and good marksmanship could spell the difference between life and death for himself and his family. Besides, the bear was considered an enemy of man and his works, as well as a source of meat and fat for family use.

But the early hunters did not pursue game out of necessity alone. They no doubt considered bear hunting an exciting sport. If a buckskin-clad hunter wanted to earn a name for himself as a truly skilled woodsman, he knew that the quickest way to local fame was to kill a bear—or several of them. Killing a bear would bring smiles from the frontier maidens and approval of neighbors who were universally convinced that there was not room in the same country for both bears and people. Besides, many of the people were scared out of their britches by the very thought of encountering a bear in the surrounding woods.

FAMOUS BEAR HUNTERS

This age-old conflict between man and bear gave the bear an irresistible appeal to hunters, as they found their way across the mountains into Ohio, Kentucky, and Tennessee when that was the western frontier. Early storytellers recorded the exploits of noted bear hunters, among them the legendary John Houchin, who discovered one of America's most famous natural wonders one day in 1799, when tracking a bear near Kentucky's Green River. Houchin overtook and shot the bear, then crawled into its living quarters. He found, with some help from the bear, what stands today as the world's largest known system of caverns, Mammoth Cave.

About the same time, Samuel Pope, an early arrival on the frontier of southern Ohio, became locally famous for killing three bears in one day. But the bear hunt he remembered most vividly involved the biggest bear he ever saw in those woods. As bear and hunter faced each other, Pope hoisted his gun to his shoulder and managed a fast shot. But the giant bear, only superficially wounded, let out a squall and loped off into the woods with the hounds in full pursuit.

Pope soon arrived where his dogs held the beast at bay, and excited now by the chase, the hunter waded in much closer to the hard-pressed animal than a cautious man should. Pope was so outraged when the old bear grabbed his favorite hound that he walked right up and placed the muzzle of his gun against the bear's head. When the infuriated hunter pulled the trigger and the gun failed to fire, he knew he was in deep trouble. The bear promptly dropped the dog and lunged at the hunter.

Pope back-peddled, at full speed, and kept on back-peddling until he tripped over a log and fell over backwards with his feet kicking the air right in front of the bear's jaws. The bear caught Pope by a heel, but at this moment, the dogs lunged back into the attack and hung on with such tenacity that the bear dropped the hunter and again struck out at the hounds.

This gave Pope the opportunity to bounce to his feet again. As he rose, he pulled his tomahawk from his belt, and with repeated blows simply chopped the bear to death.

By this time, the exhausted hunter was so injured that he had all he could do to crawl back to camp, leaving the dead bear right where it fell. He spent the next three weeks, so it is written in an old country history, on his back, "with his foot swung up to a sapling."

Pope's exploits, including his three-bear day, was topped later by the story of Barley Monroe, another hunter on the early Ohio frontier. Monroe may have been the only male citizen around that day who was not helping Izaac Bonser raise his new grist mill. A mill was vitally important to a settlement in those days, and word had gone out to the neighbors. All the able-bodied men who possibly could, left their homesteads to the care of their wives and went to spend the day helping Bonser.

The mill site was far enough from the Bonser homestead that Mrs. Bonser could not summon her husband easily, and she was feeling a mite lonely when her neighbor, Mrs. Lindsey, came over for a visit.

The two ladies were standing in the clearing before the Bonser cabin, looking down the slope to the broad Ohio River flowing gently past, when they saw a bear come out of the woods on the other side of the stream. This was not astounding, but they did consider it a bit unusual when four more bears joined the first one and all five Kentucky bears waded into the Ohio and began swimming steadily across the river toward them.

The women were without weapons because their husbands had carried their guns along to Bonser's mill. As the bears drew closer to the Ohio shore, Mrs. Bonser summoned her dog, Watch, grabbed him by the scruff of the neck, commanded him to silence, and they all stood quietly awaiting arrival of the Kentucky invaders.

As the bears scrambled out of the water, Mrs. Bonser said, "bear!" and turned the dog loose. Old Watch was no stranger to bear fights and he carried the scars to prove it. He bounded down upon the bears and his howling and snarling soon brought the other Bonser hounds, all of which pitched into the fight. The bears, perhaps fatigued by their long swim, chose not to stand and fight, even though the five of them together should have held an excellent chance of overpowering the dogs. Instead, all five bears promptly climbed into the trees.

Why Barley Monroe was lurking around Bonser's place when all the other able-bodied men were off at the mill site was never explained, but he was in the woods hunting when he heard the commotion. Monroe understood hound talk and, realizing that an event of importance was underway, trotted off toward Bonsers.

When he reached the little clearing, he knew what had to be done. He quickly dropped one of the invading bears out of its tree, then began reloading and killing bears until, within minutes, all five bears lay dead. Monroe, it is said, touching his coonskin cap, nodded politely to the ladies, then vanished into the forest again. The bear meat and grease were divided among the families of the local settlement, and Barley Monroe became a living legend throughout the frontier country, so much so that his five-bear event is recalled to this day.

For some, there was pride in numbers, and pursuit of the bear became more compelling with each conquest. Perhaps no hunter of the black bear ever exceeded the record of a Civil War general, Wade Hampton, who frequently laid aside his gun and did the job with his knife. Hampton, who succeeded Jeb Stuart as commander of the Confederate cavalry in Virginia, did most of his bear hunting on his plantations in Mississippi and South Carolina. His bear hunting was re-

General Wade Hampton

markable enough to attract the attention of Teddy Roosevelt, who told of Hampton's exploits in his book *The Wilderness Hunter.*

Hampton always had the help of a pack of hounds, sometimes forty in number. When he heard the dogs holding a bear at bay, he rode up and urged them to close with the animal. Then as the dogs worried the bear, Hampton ran in close, reached across the animal and stabbed it behind the shoulder on the opposite side.

This hazardous system worked so well that Hampton, in killing between thirty and forty bears with his knife, was injured by only one of them which managed to rip open the general's forearm.

According to Roosevelt, the general personally accounted for more than three hundred bears and participated in the taking of two hundred more. During one pre-Civil War period in Mississippi, he killed sixty-eight bears in five months. His largest daily bag was four. Most of the bears taken by Hampton were killed in South Carolina. Although partial to the knife, Hampton took his two largest bears with a gun near Greenville, Mississippi. One weighed four hundred and ten pounds, the other a couple of pounds less, and both were actually weighed on the scales.

FRONTIER BEAR TALES

To the frontiersman, the oil of the bear was almost as important as the meat. "The fat," says one old record, "was rendered into oil then put away into deerskins neatly cleaned and dressed for the purpose. The oil served many valuable purposes. It could take the place of butter and hog's lard for frying venison and turkey, and it was admirable sop for the corn dodger." Or, bear grease mixed with venison and dried corn was regarded as one of the greatest delicacies of a hunter's larder. Sometimes, as in the case of Ben Reed, bear grease could be collected right outside the cabin.

Ben and his wife Patty came out to the Ohio Country in 1805. Ben cleared a patch of woods for planting corn, and built a cabin, while shooting deer and other wild game for meat. He brought with him to Ohio one large black pig which now lived in a pen built of poles. Reed soon purchased a white hog as a mate for the black one.

When he brought the new white hog home and installed it in the pen, evening was coming on. Reed went into the cabin and lowered himself wearily onto a bench while waiting for Patty to finish preparing supper. It was during supper that he heard one of his hogs squealing as if butchering day were at hand.

Reed rushed out of his cabin without even taking his gun along and saw what he thought at first was his black hog dragging his white hog around the pen. Then, he understood what was happening. A large black bear was in the pen, attacking his new white hog. As Reed rushed in to save the pig, the bear dropped the hog and turned for its owner.

Reed was never sure about the order of affairs, but one of them chased the other out of the pen. At this point, Reed's dog joined the melee and, within minutes, they had put the bear up a nearby tree. Now Reed began yelling for Patty to bring the gun, which she did and, said Reed, "with well-directed aim, I brought him down." Not only had he saved his new pig, but he had also added a fresh supply of meat and cooking oil to the family supplies.

A few years later, John Farney, who lived in Jackson County, Ohio, had his most widely publicized encounter with a bear when he met an old black bear on a woodland trail. They saw each other in about the same instant and both were thoroughly surprised. The bear wasted no time, but charged Farney at full speed. Even then, Farney was not especially worried. He had confidence in his gun as well as in his marksmanship. He drew the gun smoothly to his shoulder, sighted on the approaching bear's eye and pulled the trigger.

The gun failed to fire. Farney then drew his tomahawk and threw it with all his force straight at the oncoming brute's head. He watched the tomahawk glance off the broad skull harmlessly as the bear continued on course.

By this time, the bear was close enough so Farney could feel its breath. As the creature reached for him, the hunter drew his knife from his belt, determined to defend himself as best he could. The broad paws of the bear swiped at him and claws raked through his buckskin shirt. Time and again the knife struck home as bear and hunter rolled upon the ground in their all-out contest. Gradually, the blade slowed the bear, which finally fell into a heap of black fur at Farney's feet.

The hunter, now weak and exhausted, slumped to the forest floor and rested until he regained strength enough to set off for home. Farney not only survived this close-range fight with a big black bear, but lived to be an old man in his community. He seems, however, to have lost his atavistic urge to tangle with bears. As history records it, "He never sought another bear fight."

In the same county, in 1826, James Samuel and Smith Stephenson came to grips with a bear probably even larger than Farney's famous antagonist. The two settlers were working in the woods when their two hunting hounds, well trained and Virginia bred, opened up with loud and serious baying at the base of a giant hollow tree.

Samuel believed the dogs had treed a possum, but when he stuck his head into the cavity for a look, he quickly drew it out again. His eyes were as big as teacups. While he and the dogs stayed to keep the bear in the tree, Stephenson ran off to fetch a gun.

Before he could return, the aroused bear came out of the tree and attacked the hounds, then tried to escape. Rather than see the bear get away, Samuel took up his pole ax and aimed a solid blow at the animal's head. The bear bawled in pain and leaped backwards, still fighting the dogs, while Samuel jumped in and delivered a second blow that dropped the bear in its tracks.

When Stephenson returned, he brought along a horse, as well as a posse of local citizens, always ready to take part in a bear killing, only to find Samuel quietly sitting on the trophy, waiting. The bear was hoisted across the saddle and was said to have dragged the ground on both sides of the horse, which indicates a large bear or a small horse, or both. Later, the hunters determined that their bear weighed four hundred pounds, which was enough to feed bear steaks to the whole settlement.

Another hunter who told of killing a bear in a hollow tree was Ruben Dickason, in a time when the bears were already becoming scarce under the incessant pressure brought upon them by the settlers. Dickason's relaxed hunting technique was to sit on the cabin porch, listening to the hounds and only follow the chase if and when they treed game.

One evening, as the sun was lowering, his neighbor, Bill Kessinger, came down the path to join Dickason in his porch sittin', and the two friends were talking and sipping a bit of Old Monongahela when, off in the distance, Dickason's hounds set off the biggest ruckus he had ever heard them make.

The two men, who were instantly off and into the woods, raced down to the creek where they came upon the dogs, holding a bear at bay in a huge hollow sycamore. The one muzzleloader they had between them was soon loaded, pointed up into the dark interior of the tree, and discharged. Then, for good measure, they reloaded and sent another charge into the regions where the bear was believed to be, and word soon spread through the settlement. The two had killed a bear.

But black bears were rapidly disappearing. Fewer were killed with the coming of each new year. As opportunities to take bears diminished, any sighting was discussed with increasing excitement, and the rarer the bear became, the more coveted the trophy. On occasion there was some question about whose shot actually brought the bear to earth and such a case could end up before the magistrate, as it did one day in 1831.

The contested bear was said to have been the last one ever killed in the hills of Jackson County, Ohio. First to see the bear were the Massie boys, who had time to get off one fast shot. The shot wounded but did not kill the bear, which raced off into the distance. There was light snow on the ground and the Massie brothers trailed their bear throughout the afternoon. In the process they managed to push it right past Bill Whitt who, of course, shot it. By the time the Massie boys arrived, Whitt was skinning the bear.

A heated argument followed, with Whitt claiming that the bear was rightfully his because he had fired the fatal shot, while the Massie boys claimed it was their bear because they shot it first, slowed it down, then spent hours trailing it. Whitt, outnumbered, finally gave in and allowed them to take the bear.

He brooded about the bear for days until he became so convinced that he had been wronged that he decided to sue the Massie boys for taking "his" bear. The old account does not enlighten us on the court's decision, but if the records are correct, the question was moot because the Massies had, by then, consumed the bear anyhow. What the story does tell us is that the once abundant bears had become rare enough in a few decades that the question of ownership of a dead black bear was enough to take people before the judge.

Only on rare occasions did a bear make its appearance, then escape its human pursuers. The year after the Massie boys had been taken to court, a bear appeared a few counties to the northeast. On a fall afternoon it was seen by the merchants and customers of St Clairsville, Ohio, who rushed to the shop doorways to investigate the commotion.

Down the main street came what appeared to be most of the people in the township, with their children and dogs, all rushing along pell-mell, making an ungodly noise. Leading the throng was Izaac Ruby, astride his big gray horse, waving his hat above his head and shouting at the top of his voice, "Bear! Bear!", while out in front of Izaac Ruby's horse a fair distance was a large black bear, coursing along Main Street under full power.

Later estimates placed the number of people who had chased the bear through St. Clairsville, at one hundred and twenty. The bear chase was disrupted by a funeral procession that came down a side street and slowly crossed the main street ahead of the bear. With his escape route cut off by the horse-drawn hearse and mourners, the bear wheeled to the left and leaped into the Episcopal graveyard, then went over the fence onto John Thompson's farm and made for the woods.

It was while the confused posse was crossing Thompson's field that Andrew Orr and his dog drew relatively close to the bear, and Orr ordered his dog to attack. But the dog, like most of the people assembled there, had never before seen a bear and wasn't sure what he was supposed to do. He solved his dilemma by grabbing a calf instead. "The chase," says the old account, "was somewhat impeded by trying to get the dog away from the calf."

The bear now had the edge, and it quickly put distance between itself and its pursuers, escaping into the woods never to be seen again. "Mr. Orr's dog," wrote the historian, "was never afterward looked upon as being worth much for bears, even by his owner." No matter, the bears were all but gone anyhow.

Any story of a frontier bear that made good its escape recalls to mind the strange case of the bear that took command of George Cochran's boat. Cochran, an early frontiersman who was in the Ohio country by 1799, told the story on himself. One day he discovered a bear swimming across the Scioto River, which comes down from the center of the state to empty into the Ohio at Portsmouth. Cochran thought he had an easy bear, even though he had left his gun back at his cabin. He feared that if he went to fetch it, he would allow the bear time to escape. He ran to the river's edge, pushed his boat into the current, grabbed a paddle, and swiftly closed the distance between boat and bear. He was planning simply to cut off the animal's escape route and either hold it under with the paddle or make it swim until it became exhausted and drowned. Then, he would drag his sodden trophy from the river.

This might have worked except that the bear, instead of swimming away from the boat, turned toward it. The bear climbed into the boat on one side, and Cochran frantically climbed out on the other. He stood chest-deep in the Scioto, watching helplessly as his boat, with a bear aboard, drifted around the next bend and out of sight.

The wonder is that more of these early bear hunters did not suffer tragedy in the pursuit of the coveted animals. One who came close was Samuel Jackson, who, one fall day in 1809, was hiking along the trace that followed Sunfish Creek three miles east of Sinking Springs, Ohio, when he met a huge bear. Jackson's thoughts turned at once to possible schemes for taking the bear, which was fat from its heavy fall feeding. When the bear wandered into an opening in the rocks, Jackson thought he saw his opportunity.

But he would need help to kill the bear and bring it out of the cave. He dashed off toward the nearest cabin where he found John Lowman, who quickly joined in the pursuit. When they hurried back to the cave, Lowman carried along a glowing ember from the fireplace.

First, they piled dead leaves at the entrance of the little cave.

When all was in readiness, Lowman touched the fire to the leaves, and both stationed themselves some thirty yards from the cave's entrance, their muzzleloaders trained on the spot where the bear would have to emerge. As the burning leaves filled the cave with heavy smoke, the bear rushed out and one of the hunters succeeded in injuring it. This caused the bear to turn back and squeeze into a still smaller cave.

Again the hunters stuffed leaves into the cave's entrance, set their fire, and took up their positions. Smoke curled up and around the rocks and into the cave. But the bear did not emerge. An hour passed and, although the men realized that they would have to take drastic measures, they were reluctant to crawl into a black cave looking for a bear, so they decided to go home and think about it a while.

That evening, back at the cave, they found no evidence that the bear had come out. There was only one way to get this bear, and Jackson volunteered. Taking a torch in hand, he lowered himself on hands and knees and began working his way into the cave, planning to force the bear out with the aid of the torch.

Once inside the cave, Jackson met the bear face to face. To the hunter's intense relief, the huge animal was stone dead from the earlier shot. Now, the only remaining problem was how to get the bear out of this tiny cave.

Lowman crawled into the cave with Jackson and the dead bear. With Lowman in front pulling, and Jackson behind pushing, they inched the bear toward the entrance. Although the bear had squeezed through the hole when alive, getting it back through, as dead weight, was a problem. Lowman was out in the fresh air pulling while Jackson was still behind pushing, and the more they pushed and pulled the body, the tighter it wedged into the cave entrance.

Meanwhile, Lowman, struggling to get the bear out, did not notice that his actions were rekindling the smoldering leaves from the earlier fire. Inside, Jackson, coughing and lying flat against the cave's floor, was alternately praying and pleading with Lowman to save him from suffocation.

Finally, Lowman thrust his hands between the bear and the rock and gradually succeeded in opening a small space. Then in one final Herculean effort, lying on his back and bracing both feet against solid rock, Lowman took a desperate grip on the bear and tugged with all his force. There are many reports of people rising to superhuman efforts in such emergencies and moving weights far in excess of what they might normally lift or pull. Finally, Lowman had the bear's body inching toward him. He soon had it clear of the entrance, and the choking Jackson pushed past him to lie in the dirt, gasping for air.

Lowman lived to be an old man. After the bears were gone and only the memories remained, he often retold the story of how he had helped kill one of the last bears in Jackson County.

On occasion, southern Ohio outdoorsmen still hear stories of bears being found in these rugged hills along the Ohio River. Mostly they are rumors about a farmer who found bear tracks over by Peach Mountain, or the farmer deep in the hollows who watched a bear and her cubs eat ripe apples beneath his tree, or a bear spotted while it swam across the Ohio River from Kentucky or West Virginia.

We hope there is substance to these stories because it would be good to know that the bears still roam these shaded hills as they did long ago. Bob Donohoe, Ohio's forest wildlife biologist, who has lived and worked with wildlife in these hills for more than a quarter century, places little credence in these reports or at best considers any bears spotted only transients passing through.

"If there were as many bears in Ohio as you hear reported," he says, "you would see them on every garbage dump." Then, he admits answering an unusual call from a party reporting a bear in Meigs County, which is one Ohio county with hills and woods still rough enough and remote enough to shelter a bear. Donohoe figured he might as well go set the people at ease by telling them there was no bear. "Sure enough," he grins. "There was a bear." Presumably, the same animal was later seen in other counties, making its way, as Donohoe believes, toward the state border.

In Ohio, as elsewhere, the rising human population quickly eliminated the bears, leaving only stories of unforgettable bear hunts.

Chapter 17

Unforgettable Hunts

Campfires grow cold, and stories of memorable hunts fade gradually from the minds of old outdoorsmen to be lost for all time. But those hunting tales which were unusual enough, even then, to be written down, still evoke visions of bear hunts in times now gone. They give us glimpses of the bears, the land where they lived, and the men who pursued them, all contrasting vividly with what the world of man and bear has since become.

Wherever the pioneer came into the wilderness, he brought no special love for wildlife for wildlife's sake. The animals were there for the taking. As William Bradford wrote of the Pilgrims in 1620, "What could they see but a hideous and desolate wilderness, full of wild beasts and wild men?"

We should not be surprised that, out of this attitude, grew such events as the remarkable mass hunt staged south of Cleveland, Ohio, the day before Christmas, 1818. This event brought out a multitude of hunters for what may well have been the largest group hunt for wild animals, as well as the most indiscriminate one, ever conducted in the Midwest. The giant drive had begun as settlers met and talked at mills and church meetings. When times are hard, human nature asks something to blame the troubles on. Wilderness was the enemy.

Old records tell the bloody story of six hundred men and boys, assembling from miles around, forming a gigantic circle enclosing twenty-five square miles, then, on a signal from the leaders, beginning to move. They yelled, shot off guns, blew horns, and banged on kettles until the animals of the forest raced off in terror. The noose tightened, and wilderness animals began crowding toward the center of the ring.

Two hunters and a townsman display a 252-pound black bear in this 1910 photo taken in Saltese, Montana. Bear hunting was always a popular sport in the West, and the subject of many tall tales around the cracker barrel.

In the early morning light, as the lines of men moved toward each other, eighty sharpshooters took positions in trees where the hunters would converge. Their assignment was to kill wild animals and avoid shooting people. Soon they were firing as fast as they could reload, killing and wounding all manner of frantic animals in the big ravine before them.

The final tally was three hundred deer, sixty-seven wild turkeys, seventeen wolves, and uncounted foxes, raccoons, skunks, and squirrels. In a single day the hunters had also removed twenty-one of the black bears from their community. That night, four hundred and fifty of the hunters spent Christmas eve in the forest, eating, drinking, and celebrating their success.

DAVY CROCKETT

One of the best remembered of all bear hunters was a lean six-footer who pursued the black bears through the frontier woodlands and canebrakes of west Tennessee. David Crockett came from a frontier family, and although he claimed that he never learned to read until he was a grown man, and then not too well, he eventually wrote his autobiography and in it an account of the spectacular bear hunting that occupied him in the fall of 1825 and the following spring.

For a man who loved bear hunting, Crockett had one big advantage; he lived where bears were perhaps as abundant as they were anywhere. That fall he laid his other work aside to hunt the bears and accumulate a supply of winter meat for his family. Crockett had help. "I asked a bear no favors, no way, further than civility", he said, "for I now had eight large dogs and fierce as painters."

Crockett had soon killed and salted down all the bears his family would need for the winter, but the pure love of the chase was strong in him, and when a neighbor who lived some twenty-five miles away asked for help killing bears, Crockett was ready to oblige. "We were out two weeks," he said, "and in that time killed fifteen bears." With this done, he returned to working on a boat he was building, but his mind was still in the woods with the bears. "I couldn't stand it any longer without another hunt," he wrote. He answered the call this time by taking his son, crossing a lake, and on the first evening, killing three bears in "little or no time."

The following morning they built an elevated platform to store the dressed meat out of reach of the wolves, then went hunting again. This time, the dogs split and pursued two bears through the canebrakes. While Crockett went in one direction his son set off following the other dogs.

"I got to mine first," said Crockett, "and found my dogs had a two-year-old bear down a woolin' away on him; so I just took out my big butcher and went up and slapped it into him and killed him without shooting. In a short time I heard my little son fire at his bear;

when I went to him he had killed it too. In a short time, we heard my other dog a barkin' a short distance off, and all the rest immediately broke to him. We pushed on too, and when we got there we found that he had still a larger bear than either of them we had killed, treed by himself. We killed that one also, which made three we had killed in less than half an hour."

They next began searching for a good camping spot, but before they could locate a suitable place, the dogs struck a fresh trail and, as Crockett said, "away they went like a thundergust, and was out of hearing in a minute."

The following day the Crocketts killed four more bears, and by the end of the week had taken a total of seventeen. This was the week between Christmas and New Years Day, and now most of the bears were settled into their winter dens. But the bears of West Tennessee were still not safe from Davy Crockett.

Moving through the timbered bottomlands, Crockett came upon a large black oak with a bear-sized hole. "I discovered that a bear had clomb the tree. I could see his tracks going up but none coming down, and so I was sure he was in there." Crockett explained that an experienced woodsman can tell, "easy enough when the varmint is in the hollow; for as they go up they don't slip a bit, but as they come down they make long scratches with their nails."

The den tree was attacked with belt axes, but the task was interrupted by the baying of Crockett's hounds, which had come upon the trail of one late denning bear, then another. Both of these bears were shot and brought back to the den tree where the disturbed bear eventually came from the hollow tree into the midst of the dog pack. Crockett ran up and, as he said, "putting my gun against the bear, fired and killed him." Again they had killed three bears in a short hunt and, as Crockett asserted convincingly, this was the truth or, "I wish I may be shot."

The wildest night Crockett had in these months of bear hunting came in the canebrakes that grew thick as hair and higher than a horse, across those western Tennessee riverbottoms. By the time the dogs treed the big bear, the land was in full darkness. Crockett came upon the scene and could scarcely make out the dark lump in the top of the tree. He tried firing anyhow; the growling gnashing bear came down among the yapping dogs and the fight went on all around the hunter who stood ready with his butcher knife in hand, in case he was attacked. All he could see was his single white dog. The other yapping dogs and the maddened bear were lost to the blackness of the night.

People of west Tennessee still remembered vividly the New Madrid earthquake of 1812, the strongest earthquake ever to hit the continent in historic times. Crockett knew that the quake left numerous trenches in the earth and was not too surprised when the bear tumbled into one of these cracks about four feet deep and became stuck in the bottom of the pit. Said Crockett, "I could tell the biting end of him by the hollering of my dogs."

The hunter, guessing at the bear's location, shot him in the foreleg, then for a while punched him with a pole, and finally decided he would have to get down in the pit with him. "It might be that he would lie still enough for me to get down in the crack and feel slowly along 'till I could find the right place to give him a dig with my butcher." While the dogs kept the business end of the bear occupied, Crockett felt along the rump and forward until he knew where he was; then, with a single thrust to the heart, he killed the bear.

That fall, he killed fifty-eight bears, and the following spring, with the bear hunting urge still unsatiated, went after the "varmints" again as soon as they began emerging from their winter quarters. In a month he had killed another forty-seven—a hundred and five bears in half a year. "If that's not true, I wish I may be shot."

Bears did more for Davy Crockett than supply his family with meat. His fame as a bear hunter helped elevate him to the halls of Congress and bring him fame that would live long after the last bear had vanished from west Tennessee. There may have been hunters who killed even more bears than Crockett did in those years of abundant game when there were no limits set by law or conscience.

TEDDY ROOSEVELT

Theodore Roosevelt was a determined bear hunter also, although he never killed large numbers of bears. He was a careful observer of the natural world around him, a good hunter, and the stories and books he wrote describing his hunting experiences provide excellent adventure even for today's readers. One of his best remembered bear hunts occurred in the canebrakes of northern Louisiana, in habitat similar to that hunted by Davy Crockett. "I was especially anxious," he wrote in *Scribner's Magazine*, "to kill a bear in those canebrakes after the fashion of the old southern planters, who for a century past had followed the bear with horse and hound and horn in Louisiana, Mississippi, and Arkansas."

In October 1907, the President arrived in Mississippi, and his group set up camp on Tensas Bayou, where they found no bears. Roosevelt took note of the other wildlife of the swamps, notably three giant ivory-billed woodpeckers, now believed to be extinct.

The second day they were in camp there emerged from the woods a quiet, lanky man with a full beard and deep blue eyes. The woodsman, who was followed by a couple of rangy hounds, appeared to be in his fifties and he talked little. Roosevelt learned that the man had not eaten for twenty-four hours, and he had drunk no water because he did not like swamp water. He carried no shelter and spent the rainy night perched in the crotch of a tree, "much as if he had been a wild turkey." The newcomer was perhaps the most skilled bear hunter anywhere and already a legend. His name was Ben Lilly, and he had come in response to a telegram to help guide the President on this bear hunt.

On the trail, Ben Lilly was a driven man, never yielding to discomfort of weather or hunger. He did not drink, swear, or work or hunt on Sunday. He preferred sleeping on the ground to slumber in the finest feather bed, and even when living in a well-equipped hunting camp, might cook his own simple supper of corn meal.

In Louisiana, Ben Lilly was in country he knew well because he had a farm and family here, according to famed Texas folklorist J. Frank Dobie, who wrote that Lilly's wife once asked the woodsman to take his gun and shoot a chicken hawk. Lilly was gone for the next year. "That hawk just kept going," he explained.

He had worked as an agent of the federal government, killing predatory animals, could read sign as if the outdoors were an open book, and would stay on a trail for days or weeks until he found the animal he pursued. Bear hunting was his favorite. Teddy Roosevelt was much impressed with Ben Lilly, and Lilly was always proud of having hunted with the president.

Also in the Louisiana camp that October was Holt Collier, a sixty-year-old ex-slave who, it was said had, in half a century of hunting, either killed, or assisted in the killing of three thousand bears. Roosevelt mentioned him in his writings. Collier may hold the record for the sheer number of bears dispatched by one man.

Eighty-two years before this hunt, Davy Crockett had killed seventeen bears in similar canebrake country in a single week, but the party in Louisiana was having no success, and after a week on the Tensas Bayou, with little sign of bear, Ben Lilly figured it was time to move. Teddy Roosevelt and the party set off for a new camp on the shore of Bear Lake, where their chances seemed to improve, especially after, as Roosevelt reported, "We had seen the tracks of an old she in the neighborhood, and the next morning we started to hunt her out."

The hounds eventually announced that they had located the trail, and the hunters galloped off. "The tough woods horses," Roosevelt wrote, "kept their feet like cats as they leaped logs, plunged through

This photo from a 1905 issue of Scribners magazine shows Teddy Roosevelt standing over a black bear he killed on one of his many hunts.

bushes, and dodged in an out among the tree trunks." After two hours of being whipped by vines and briars, they came to the scene in the thick-growing cane where the dogs were holding the bear at bay.

They leaped from their horses and began working closer to the bear. "Before we were within gunshot, however, we could tell by the sounds that the bear had once again started, making what is called a 'walking bay' ". They worked to a spot where they thought the bear would be intercepted. "Then we crouched down," wrote Roosevelt, "I with my rifle at the ready. Nor did we have long to wait. Peering through the thick-growing stalks I suddenly made out the dim outline of the bear coming straight toward us; and noiselessly I cocked and half-raised my rifle, waiting for a clearer chance. In a few seconds it came; the bear turned almost broadside to me, and walked forward very stiff-legged, almost as if on tiptoe, now and then looking back at the nearest dogs."

Moments later the President had his shot. As he aimed for a point behind the shoulder and squeezed of the shot, he felt good about it. The bullet passed through both lungs and out the other side of the bear. The old bear was lean and weighed two hundred and two pounds.

The news reached the outside world by telegraph. *The New York Times,* on its front page, carried a modest story announcing "Roosevelt Gets A Bear." The Times called it a "great, big bear" and explained that the President went into the thicket after it.

There are still memorable bear hunts, but the modern hunter, equipped with four-wheel-drive vehicle and two-way radio communications, may, if he is fortunate, take one bear in a lifetime.

Chapter 18

Rascals and Rangers

Visitors and park rangers alike, in Yellowstone, Great Smokies, Shenandoah, Yosemite, and elsewhere, repeat bear stories until the bear becomes a wildlife folk hero. Typically, these stories stem from conflicts between bears and people, and the fact that rangers, who take very seriously their joint responsibilities of looking out for the welfare of both bears and people, cannot be everywhere at once enforcing the rules.

Even though there are fewer bears by the park roadsides than there once were, the feeding goes on. Panhandling bears establish their beats along favorite stretches of park roadway where they are conditioned to the hand delivery of human foods. The more successful a bear is at panhandling, the more fixed this behavior becomes. Furthermore, the female brings her cubs to the roadside, indoctrinating the next generation to a lifetime of begging. There is no effective cure for this except cutting off the food sources. In years past, when feeding regulations were less strictly enforced, the panhandling bear was more of a problem than it now is.

Bears can no longer break into cars as easily as they once did. Years ago, when cars had tops made of canvas and wood, bears slashed the tops to gain entrance and reach food supplies locked inside. Bears have also been known to knock windshields out of cars and pick-up trucks, and one bear in Great Smoky Mountains National Park even pried and bent open the locked door of a car to obtain a loaf of bread lying on the front seat.

Another bear episode occurred when a visitor in Great Smoky Mountains National Park left his sports car at a trailhead and hiked off on an overnight camping trip into the backcountry. That night a human thief broke into his car and left the windows down. Next came a bear who crawled in through the open window, and finding nothing to eat, tore the upholstering apart. The bear then dug through the back seat into the trunk and opened and emptied eight cans of motor oil.

One woman lured a bear into her car for a picture, then couldn't get the animal to leave. Instead of departing quietly, the frustrated bear bit and scratched the woman. There is also a classic story, probably true, of the ranger who intercepted a tourist trying to push a large black bear into his car so he could make a picture of it "driving" as his wife sat beside it.

This desire to get a brag photo to show friends and neighbors back home has brought tourist and bear dangerously close together many times. Rangers found one park visitor coaxing a bear to lick chocolate off his child's face while he made a picture. Rangers insist that many people have instructed their children to "pet the nice bear" while they make a picture. Others have attempted to make pictures of their small children sitting on the backs of bears. The maker of home movies is sometimes seen, camera to eye, backing away happily as a large begging bear follows within striking distance.

One ranger tells of the visitor who saw a bear beside the road, screeched to a halt, grabbed his camera and climbed from his car so quickly that he forgot to set the brake. He discovered the oversite when he heard the car crash on the rocks in the creek below.

At Mt. LaConte Lodge, in the Great Smokies, where black bears are numerous, a large bear once walked into the kitchen, selected its food, then wandered into the dining room to eat. He was chased out before he could finish his meal.

Rangers remember also the man who came sheepishly into the visitor center, asking for a first aid kit. When questioned about what happened he held his bald head down displaying four long gashes. His explanation? "I ran out of crackers."

Another park visitor who displayed a remarkable lack of respect for the size, strength, and unpredictable temper of the black bear, rushed into a Yellowstone visitor center and set his bleeding two-year-old son on the counter. The distraught father was calling on all present to "do something" about the bear that had caused it. Asked how the incident occurred, the father admitted that he was "trying to get the bear's attention. But all I did," he insisted, "was slap its face."

When a concessionaire first installed candy machines in Cades Cove in Great Smoky Mountains National Park, rangers warned that the bears might break into the machines. Any doubts the concessionaire harbored about the animal's ability to accomplish this vanished the following morning when he arrived to find the candy machine broken open and all the candy bars eaten. He set up another machine, but this time secured it by wrapping a heavy chain around the machine's door. The bear, unable to break the door off, forced its claws behind the edge of it and simply folded it down to get to the candy.

California bear biologist Tim Burton, who can testify to the strength of the black bear, tells about the seventy-pound yearling, taken from a trap by two strapping biologists, weighing a total of three

A black bear caught rummaging through a garbage can in a 1905 stereophoto taken in Yellowstone. From feeding on garbage, the bears eventually progressed to panhandling.

hundred and forty pounds. Instead of drugging the young bear, the biologists decided to simply drag it from the trap and spread eagle it on the grass long enough to check its measurements. The bear took the two husky biologists cartwheeling all the way to the bottom of the hill before they finally overwhelmed it by sheer weight.

The black bear's remarkable strength forced the Park Service to design a garbage can with a steel top, equipped with a drop door, resembling those on streetside mailboxes. As an economy measure, one concessionaire used the newly designed bear-proof tops on aluminum instead of steel cans. A bear, promptly named "Crusher," learned to plant its feet firmly, put its shoulder against the can and mash it, forcing the edge free of the iron top.

Wildlife biologist Bill Cook on the staff of Great Smoky Mountains National Park likes to recall the peculiar traits of a favorite male black bear called Big Boy. "We captured him once and while we had him, we tried to weigh him. Our scales only went up to five hundred and fifty pounds. He weighed more than that."

Big Boy was a lovable old bear, except that his specialty was breaking open picnic coolers, a task that became simpler as he standardized his technique. He learned to tip the cooler over on its side, then slap his two paws against either side of it so hard that the latch snapped open and often flew off completely.

"Then, Big Boy would take the front edge of the cooler in his jaws," Cook explains, "and waddle off up the hill to eat while the open lid bounced against the top of his head each time he took a step. As the lid banged him on the head, Big Boy would growl and grumble." Big Boy amused people, as long as the cooler he took belonged to somebody else.

Then, suddenly the giant bear vanished, and nobody on the park staff ever saw him again, or any part of him, or his tracks. "We think we know who it was," says Cook quietly, and you get the impression that whoever potted Big Boy is being watched.

A solitary little black bear appearing along a two-lane road in a busy national park can back up traffic half a mile or more in what rangers have long called a "bear jam." Park visitors cannot resist stopping to see whatever it is that other people have found of interest.

Dale Nuss, retired chief ranger in Yellowstone, remembers the summer day in 1970 when he had an early errand to run over at West Thumb. "The bears didn't usually come out to the roads until around nine o'clock," he explains, "and I thought it was too early to have trouble with a bear jam, but I came to this female and two cubs, and the traffic problem wasn't too bad, so I worked my way through and went on about my errand.

Black bears begging for food in Glacier National Park. The female often brings along her cubs and teaches them the game.

"An hour later, when I came back, the bears were still there and cars were stopped everywhere. The bears were completely hidden by cars. I couldn't let this go. I don't know why I did it, because I didn't usually do it, but this time I reached down and picked up my bear club when I got out of the car." Carrying the night stick, Nuss, made his way to the large black car with New York licenses plates from which marshmallows were being tossed out "like a snowstorm."

To his surprise, the female bear charged him. "I drew back," says Nuss, "and laid the club on the side of her head and decked her." A minute or so later the old bear staggered to her feet, shook her head, and went off into the forest with her cubs. Nuss is convinced that she was not making a bluff charge. The bear jam broke up, but Nuss had not won any popularity contest. "That whole line of people booed and hissed me," he says, "and I just slipped away as quietly as I could."

Yellowstone assistant chief ranger Gary Brown knows how Nuss felt. One day a couple of years earlier, Brown came upon a monumental bear jam at Grant Village. He worked his way toward the head of the line where he could see the food items flying. "There at the front of the line," he recalls, "were two little elderly ladies, feeding cookies to a two-hundred-and-fifty-pound black bear, so I got them to get back into their car and was leaning over explaining that feeding bears was contrary to park policy, and that it was harmful to the bear, and just then that bear ran back out of the woods and hit me with his snout right behind the knee. Without thinking about it, I just wheeled and kicked the bear a good one right in the soft underbelly. That bear bellowed as though he was mortally wounded, and that whole line of people began booing me." Brown, too, slipped away as quietly as he could. In later years, after the rules against feeding were more firmly enforced, a ranger would have made arrests under such circumstances.

Bears quickly learn to recognize Park Service vehicles and run away at the rangers' approach. Bears can even spot the Smokey Bear hat that rangers wear. Rangers in the Great Smokies insisted for years that, in plain cars and without their hats, the bears still knew them instantly. Some even speculated that the bears were reading the "I," for Department of the Interior, on their license plates.

Brown recalls a special day when he was working in Glacier National Park and came upon a bear jam. As he drove up, the bear spotted him and dashed to the nearest tree where it climbed up out of reach. The crowd of tourists began giving Brown a rough time for breaking up their bear party. One camera carrying visitor was especially abusive toward the ranger and continued to berate Brown, even as he carried his camera toward the bear tree, apparently determined to get one last picture from directly beneath the animal. While the other tourists, and the ranger, watched from the sidelines, and the angry tourist peered up through his view finder, the bear emptied its bladder all over the man's head. "It was", says Brown in retrospect, "a little difficult to keep from laughing."

Along the remote hiking trails in the backcountry of Great Smoky Mountains National Park bears are frequent visitors at the overnight shelters where rich odors of frying bacon drift through the forest. The bears became so bold, and the potential for accidents so ever-present, that the Park Service began enclosing its trailside shelters in bear-proof fences. The rangers refer to this as a "zoo in reverse," because the bears running free on the outside can look through the fences at the people crowded into their pens for the night.

Even this precaution does not always thwart the intelligent bears. One bear stood guard outside the fence, refusing to allow anyone to escape, despite Sierra Club tin cups banging on the fence. Eventually, a member of a bear research team arrived and chased the bear off into the forest.

Backcountry bears learn quickly that hikers' packs contain special treats, and hikers who drop packs to divert pursuing bears reinforce the bear's experience, bringing it one step closer to becoming a back-pack specialist. All the bear has to do is follow a hiker long enough and close enough, and he is given the pack.

This happened to a camper in Yellowstone who was carrying his four-hundred-dollar Nikon in his pack. According to *Audubon* the magazine of the National Audubon Society, the camper returned to the park visitor center in a bad mood, claiming that, because a bear had made off into the forest with his camera, the federal government owed him for the equipment. The young lady ranger on duty saw it differently. Flashing her prettiest smile, she said, "Sir, encountering a bear is all part of your wilderness experience."

Beyond the park boundaries, businessmen, farmers, and home-owners too occasionally call on rangers, sheriffs, and wildlife officers to help them combat pesky bears. Some years ago a Colorado wildlife officer was called to deal with an unruly bear that had been disturbing motel owners and guests. The officer, knowing that the bear was a repeat offender, already captured and moved several times unsuccess-fully, decided that he must eliminate the animal.

In the evening the officer arrived with a bucket of fish guts from the local hatchery, set the bait out in the backyard, and took up his vigil. He soon discovered that the room right in front of him was occupied by newlyweds who forgot to pull the shades, although at one point they did turn the lights out for a few minutes.

The officer could not figure out why the bear didn't appear at all that evening. "Maybe it was because those two were in plain sight," he said, and not until the lights finally went out for the night did he discover that the bear had eaten the whole bucket of fish and departed, undetected. "I was so damn mad at that bear," he said, "I couldn't think straight."

Bears frequently wander into town where people sometimes do not know what to do about them. A dubious Missouri conservation officer was called out one day to a property east of Kansas City to deal with a bear. The surprised officer arrived to find that there actually was a bear, a very rare occurrence. An armed crowd had gathered, and the situation was volatile. Although the officer did not want to destroy the bear, one hundred men surrounded the nervous animal, each of them itching to be the one who would shoot it. When the officer heard someone speculate that the person killing the bear would get the hide, he figured it was time to act to save the people from each other, and promptly shot the animal himself.

Another bear came into a Pennsylvania town several years ago at a somewhat safer time. Two of the village women saw the animal, and according to *Pennsylvania Game News,* hurried off, seeking someone to shoot it. Their search for help was fruitless; every able-bodied male in town, and perhaps some of the females as well, were off in the woods celebrating the first day of the bear-hunting season.

In Manhattan, Kansas, a black bear had to be moved from the zoo because of a fire and the only place available to hold the animal was an empty cell in the jail. The bear, accustomed to people, adjusted better than the other inmates, who claimed that the bear had a bad odor and requested that the authorities either let the bear out or let them out.

As bears and people are brought together in increasing numbers, this closer association may be changing the nature of the bears. This may be especially so in the parks, and around summer home developments, where hunting is prohibited and the adaptable animals learn not only that people have food, but also that people are not a serious threat.

Chapter 19

The Black Bear's Secrets

The black bear has risen above its old role of varmint, and is no longer classed with the creepy crawlies, or viewed as a pest to be eliminated by plinkers, amusing themselves at the city dump. This new status for the black bear had its beginning in the 1950s and 1960s, as pioneering biologists began probing the mysteries of the bear's life. Among the first of these researchers, in the early 1950s was Albert W. Erickson, working in Michigan. In those years any biologist, setting off into the woods to study bears, had to devise his own methods and his own tools, and the first task was the formidable one of capturing the bear alive, without injury to bear or people.

TRAPPING THE BLACK BEAR

Some bear biologists began capturing bears with steel traps, hoping that the trap did not injure the bear seriously. Wisconsin bear workers found late in the 1950s, that twenty-three percent of the bears they captured in steel traps suffered from one to three fractured or dislocated bones, plus assorted lacerations.

A better tool was the live trap, fashioned from a length of culvert with doors of iron grating welded on both ends and the whole contraption mounted on wheels so it could be trailed behind a pick-up truck. In the woods, this trap is baited with fish or meat, and the bear that goes to the back of the trap and pulls on the bait releases a trigger that drops the door.

Early versions of this trap were made by welding a couple of fifty-five-gallon oil drums together. Bears larger than three hundred pounds have been taken in these barrel traps, and one three-hundred-

and-three-pound Wisconsin male black bear even turned around inside a barrel trap.

An up-dated version of the ancient Stone Age trapper's snare offers modern biologists one of the best of all methods of capturing bears. This state-of-the-art snare had its origin in the deep green coniferous forests of Washington where black bears damage valuable forest trees by stripping away the bark and eating the life-supporting cambium layer, perhaps for its sugar content. Tree damage by bears became so troublesome in this century that western timber companies hired bear hunters to kill the animals.

For years, these hunters pursued the bears with traps and hounds. Then one of them, Jack Aldrich, decided that there should be an easier way. His solution was a loop of steel cable that could be arranged on the ground around a trigger. When a bear steps on the trigger, as it tries to reach a bait, a spring throws the loop of cable over its foot and secures it. There are several advantages: the snare is harmless to people, lightweight, and inexpensive.

In Washington State, the Aldrich Spring Activated Snare is used selectively to capture bears that develop a serious hunger for the inner bark of trees. A handful of forest industry workers cruise their snare lines in pickup trucks in the season of greatest damage, listening to their radios. Each snare is equipped with a miniature radio transmitter that flips on whenever the snare is tripped. The broadcast signals carry for a couple of miles, and the trapper hurries to the scene as soon he hears the signal. The Aldrich trap is also widely used by bear biologists who need to capture bears to study and mark them.

Once captured, the bear must be subdued, and for this the biologists employ a lengthy list of drugs. Some of Erickson's earliest efforts called for wrestling a snared bear to the ground and slipping an ether cone over its nose, a procedure at least as hazardous to the people as to the bear. Then came the drug-loaded hypodermic shot from a gun, a welcome addition to the bear biologist's arsenal. A modern variation of this is the jab stick five or eight feet long that a person can carry into a den to inject a sleeping bear.

In four years Erickson captured more than a hundred bears by using culvert traps and foot snares. Each sedated bear was measured and marked so Erickson and his crew could recognize it if it was later taken by a trap or reported by a hunter.

Another pioneering scientist studying bears by the 1950s was Charles Jonkel, who became internationally recognized for his work with polar bears and grizzlies. In addition to gathering new information on the ecology and behavior of bears, these early researchers found that the black bear, far from being the fierce and dangerous animal often portrayed, is really a chicken at heart and most reluctant to attack people, especially people who seem aggressive toward it.

In the late 1950s, biologist George J. Knudsen, and his coworkers, probing for secrets among the black bears of Wisconsin, captured one hundred and thirty-seven bears in three summers. Each bear was weighed, measured, and marked, and Knudsen reaffirmed the earlier findings about the nature of the bear, reporting that most trapped bears remained calm even when approached by people. An occasional bear was so timid that, under the stress of associating with people, it would hide its head beneath its body and do somersaults. One bear, taken in a steel trap by Knudsen, stuck its head into a hole, hiding the trappers from its view even while they injected it with a tranquilizer drug. Some bears were excitable, some antagonistic, and there was no standard behavior pattern that applied to all.

George J. Knudsen, Wisconsin biologist, observes a black bear captured in a live-trap made from a length of steel culvert. The trap is baited with fish or meat and the door triggered by the bear when it pulls on the bait.

BIOLOGISTS STUDY THE BEAR

As respect for the black bear increased, hunters who had killed most of their bears incidentally while deer hunting, began taking a new interest in hunting the bears for themselves, and this brought the black bear added attention from state wildlife agencies. State after state sent its biologists out to study the lives of the bears and gather details that would lead to sounder management of these animals. Today there are dozens of biologists studying the black bear. For years, Dr. Lynn Rogers has studied black bear denning in Minnesota, while Dr. Mike Pelton concentrated on the bears of the Great Smokies, and Dr. John Beecham probed the secret lives of Idaho's black bears. Other bear studies continue in West Virginia, New York, Washington, Colorado, and elsewhere. The conferences at which these workers assemble regularly bring together more than two hundred wildlife professionals from across the country.

Among them will be Gary Alt, whose work is widely recognized in bear research circles. Alt, a young man of medium size, with sandy hair and a small moustache, has pursued the black bears of Pennsylvania for a dozen years, during which he has captured and handled more than two thousand bears.

He was finishing work on his Bachelor of Science degree at Utah State University when word reached him that his native state was about to hire a bear biologist. "I came right back," he says, "cut my hair, shaved off my beard, and appeared for my interview." Near the end of his interview, an inch-thick sheaf of applications was placed on the table before him and he was asked why he was better qualified than these other applicants. "I just hoped he had a sense of humor," Alt recalls, "I knew there wasn't any use giving him the same answer all the others had given. I just told him, 'I'd eat a bushel of rocks to get this job.'" Gary Alt became Pennsylvania's bear biologist.

He spent most of that summer trying to live-trap his first bear in a culvert trap, and after the first one, they came easier. He took seventy the first year and began working out the techniques he has since perfected.

A high point in Alt's year comes in early spring before the bears emerge from their winter dens. Through the winter he usually knows the locations of at least thirty adult females with newborn cubs and another thirty adult females with yearlings. Before they leave their dens, he must visit each one and record the vital statistics about both females and their offspring.

Depending on the nature of the dens, his inspection of the slumbering bears can be either relatively simple or potentially hazardous.

Occasionally, he must follow a denning bear far back into a rocky cervice, sometimes turning a ninety degree corner and ending up in an area of total darkness, depending on his fellow workers to help pull him out in case of trouble.

When he sets off to inspect denning bears, Alt and his crew are often accompanied by one to two dozen reporters, local farmers, and sportsmen tagging along for the show. On one such venture, three four-wheel-drive vehicles, carrying fifteen people, departed from the Pennsylvania Game Commission's southwestern regional office in Ligonier at nine a.m., an hour that gave all the bear watchers time to arrive from various starting points.

Before going into the woods, Alt, assisted by land management supervisor Dennis Jones, loaded enough darts to immobilize several adult bears and cubs, their drug dosages carefully measured to correspond to the estimated weights of the bears. The drug is a mixture of a muscle relaxant and a sedative that puts the mind to sleep.

The little convoy wound along a succession of secondary highways and country roads, passed through quiet villages, and finally turned into a narrow rutted road, leading upward through forests of hemlock, birch, maple, and beech. The line of vehicles crossed creeks swollen by recent snow melt, then climbed into an old stripmined region, now reforested.

Alt and his two helpers shouldered packs carrying equipment needed for tranquilizing, weighing, measuring, and blood-testing bears. Each man carried a loaded dart gun that resembled a single-shot shotgun.

The accompanying observers moved quietly to the top of a forested slope that dropped sharply to the bench a hundred yards below. From here, biologist Jake Stunzi, carrying a radio receiver, swept the hillside with his hand-held antennae and picked up a steady beeping that told him that the female was still in her den down on the bench.

As the observers waited silently on the logging road, the three bear workers began their stalk down the rocky slope, converging on the thick top of a fallen hemlock tree.

There was always the chance that the old female, hearing them sliding down the hill, would leave her den, or that once shot with a dart, she might have time to escape into heavy cover and become lost. Because of this, a game commission helicopter clattered in over the ridges and began circling above. If she escaped, the crew could keep her in view until the drug slowed her down.

Looking through the leafless forest, the observers could see the men with their dart guns as they approached the den from two sides. Suddenly, a yearling bear bolted from beneath the deadfall, passed a team member who did not try to block its escape, scrambled up the hill, bypassing the observers, and was soon out of view.

An instant later a large bear rushed from the brushpile in the same direction, and there was a barely audible report from a dart gun. Then, the old female did an unusual thing: she wheeled about and dashed back into her den, beneath the fallen hemlock.

About the same time, Gary Alt heard the crying of small cubs, sounds he would never have expected from this den. The crew waited for ten minutes until the drug took effect, and it became safe to enter the bear's home.

As his eyes adjusted to the darkness, Alt saw the still form of the old bear, her head stretched out on the ground. Then, he saw three tiny cubs, huddled together in the nest. In returning, the sow had shown a remarkable display of maternal loyalty to her cubs. Alt invited a visiting photographer to crawl into the den with him and make a picture. "You are lucky," he said. "You're seeing a rare sight. This has never been reported before. This is the first documented case of a black bear wintering with cubs from two successive years."

He knew the bear's history because the transmitter on her collar had been there for two and a half years. The previous winter she chose as her den a tall hollow tree and spent the cold months crowded into the cavity far above the ground, insulated from the wind and away from other bears that might threaten her cubs. That den site, perhaps two and a half miles distant as the crow flies, was the birthplace of the yearling cub that escaped.

There is no explanation for the bear's choosing such a variety of winter shelters. "Denning sites," says Alt, "are no limiting factor for the bear population. None at all." If the bears find no suitable den, they may spend the winter lying in a depression right out on top of the ground, sometimes at the base of a tree in the open woods where a man in a low-flying aircraft can spot them easily against the snow. Even the pregnant females sometimes winter in these exposed situations, bearing their new cubs in subzero weather, exposed to rain, snow, and frigid winds. Very rarely will a bear return to an old den used in previous years.

With the record-setting bear immobilized in her den, Alt motioned the spectators down the hillside. Three of them tucked the small shivering cubs inside their down jackets to keep them warm while Alt and his crew worked with their mother. She was dragged carefully from beneath the downfall into the open where she lay on her back, her legs sprawled, and her pale pink tongue protruding.

Her old transmitter needed replacing, and the bear workers cut

Bear biologist Gary Alt and one of the anesthetized female bears that serves as a subject for his Pennsylvania research.

This special gun fires drug-loaded darts for anesthetizing bears located by Gary Alt and his co-workers in the forests of Pennsylvania. Each dart is carefully loaded with the amount of drug needed for bears of estimated weights.

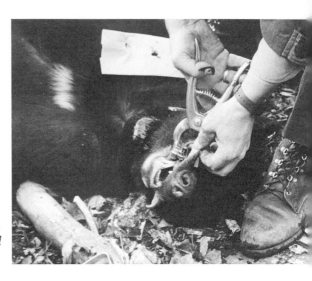

A drugged bear is tatooed on the lip for permanent identification. Whenever the bear is recaptured in the future, it can be identified by this mark.

Biologists take samples of the bear's milk and blood for use in laboratory experimental work.

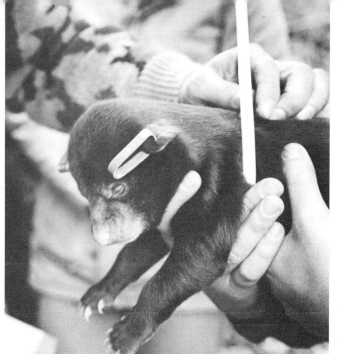

Black bear cubs weigh about three pounds. This one is equipped with an identifying aluminum ear tag large enough for the little bear to grow into.

While biologists work with the mother bear, drowsy cubs are kept snug inside the down jackets of observers who tag along for a close-up view of the bears.

the leather collar off and installed a new transmitter, checking it to be certain that it worked well.

Then, they began a whole series of procedures on the immobilized bear. One biologist opened her lower lip and tattooed a permanent identifying mark on it. Next, Dennis Jones pried out one of her small pre-molars from just behind the canine tooth. This would go to the laboratory to be cross-sectioned so the biologists could read the annual rings, as a forester does with a tree stump, and determines the bear's age. "It's not a perfect method," said Alt, "but it is the best we have."

They also drew a blood sample from the bear, and even stripped warm milk from her teats into small vials. The milk was destined for the National Zoo in Washington, D.C. where research biologists want to determine what the content of milk should be for raising cubs of the closely related endangered giant panda.

The blood was later placed in a centrifuge and rotated until the blood serum separated into a clear band of liquid above the red blood cells. "If we injected some of this into you," Alt said, "you might go into hibernation." This fluid, titrated off into clean vials, was shipped to university laboratories where scientists study the mysteries of hibernation.

The bear was also measured, and finally she was weighed by tying her legs together and suspending her from scales by a rope. Four men pulled the dead weight up free of the ground and this raised the scales above eye level. Alt shinnied up the tree until he was high enough to read the scales. "A hundred and ninety-seven," he said.

Finally, the sleepy cubs were processed. They weighed from three and a half to four and a half pounds and were all chubby and healthy. A numbered aluminum cattle ear tag was clamped onto each ear of all three cubs and, for each ear punctured, there was a loud squawl which, had the mother been awake, might have brought her swiftly to the infant's defense.

Five men then assumed pallbearer positions around the old female, carefully lifted her and carried her back into the darkness of her familiar den where she was arranged just as they had found her. After another hour of sleep, she would awaken, probably to find her hungry cubs nursing. The den might still be filled with human odors, but the female would pay them no heed because Gary Alt, as his final precaution, had employed a trick learned some years ago; he rubbed Vicks into each of her nostrils and by the time the sharp odors of the salve wear off, the human odors have dissipated.

The Vicks trick has been a part of Alt's highly successful research with orphaned bear cubs. Cubs, orphaned when their mothers are killed, can be a problem to state wildlife agencies any time. For years, state officials had little they could do with orphaned black bears except to try to find zoos that would take them, and zoos quickly fill to capacity with bears. One year, long before Alt learned how to manipulate orphans, the Pennsylvania Game Commission had more than a dozen cubs. It tried releasing into the wild the last five that it could not give away. The results were disastrous.

One was hauled into the wilderness where it was released after firecrackers were dropped into its crate in an effort to condition it against people. It departed at full speed, but a short time later was seen coming down the trail, nose to the ground, tracking the car's tires, "like a hound after a rabbit," said the state's chief wildlife official.

Two others were destroyed because they pestered fishermen for food, and another was shot when it entered a farm kitchen and tried to steal a fresh-baked apple pie. The last one had to be destroyed after it moved into a village where it insisted on panhandling in one store after the other.

Wildlife workers had observed female bears with cubs of varying sizes and concluded that there may be instances of wild females adopting orphaned cubs of other bears. To Alt, and a few others, this promised some practical applications. A New York biologist successfully introduced a bear cub into a foster mother's den, and the following year Alt set in motion his own adoption agency for Pennsylvania bears.

Many cubs are brought to him during the spring and summer when the bears are no longer in their dens, and Alt hoped to palm these cubs off on foster mothers. When there was a cub up for adoption, Alt and his crew tracked down a radio-equipped female, chased her away, and chased her cubs up a tree. Then the new cub was sent up the tree with the other young.

In early experiments, the returning mother, using her highly sensitive nose, quickly picked out the cub, carrying a strange bear scent, and killed it. This prompted Alt to search for an agent to mask the odor, and he eventually found that Vicks rubbed on the cub and in the sow's nostrils kept her from detecting the new cub. Alt believes that by the time the Vicks wears off, she has licked the cubs and they all smell the same to her as she pads off through the forest with her enlarged family. Cubs that have lived in captivity more than a few days, put out with strange females, tend to run off into the woods and stray from their foster mother, but Alt found that if he first confines them until they become hungry, they feed and, having nursed, stay with the sow thereafter.

Using his adoption techniques, Alt has moved orphaned cubs across the state from the Pocono Mountains to the hills of southwestern Pennsylvania to reinforce the bear population there. He can manipulate the bears by bringing in a preponderance of females to build the population more rapidly.

Alt's record number of cubs raised by one sow is seven—four of her own plus three adopted ones. The bear adoption system has also been widely used in Idaho by bear biologist John Beecham. Biologists were soon considering the more hazardous challenge of employing the plan with grizzly bears. Furthermore, Alt and Jonkel saw promise in farming out grizzly cubs, perhaps those born in zoos, with lactating black bears to bolster the threatened grizzly's numbers.

Alt also worked out a system for transplanting adult bears. By taking the bear from the winter den and installing her in a wooden crate with hay and straw bedding, he allows the bear to complete her hibernation in the crate. During the winter, she gives birth to cubs. When spring comes, and the cubs are old enough to travel, the crate is opened. The mother accepts the new territory, which may be hundreds of miles from her old home.

The end result of this, or most other black bear research across the country, is to amass a store of facts on which managers can base their efforts to restore bear populations, or establish sound hunting regulations.

Manipulation of hunting regulations becomes a prime management tool. The radio tracking of bears in Pennsylvania, the Catskills of New York, and elsewhere told biologists that the females go to their dens well ahead of the males, enabling wildlife officials to set the hunting seasons after the females are in their dens and before the males have gone to their winter quarters. In this manner, the kill can be tilted toward the males, leaving the females to build the population. Pennsylvania, following Alt's advice, has a carefully timed annual bear hunting season, usually one or two days a year.

As a result, Pennsylvania's bear population is in the best condition it has been for many years, and as the bear population grows, so does interest in bear hunting. In recent years the one hundred thousand or so Pennsylvania bear hunters have taken record numbers of fifteen hundred or more bears annually.

Part of this success can be traced to the fact that the bears of Penn's Woods find the food as plentiful as anywhere on the continent. "Our forests are remarkably productive," says Alt. "There are abundant crops of acorns and other foods, and if there are failures of natural foods, the bears search out human foods." Bears in the Pocono Mountains of northeastern Pennsylvania feed on farm crops and even visit the backyard feeding stations which the bears' admirers maintain in surprising numbers.

This superior nutrition explains to Alt's satisfaction the high reproductive rate of Pennsylvania bears, and he compares his state's bears with those elsewhere to make his point. The average fall weight of adult male bears in Pennsylvania is four hundred and eighty-six pounds, about twice the national average.

"The average weight of the pregnant female bear in the United States," Alt adds, "is a hundred and fifty to a hundred and seventy-five pounds, but in Pennsylvania it is three hundred and fourteen pounds.

"Furthermore, most female black bears nationwide have their first young when four years of age and, in the West, maybe five or older, but here thirty-eight percent have their first litters when they are three years old." Pennsylvania's bears average two and nine-tenths cubs per litter, about fifty percent higher than the national average, and while western bears may go three or four years between litters, Pennsylvania black bears regularly have young every second year.

This success in churning out young bears, plus management based on modern research, caused Pennsylvania's bear population to more than double in less than a decade, and without any of the loss in average size or growth rate that the biologists might ordinarily look for, again telling Alt that his bears have abundant food.

Under these conditions, the long range factor that sets the upper limit on the number of bears becomes a question of how many bears people will tolerate. "We used to believe," says Alt, "that bears could not exist in populated areas, but we have documented many cases of them living, and even denning, in backyards. The bears adapt quite well. It is the people who have difficulty adapting. Often it is not what bears do that get them into trouble, but what people think they might do."

Concern for the black bear is overdue. This resilient and adaptable beast of the deep forest is faced with steady losses of habitat and, to help it survive and prosper, we must understand its habitat needs. Only scientific research can continue to fill the long-standing gaps in our knowledge of what one writer called "everybody's bear."

Chapter 20

The Bear Poachers

The night was black and cloudy and no stars hung in view above the forested slopes of Great Smoky Mountains National Park. The hunter put his hounds into the back of his four-wheel-drive vehicle and started the slow grind up the long, steep road to Cove Mountain Ridge. A November chill was on the woods as the man released his dogs. Moisture from the recent rain would keep the bear's scent sharp in the old Bluetick's nostrils. Dog and bear should run well.

One of the dogs soon picked up a trail, and the hunter heard the baying hound send his message down the wooded slope. The man stood and listened for a bit to the sweetest music in the world, until he knew which direction the bear was moving. Then, he set off, following the dog toward the ridge above. Long experience told him where the bear was headed, and he understood the risk of following, but a man couldn't leave his dog, could he? Besides, he had never been caught and, more than once in the darkness, he had been within spittin' distance of the rangers.

As he neared the top of the ridge, he stopped for a breather. His hound had done exactly as he expected; dog and bear had both, as the bear hunters say in these mountains, "crossed the road," meaning that the hunt had crossed the ridge into the forbidden sanctuary of Great Smoky Mountains National Park. Then he understood that the hound was sending a new message. The bear had sought safety in a tree, and the dog was telling his master to come and take over.

For half a century this magnificent region, covering an area fifty-four miles long by nineteen miles wide at its widest point, has been a splendid national park, straddling the mountains that separate Tennessee and North Carolina. In these eight hundred square miles, there were hundreds of black bears flourishing before the land was settled. Then, by the 1920s, the small-scale logging grew into a large operation, and as the trees vanished, and the number of people increased in the valleys, bears were seldom seen anymore at low elevations. Dogs were used increasingly for hunting, and hunts became party affairs, rather than the one-man adventures they had long been.

Then came the national park, still not welcomed to this day by some people whose granddaddies settled in the hills. Gradually, the woods returned and so did some of the wildlife of the forests, including the turkeys and the bears. Although the bears may never again number what they once did, Great Smoky Mountains National Park is now a reservoir from which black bears move off to stock the surrounding hills. Some wildlife workers believe that without the national park, the bears would be gone from these hills.

Without giving it much thought, the hunter, following his dog, crossed into the park on Cove Mountain. What he did not yet know, however, was that he was not the only person marking the location of his hounds at that moment. The National Park Service rangers protect the bears, day or night, if they can, and they know the hills almost as well as the poachers do. They understand which hollows are the favorites of the best known bear poachers.

This poacher, a young man long on the rangers list of known outlaw hunters, but still without any record of prior arrests, hurried on toward his dogs. He flashed his light into the tree, located, and shot the medium-sized bear looking down at him.

At this point two men came out of the dark, guns out of their holsters, and announced that the hunter was under arrest for hunting in the national park and for the illegal shooting of a black bear. They began reading his rights to the outlaw, but instead of submitting quietly, the man, as one of the rangers said later, "tried to rabbit." He was a mite too slow and the rangers dragged him to the ground. "He fought us every inch of the way," the ranger said. "Tore up the ground like a bunch of hogs had rooted through." He was, however, overpowered, and as a result, made his first trip into court where he was convicted as charged. This was only one of the recent illegal bear-killing cases in Great Smoky Mountains National Park.

HUNTERS VS. RANGERS

Wherever bears, both grizzly and black, live, poachers are usually a threat. The Great Smoky Mountains is a perpetual hotbed of bear poachers for several reasons.

For one, bear hunting is traditional in these hills. Some of it is done for spite. "Granddaddy hunted these hills and by gawd, I can hunt 'em too." There is a macho satisfaction in "beating the man"—outwitting the rangers. A few years ago, park service personnel found a bear paw nailed to one of the park signs, and a bear head tossed out in the yard at park headquarters.

Another reason they hunt park bears is ownership of a bear dog so good that other hunters up and down the hollows admire and talk about him. One long-time poacher admitted that the love of good dogs was the real reason for hunting bears, as if the dog deserved to hunt. "I tree a lot more bears than I shoot," he said. "Run 'em for the sport of hearing my dogs."

Another man, a reformed poacher, tells about his all-time favorite Bluetick hound. "He was just like one of us. Best dog I ever had. Kept me outa jail more than once. He wouldn't hunt very far from me, and never run nothin' but a bear. I've been so close to the law that I could reach out and touch 'em when they passed. But Old Blue knew when we got close. Even if we was runnin' up on a treed bear, if there was anybody else around, he'd kinda whimper and turn off in another direction, leaving that bear alone. I always knew what Old Blue was sayin'. And Old Blue knew where the park boundary was as well as I did."

This man, living with his memories, believes that there may not be as many bear poachers in those hills as there once were. "They're too lazy today," he says. "Oh, if there's a bear out beside the road, they'll take him, but they're not fer gettin' very far from their fancy four-wheel drives. Besides," he adds, "it's got too costly to keep dogs."

There may be an element of truth in this observation, but the fact is that bear poachers around the Great Smokies are still far more numerous than they should be for the good of the bear. Besides, there is a different breed of hunter out there, as the wildlife officers will verify. "They're more sophisticated than they ever were before," says one officer with a long history of arresting bear poachers. "Their cars are equipped with two-way radios. If I drive a Park Service vehicle back one of these roads in the evening, word gets up in the hills in minutes."

Even the dogs are radio equipped. Some owners now fit their favorite bear hounds with collars, carrying miniature radio transmitters which cost about two hundred and fifty dollars each. Then, using receivers, the owner can locate his lost dogs or quickly move right to them when they tree a bear.

The everlasting cat-and-mouse game goes on. On one occasion, the officers captured a radio-equipped dog inside the park, tied him to a tree and waited in ambush for the hunter to arrive, then arrested him for hunting.

The dogs used for bear hunting can be costly animals. A price tag of five hundred dollars for such a dog is common and the hunter's pack may include anywhere from a single hound to half a dozen dogs. One man paid five thousand dollars for a dog to use for stud service. Most famous of all the bear dogs ever used in these hills were the Plott hounds, first imported from Germany by Jonathan Plott in the 1700's. Noted for their strength, stamina, and viciousness, Plott hounds are still being used today for bear hunting, both legal and illegal. Increasingly, however, the officers chasing bear poachers over the Great Smokies are encountering pitt bulls, airedales, and now Dobermans.

If there is big money going into the bear poacher's equipment, there is also the promise of realizing more from the bear than ever before. Strange new uses have been found for the poached bears. Claws, teeth, and hide can all be sold if seller and buyer want to take the risk, and they still do. Bear claws, used for making jewelry, may bring the poacher five dollars each, while a grizzly claw is worth much more.

One case that attracted wide attention from the press around the Great Smoky Mountains in 1983 involved a Gatlinburg businessman who made the mistake of doing business with an undercover wildlife officer. "He had two freezers full of bear parts," the officer said. "He bragged about killing eighty-five bears in the park, and I believe him because I bought enough paws from him that I knew he killed seventy-five bears."

Did the poacher go to jail? Not likely. "He paid a fifteen-hundred-dollar fine," said the officer with a touch of bitterness in his voice. "They don't ever do time here." In 1980, a North Carolina offender, after selling claws to an undercover agent, and testifying in court that he supplied five hundred claws to a jeweler, was fined three hundred dollars, then had his ninety day sentence suspended.

Mounted canine teeth sell at ten dollars each. If the poacher wants to sell the mounted head, the bear's teeth can be replaced with plastic falsies, ordered from a taxidermist's catalog. The fur can also be peddled separately.

POACHING LIVE BEARS

But there are sometimes ways to sell the live bears as well. Although both Tennessee and North Carolina forbid the keeping of bears in roadside cages, wildlife officers believe that cubs are still being taken and sold. Sometimes they cross state lines, making the theft a federal offense under the Lacey Act.

There once were, and may still be, a few bear chasers far back in the hills who keep a bear tied to a tree, or secured in a pen, so they can test their bear dogs against the animal. "One man I knew," said a reformed poacher, "charged a dollar to put your dog with the bear. You could tell right off if he was any good for a bear dog. If he was afraid of the bear, you killed him right there."

A more shoddy version of this developed into a contest of sorts in which a bear was pitted against dogs while the observers worked themselves into an orgastic lather, betting on the outcome. To protect the costly dogs in such a match, the bear would be handicapped by a combination of methods, including extracting its teeth, pulling its claws out without benefit of anesthesia, and sometimes breaking a front leg, or cutting a tendon, so it could not strike. The bear's lower jaw could also be broken so it could not bite. As one final precaution, the mutilated bear was chained to a stake.

Did this entertainment, reminiscent of a Roman Circus, go out with the arrival of more enlightened times? Not quite. In October 1982, according to North Carolina newspapers, twenty men were arrested in the act of pitting bear and dogs against each other.

Live bears, believed to be poached from the park, may be used for rigged bear hunts. One wildlife officer, working for the Park Service, said of a recent case, "I was working undercover. I was a 'rich hunter' from the East. I asked around until I finally arranged a guaranteed hunt for a bear. The fee was a thousand dollars, but you have to understand that it can go to several times this when they begin adding extra for making the skin into a rug, mounting the head, and the other services a hunter might want."

Finally, the "hunter" was led to a remote location where there was a culvert trap in plain view. The object was to shoot the bear when the door went up. It came out of the dark trap, blinking in the bright light. "I didn't shoot," admitted the officer. "I pretended to slip, and slid down the hill." The guide shot the bear and was later convicted.

Another supplier of captive bears for phony hunts already had one ratty looking seventy-five-pound female black bear he was trying to fatten up when caught using a bear trap inside the park. He was fined a thousand dollars, lost his hunting and fishing privileges for five years, and was given five years probation. But, typically, his eleven month and twenty-five day sentence to jail was suspended.

There are also available illegal, guided commercial bear hunts inside the boundaries of Great Smoky Mountains National Park. One of these came to light the day a U.S. Fish and Wildlife Service agent called the park headquarters and asked for Bill Cook.

Bill is a burly young man of pleasant countenance, but has a low boiling point where poaching is involved. The federal agent had picked up a clue that told him the name of a man offering bear hunting inside the park. Cook put the name into the Park Service computer, compared some notes, and figured out which watershed the man preferred for his hunting. When the visiting sport was eventually led to his animal in the dark of night, a team of officers emerged from the shadows. The sport was caught. "But the guides rabbited," said Cook. "We caught one of the dogs, but the collar it was wearing belonged to a dead man. Park rangers were not surprised when the dog went unclaimed and had to be destroyed by the Humane Society.

The client, meanwhile, was charged with possession of firearms in the park and hunting in the park. He paid fines totaling three hundred and fifty dollars and was sentenced to thirty days of which he served only ten, and that on weekends.

The real punishment for those caught poaching bears in the park may be the disgrace suffered in the eyes of their peers. They got caught, and that says something about their lack of woodsmanship, wits, and wisdom.

Traps remain a favorite bear-capturing method. One of the more common is cobbled together from two or three fifty-five gallon metal drums, welded together into a tube. The trap is carted off to a remote area of the park in the dead of night, staked down, baited, and set. The bear follows its nose to the sardine or decaying meat baits, crawls in, and trips the trigger causing the door to drop.

Within the memory of some park workers, the old-fashioned giant steel leghold traps were still being found on park trails. These bear traps were once made by frontier blacksmiths and widely used in this country, especially by stockmen and their agents. In the twenty-year period between 1932 and 1952, park rangers confiscated two hundred and thirty-one of these bear traps inside the national park. They were still used regularly in the nineteen forties. North Carolina law enforcement officers were always understandably furious whenever they found a bear-sized leg-hold trap in the middle of some little-used forest trail. One officer stepped in one, putting his foot firmly down on the pan before he realized what he had done. Fortunately, the day was cold and the trap mechanism, frozen in place, did not spring.

The cruelist traps were made of hollow logs, with a ring of long horseshoe nails driven into them at an angle that would not let the curious bear withdraw its head once it had investigated the bacon with which the trap was baited. Once abandoned, this trap killed again and again, when curious bears were baited by the heads of previous victims. Deadfall traps that break the bear's neck have also been used.

All this takes its toll. Nobody knows how many bears are stolen from Great Smoky Mountains National Park, or other lands, both public and private, where bears still live, but Chief Ranger Dick Moeller estimated in the mid-seventies that the figure was two hundred in one year. This estimate may now be high because, according to some observers, bear poaching may gradually be losing some of its former respectability.

THE ORGAN BUSINESS

But new threats to the country's bears continue to surface. In recent years wildlife law enforcement officers of the California Department of Fish and Game uncovered a widespread poaching operation aimed at supplying the peculiar superstitions of ethnic groups who believe they must have bear organs to keep them healthy. After two centuries of taking bears for every reason, and often for no reason, men still kill them to obtain the gallbladders.

These organs are shipped half way around the world, as well as to ethnic groups in a few large cities in this country. The bile is considered a medicine for various maladies and, although it could be concocted in the chemistry lab, ancient tradition demands that it come directly from the bear's gallbladder.

This gallbladder cure-all, known among people of Korean ancestry as *ungdam,* is described by journalist Dennis G. Hanson, writing in *Audubon* the magazine of the National Audubon Society, as "something that looks like a wet sandwich bag filled with gooey, green slime." But the price for the dried gallbladders, properly prepared, may go to three thousand dollars a pound. In addition, the suppliers of this material are also shipping abroad bear claws, hides, and paws. Meanwhile, West Coast oriental restaurant owners sometimes serve bear paw soup as a special delicacy.

When word of these illegal uses of bear parts reached the California Department of Fish and Game, that agency's law enforcement agents began planning a massive undercover operation. They had a law that could back them up. Under California law, the selling of bear parts can bring an offender up to one year in jail and a five-thousand-dollar fine. According to Captain Wayne Klein who supervises the state's wildlife law enforcement in northern California, the officers soon learned that they were dealing with outlaws who are interested only in money, and have "no regard for wildlife or hunting as a sport."

For seven months in 1981, two California undercover agents infiltrated the bear poaching business, one working his way into the Korean community in Los Angeles where the demands centered, the other becoming a trusted member of the fraternity of bear houndsmen in northern California where he was even urged to run for president of the group.

The law enforcement people were not happy with what they learned about the bear houndsmen. Where they had once believed that illegal selling of parts by houndsmen might be limited to fewer than half a dozen, they soon found, according to Klein, a large percentage of them had either sold parts or had knowledge of the illegal traffic.

By the time the news of the investigation broke, California officers had seized parts of fifty-five bears, a number considered by Klein to be only a fraction of the bears killed illegally in that period. Among the numerous defendants facing charges as a result of this single small operation were houndsmen, owners of Oriental restaurants, buyers dealing in bear parts, and an herbal-acupuncturist who made the mistake of ordering a hundred frozen gallbladders, at one hundred dollars each, from an undercover agent. This individual already had twenty-three gallbladders in stock, along with several trays of elk antlers in the velvet.

This sting operation hit only a fraction of the illegal bear poaching business, but it put the pressure on and gave the outlaws warning that they might make a mistake at any time.

The officers found that the demand for bear parts far exceeds the supply, and that parts are obtained from several other states as well as from Canada.

Some California officials believe the illegal take of black bears in that state may equal the legal kill. Evidence that poachers are making serious inroads on the black bears there is seen in the age structure of the bear population. California biologists find that the state's black bears now have an average age of only four years which is at least a year shy of what the biologists consider a healthy age structure.

Wherever the bear lives in the wild, poaching threatens its life. In the late summer of 1980, a federal game agent delivered a beautiful mounted black bear, in the light color phase, to the Northeastern Nevada Museum. The donated bear was one of a dozen or so bears, believed to have been killed illegally in recent years in Nevada, where the total bear population is down to about thirty individuals. Two men were arrested for guiding illegal hunts into the Sierras for these rare and unusual bears, and fined a total of ten thousand dollars in federal court.

Some bears are poached because the person stealing the animal cannot resist the temptation to have a mounted head in his home. A bear may even be taken as a lark. Some years ago two young men, traveling through Yellowstone, pushed a bear cub into their van and sped off. By the time state troopers arrested them outside the park, the bear had completely destroyed the car's upholstery.

Poachers who go for an illegal grizzly, and some still do, face even tougher laws because of the big bear's status as a threatened species. In addition, public sentiment against bear poaching has intensified and this is reflected in such developments as The National Audubon Society's reward system for citizens who turn in grizzly bear poachers. The Society's program figured in the celebrated case of James Bibb, an Idaho man who shot a grizzly from his tree stand with a compound bow, as the bear approached bait beneath the tree.

He promptly set up his camera and shot a self-timed picture of himself holding the bow beside the dead bear. Eventually, the picture was shown around town and someone who saw it notified law enforcement agents. Bibb, who had killed one of the few remaining grizzlies in the Selkirks in northern Idaho, claimed he shot it in Canada where bear hunting was legal.

Bibb's bear picture appeared at the top of page one of *The Spokesman Review* of Spokane, Washington, in January 1984, following the sentencing of Bibb. The sentence was a hundred and fifty days of community service and a fine of fifteen hundred dollars. The informant was rewarded by the National Audubon Society with a forty-five hundred dollar payment, and was given another five hundred dollars by an organization called "Citizens Against Poaching". Irate citizens insisted that Bibb got off too lightly. Said an editorial in *The Spokesman-Review,* "Bibb's idea of hunting is not hunting at all—it's wanton, craven butchery and it gives the sport a bad name."

The matter of the court's levying light sentences against poachers is a widespread complaint of law enforcement officers. An outfitter who shot two grizzlies in Bridger-Teton National Forest in the fall of 1983, was permitted to plead guilty to a lesser charge of cruelty to animals. Instead of the twenty thousand dollars he could have been fined, he was sentenced to six months in jail, six months probation, and fined seven hundred and fifty dollars, all of which was suspended except for three months probation, which he was considered to have served before the sentencing.

Many states now have official programs offering rewards to citizens who turn in poachers. Reporting the poacher, especially the one taking endangered wildlife, is becoming not only socially acceptable, but also a civic duty, and law abiding hunters are among those ringing the bell on the poachers. Bears everywhere, along with deer, turkeys, and other wildlife, can use this help if they are to stay with us into the future.

Chapter 21

Tomorrow's Bears

The future for America's bears ranges from bright to hopeless, depending on the bears in question and where they live. The black bear, much more common, widespread, and adaptable than the grizzly, promises to be around for a long time. About half of the Lower Forty-eight states still have appreciable populations of black bears, with the total estimated at more than two hundred thousand.

They prosper best in states of the West Coast, the Northern Rocky Mountains, the Northern Great Lakes, and some parts of the Northeast. States with the largest black bear populations include Alaska, Colorado, Montana, Idaho, Oregon, Washington, California, Wisconsin, Maine, Michigan, Pennsylvania, and New York.

However, the black bear's status is spotty, and as we continue to take its habitat for our own purposes, we eliminate bears. They are essentially gone from a wide band of states across the Midwest and most of the Southeast. Throughout the coastal states, all the way from east Texas through South Carolina, there are little more than small threatened pockets of black bears left. In the swamp forests of these states, where the bears once numbered in the tens of thousands, they are down to a few hundred.

Perhaps a third of the black bears of the southern swamplands live in Arkansas in the White River National Wildlife Refuge. But Arkansas has begun to bring the bear back to its mountain country. Between 1959 and 1968, this state imported two hundred and fifty-four black bears from Manitoba and Minnesota and released them in the Ozark and Ouachita mountains where they apparently found a suitable food supply. In 1980, Arkansas opened a bear hunting season again after fifty-three years of no legal bear hunting.

Importations and releases, however, seem to hold little promise across most of the bear's former range. People resist efforts to bring the bears back because of concern over threats to people and property. Hope for the security of the black bear remains with those states that have never entirely lost their bears.

Through much of the black bear's present range, and where bear numbers permit, the black bear is a highly regarded game animal and the popularity of bear hunting is growing. The estimated total legal kill is twenty-five to thirty thousand black bears annually, nationwide, outside Alaska.

This high interest in bear hunting works to the black bear's long-range benefit. States with secure well-nourished black bear populations and hunting seasons generally have research biologists studying the animals and assembling information to guide them in establishing hunting regulations. Where the seasons are designed on a sound basis of scientific research, covering both the bear and its habitat, and legislators resist the temptation to dabble in game management, legal hunting is no threat to the long-range welfare of the bears. Furthermore, hunting seasons supply funds for continuing vital research into the lives of the bears. In states that have too few black bears to justify an open season, the bear's needs are often ignored.

In addition, a large percentage of people who do not hunt also want to see the bear prosper, and this broad-based support is the best hope the bear has for survival. No longer is it widely socially acceptable to harass bears or kill them illegally, even in those areas where old attitudes have hung on the longest.

With evolving attitudes favoring the black bear and modern sophisticated research telling us about the bear's needs and how to get along with them, the remaining question is habitat. If we can protect what is left of the world of the black bear, the animal will march with us into the foreseeable future.

For the mighty grizzly there remains cautious hope of retaining viable populations in and around Glacier and Yellowstone National Parks, and perhaps in another pocket or two of wilderness.

The basic word is habitat. Unless we can save enough habitat to support the grizzlies, there is no long-range hope for the great bear. The grizzly bear needs habitat that is extensive and varied, with safe denning areas, moist areas for spring feeding, and secure places for summer day beds. The bears require habitat at both low and high elevations, and although they must have these places for only a fraction of the year, each is essential in its season. Securing this habitat calls for constant vigilance. If we leave land that supplies the needs of the bears, they will take care of the rest. The bears know how to reproduce.

The pressures mount. We treat the habitat as if it were a cake being sliced, rationalizing that one more piece scarcely matters. In this manner we justify a new campground or lodge in Yellowstone National Park, a ski development in national forest grizzly range adjoining the park, roads into the backcountry, livestock instrusions in bear habitat, one more permit for mineral exploration, and a new subdivision, bringing bears and people closer together, until someday the great bear watches us take the last slice.

There are still sections of this country where the wilderness might still support grizzlies if they were transplanted to these regions. Biologists believe the North Cascades would support a resident grizzly population. Other areas that might be candidates for the return of the grizzly include the Gila Wilderness in New Mexico, and the High Uintas in Utah. However, people, especially ranchers, resist all efforts to move bears into country from which they have been eliminated.

One biologist of the Washington Department of Game says, "Unfortunately, most people do not like the idea of releasing grizzlies into their neighborhood. Whatever happened," he adds, "to the Wild West and all the open space?" There are other wilderness areas that seem suitable for supporting grizzly bears, but the reintroductions would never succeed without massive educational programs.

The future of this king of bears is in our hands, and the attitudes of people will determine whether or not the grizzly bear is secure, even in the national parks.

We can help the beleagured grizzly by insisting that planners give the bear the high priority that the Endangered Species Act grants it by law. There is need for programs that will help people everywhere understand the grizzly's specialized requirements. The grizzly cannot recover without broad public support. The grizzly bear research community, itself, is sometimes criticized for quibbling, jealousies, and empire building, all of which do little to benefit the bear.

Bear biologist Dr. Stephen Herrero of the University of Calgary, writing in *Bioscience,* says, "Grizzlies and man can coexist in the National Parks. However, to accomplish this, people will need to develop a more tolerant attitude. Men must go infrequently into grizzly habitat, and then as cautious and alert visitors. Man must temporarily relinquish his role as a tamer, a reducer of wilderness, and enter into an ecosystem in which he may not be the dominant species . . . Here man becomes a part of nature. This is the highest purpose our parks can serve."

Once the world of the grizzly was long and broad, stretching across the wide prairies, up into the cool mountains and on, to the shores of the Pacific. Through nearly all of its former range, there is little hope for its return, and where it still hangs on there is the real possibility that its numbers will dwindle.

We have saved remnants of the bison, trumpeter swan, bald eagle, and prairie dogs, and brought back the elk, pronghorn, and some other species in fair numbers. Someday we will know if we possess tolerance and understanding enough to do as much for the Great Bear that we inherited with this broad and splendid continent.

Picture Credits

Chapter 1: page 4, Larry D. Agenbroad; page 5, Larry D. Agenbroad.

Chapter 2: page 11, Library of Congress; page 14–15, Library of Congress; page 16, National Gallery of Art; page 17, National Gallery of Art.

Chapter 3: page 23, National Gallery of Art; page 25, Library of Congress; page 26, National Gallery of Art; page 28, George Laycock; page 30–31, Joslyn Art Museum, Omaha; page 32, National Museum of Art, Smithsonian Inst.; page 34–35, National Gallery of Art.

Chapter 4: page 38, Tom Beecham; page 39, Jess Lee; page 40, Jess Lee; page 42, Michael H. Francis; page 44, Jess Lee; page 46, Jess Lee; page 48, Jess Lee; page 49, Jess Lee; page 50, Jess Lee; page 52, Jess Lee; page 53, Jess Lee; page 54, George Laycock; page 56, Danny On; page 58, Michael H. Francis.

Chapter 5: page 60, Walters Art Gallery, Baltimore; page 63, Library of Congress; page 66, Kennedy Galleries, N.Y.; page 74, Smithsonian Inst.; page 78, Colton Hall Museum; page 80, California Historical Society; page 84, Library of Congress.

Chapter 7: page 91, William E. Weiss, Buffalo Bill Historical Center, Cody; page 101, George Laycock.

Chapter 9: page 115, Mark Henckel; page 117, Smithsonian Inst.

Chapter 10: page 122–123, Library of Congress.

Chapter 11: page 134, Kansas Historical Society, Topeka; page 138–139, LuRay Parker; page 144–145, Michael H. Francis; page 148–149, Glacier National Park.

Chapter 13: page 168–169, Jess Lee; page 171, Tom Sterling.

Page 178: Lynn Rogers.

Chapter 15: page 191, Tom Beecham; page 192, Lynn Rogers; page 195, Jess Lee; page 197, Jess Lee; page 198, National Archives; page 199, Lynn Rogers; page 201, George Laycock; page 202, Lynn Rogers; page 205, Lynn Rogers; page 207, Lynn Rogers; page 208, Lynn Rogers; page 209, Lynn Rogers; page 210, Lynn Rogers; page 211, Lynn Rogers.

Chapter 16: page 215, Library of Congress.

Chapter 17: page 221, Library of Congress; page 229, P. B. Stewart.
Chapter 18: page 233, Library of Congress; page 235, Danny On.
Chapter 19: page 241, Wisconsin Conservation Dept.; page 245, George Laycock; page 246–247, George Laycock.

Bibliography

Alt, Gary L. Results of Pennsylvania's 1983 Bear Season. Pennsylvania Game News. Dec. 1984.

Bauer, Erwin A. *Bear In Their World.* Outdoor Life Books. New York. 1986.

Brown, Don L. (Plan Leader). *Grizzly Bear Recovery Plan.* U.S. Fish and Wildlife Service. 1982.

Burk, Dale (Ed). *The Black Bear In Modern North America.* Proceeding of the Workshop on the Management Biology of North American Black Bear. Boone and Crockett Club. 1979.

Craighead, Frank C. Jr. *Track of the Grizzly.* Sierra Club Books. San Francisco. 1979.

Dufresne, Frank. *No Room For Bears.* Holt, Rinehart and Winston. New York. 1965.

Erickson, Albert W. *The Brown-Grizzly Bear In Alaska.* Alaska Department of Fish and Game. Juneau. 1965.

—*The Black Bear In Alaska.* Alaska Department of Fish and Game. Juneau. 1965.

—Nellor, John and Petrides, George A. *The Black Bear In Michigan.* Michigan State University. East Lansing. 1964.

Hanna, Warren L. *The Grizzlies of Glacier.* Mountain Press Publishing Co., Missoula, Montana. 1978.

Haynes, Bessie Doak and Haynes, Edgar. (Ed.) *The Grizzly Bear: Portraits From Life.* The University of Oklahoma Press. Norman. 1966.

Herrero, Stephen. *Bear Attacks.* Winchester Press. Piscataway, N.J. 1985.

Hubbard, W.P. with Harris, Seale. *Notorious Grizzly Bears.* The Swallow Press. Chicago. 1960.

Jonkel, Charles J. and Cowan, Ian McT. *The Black Bear in the Spruce-Fir Forest.* The Wildlife Society. 1971.

—*Grizzly Bears and Livestock.* Western Wildlands. Montana Forest and Conservation Experiment Station. University of Montana, Missoula. Summer, 1980.

Knight, Richard R. and Eberhardt, L.L. *Projected Future Abundance of the Yellowstone Grizzly Bear.* Journal of Wildlife Management, vol. 48(4), (1984), pp 1434–1438.

McCracken, Harold. *The Beast That Walks Like Man.* Hanover House. Garden City, N.Y. 1955.

Meslow, E. Charles. (Ed). *Bears—Their Biology and Management.* International Association of Bear Research and Management. 1983.

Mills, Enos A. *The Grizzly.* Houghton Mifflin Co. New York. 1919.

Moment, Gairdner B. *Man-Grizzly Problems—Past and Present.* BioScience Vol. 20. No. 21. November, 1970.

National Park Service. *Final Environmental Impact Statement Grizzly Bear Management Program.* Yellowstone National Park. 1982.

Pearson. A. M. (Chairman). Proceedings of the First Bear Workshop. International Association for Bear Research and Management. 1983.

Pelton, Michael R. and Conley, Richard H. (Chairmen) Proceedings of the Second Eastern Workshop on Black Bear Management and Research. Tennessee Wildlife Resources Agency, et. al. 1974.

Poelker, Richard J. and Hartwell, Harry D. *Black Bear of Washington.* Washington Department of Natural Resources. Olympia. 1973.

Rogers, Lynn. *The Ubiquitous American Black Bear.* North American Big Game, 7th Edition. Boone and Crockett Club and National Rifle Association. 1977.

Schneider, Bill. *Where The Grizzly Walks.* Mountain Press Publishing Company. Missoula. 1977.

Schullery, Paul (Ed). *American Bears, Selections From the Writings of Theodore Roosevelt.* Colorado Associated University Press. Boulder. 1983.

—*The Bears of Yellowstone.* Yellowstone Library and Museum Association. Yellowstone National Park. 1980.

Serveen, Chris. *The Grizzly Bear.* Audubon Wildlife Report. 1985.

Storer, Tracy I, and Tevis, Lloyd P. Jr. California Grizzly. University of Nebraska Press. Lincoln. 1955.

United States Department of the Interior. Fish and Wildlife Service. Grizzly Bear Recovery Plan. 1982.

Wright, William H. *The Grizzly Bear.* Charles Scribner's Sons. New York. 1909. University of Nebraska Press, Lincoln. 1977.

Young, F.M. (Compiler), Beyers, Coralie(Ed). *Man Meets Grizzly.* Houghton Mifflin Company. Boston. 1980.

Index